War and Social Change
in the Twentieth Century

4

# War and Social Change in the Twentieth Century

A comparative study of Britain, France, Germany, Russia and the United States

ARTHUR MARWICK

MACMILLAN

*First published 1974 by*
THE MACMILLAN PRESS LTD
*London and Basingstoke*
*Associated companies in New York Dublin*
*Melbourne Johannesburg and Madras*

SBN 333 11238 5 (hard cover)
333 11248 2 (paper cover)

*Printed in Great Britain by*
HAZELL WATSON AND VINEY LTD
*Aylesbury, Bucks*

This book is dedicated to two
distinguished pacifists who
celebrated their golden-wedding
anniversary at the time it was
being completed

W. H. and M. C. Marwick

# Contents

PREFACE  ix

1  The Nature of the Problem  1
   I  The Disasters of War  1
   II  The Causes of War  3
   III  The Consequences of War  6
   IV  Germany, Russia, France, Britain and the United States
       in 1914  14

2  The First World War: Germany and Russia  24
   I  The Stages of the War  24
   II  Germany's 'Fortress Truce', August 1914–November 1917  25
   III  Russia: Disruption of War and Growth of 'Voluntary
        Organisations', August 1914 – March 1917  33
   IV  Revolutions in Russia and Germany, 1917–19  37

3  The First World War: France, Britain and the United States  52
   I  Destruction and Disruption  52
   II  The Test of War  63
   III  Participation  73
   IV  Psychological Implications  79
   V  General Consequences of the War  86

4  The Second World War: Germany and Russia  98
   I  Totalitarianism and Democracy on the Eve of the War  98
   II  The War and German Society  108
   III  Russia and 'The Great Patriotic War'  123
   IV  The Aftermath of War  134

5  The Second World War: Britain and the United States  151
   I  The Impact of the Second World War on British Society  151
   II  The War and American Society  165
   III  New Relationships  179

6   The Second World War: France   185
  I    The Chagrin and the Pity of it   185
  II   Social Consequences   194
  III  Beauty and the Beast: Economic Recovery and the Idea
       of a United Europe   205

7   Problems and Conclusions   213

    NOTES ON THE USE OF ARCHIVE FILM MATERIAL   226

    ANNOTATED BIBLIOGRAPHY   235

    INDEX   247

MAPS
1   German Territorial Changes, 1918–38   xi
2   Furthest Extent of German Power, end of 1942   xii
3   Europe at the end of the Second World War   xiii

PLATES (*between pages 114 and 115*)

  I    Berlin before August 1914
  II   War as Sport Continued by other Means
  III  We are Making a New World
  IV   London in the Blitz
  V    The Air-raid Warning
  VI   Dresden, February 1945

# Acknowledgements

Sir W. S. Churchill, *The World Crisis* reproduced by permission of The Hamlyn Publishing Group Ltd and Charles Scribner's Sons; Golo Mann, *The History of Germany Since 1789* by permission of Chatto & Windus and Frederick A. Praeger Inc.; A. Solzhenitsyn, *The First Circle* by permission of Collins Publishers and Harper & Row Publishers Inc.; Alexander Werth, *Russia at War* by permission of Barrie & Jenkins and © 1964 by Alexander Werth, published by E. P. Dutton & Co. Inc. and used with their permission.

# Preface

This book is a product of about a dozen years' reflection on the question of the social consequences of war. As originally planned, it was intended to be a much bigger, and a much more detailed work. However, as I think a number of recent publications have shown, big books are not necessarily best. In any case, my new duties at The Open University forced me to abandon the extensive research programme which I had originally outlined for myself. At the same time, I have been able to benefit enormously from the preparation of The Open University third-year history course on 'War and Society'. It therefore seemed worthwhile proceeding to publish a book which, though largely dependent on secondary sources, many of them in translation, would at least set down the various ideas I have been grappling with for so long. No work of historical interpretation can hope to be definitive, but necessarily this book must be less definitive than most. If it stimulates some thought, and suggests a few lines of further enquiry, then it will have more than succeeded.

The main issues discusssed, obviously, concern the consequences of modern war. But it may be, too, that the book will illuminate the advantages and disadvantages of a certain approach to history, rather more conceptual than that normally favoured by the mainstream of the historical profession. I have found myself faced with some interesting problems in regard to resolving the conflicting demands of a fairly rigid analytical framework, the actual messiness of history as it happens, and the need to write what I hope is a reasonably readable and interesting narrative. It has occurred to me that of my own two previous ventures into this general area, my earlier book *The Deluge: British Society and the First World War*, which is fairly traditional historical writing, is rather more readable than my *Britain in the Century of Total War: War, Peace and Social Change*, which sticks more strictly to a hard analytical frame. This book attempts to retain a judicious balance. Chapter 2, because of the nature of events in Russia and Germany, departs furthest from my conceptual framework (though the framework *is* there all the time); the other chapters stick very closely to it.

Professor Alan Milward has commented on what he sees as the undue attention which has been accorded to the British experiences of war, given that events in Britain have not had the drama of those in Russia, Germany and France. Yet if British history seems to form a kind of base-line for this comparative study, I make no apology for that. Where there was no direct impact of invasion, occupation or defeat, some of the more subtle aspects of the interrelationship between war and social change can be most fully analysed.

Perhaps my title is not quite accurate. Certainly, I have concentrated on the two World Wars: they were, after all, the most important in fostering social change in the major countries I am concerned with. But my final chapter does suggest some lines of enquiry with regard to other wars (especially in respect to post-1945 conflicts in Indochina, Korea and Algeria).

The following have read all or part of my typescript: Professor Douglas Dakin and Professor Douglas Johnson of the University of London; Mrs Jill Stephenson of the University of Edinburgh; Mr Clive Emsley of The Open University; and Dr Neil Wynn of the Glamorgan Polytechnic. Although not always in agreement with the way in which I have set about my labours, all have commented generously and helpfully. I have learned much, too, from other colleagues and students both at home and abroad. Inevitably, though I have sometimes tried to go my own way when probably I should not have done so, I have been much influenced by those authorities who have contributed to the War and Society course, particularly Mr Harry Hanak and Professor Donald Watt of the University of London, Dr Anthony Adamthwaite of the University of Bradford, Professor Alan Milward of the University of Manchester Institute of Science and Technology, Professor M. R. D. Foot, formerly of the University of Manchester, Dr Gary Werskey, of the University of Bath, and Dr Kenneth Thompson, Senior Lecturer in Sociology at The Open University. My understanding of archive film has been greatly enhanced through working with Edward Hayward, Nick Levinson, Lisa Pontecorvo and Des Murphy of the B.B.C.–Open University production staff. My thanks, too, go to Margaret Keech, who typed the various versions of this book, and to Dr Christopher Harvie and Mr Bernard Waites, who read the proofs.

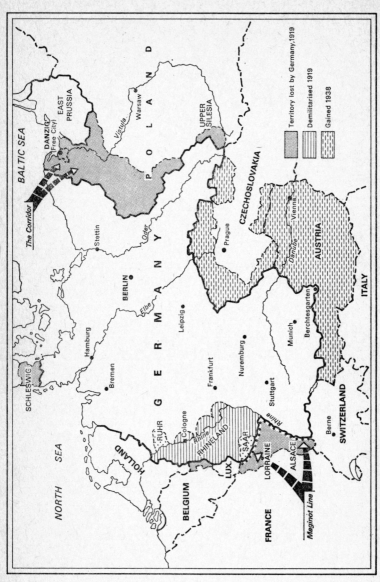

1   German Territorial Changes, 1918–38

2    Furthest Extent of German Power, end of 1942

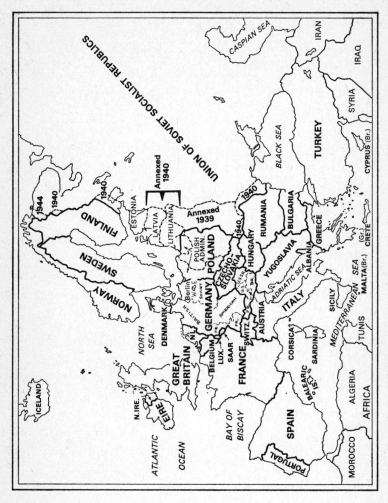

3  Europe at the end of the Second World War

# 1. The Nature of the Problem

## I The Disasters of War

Winston Churchill, to say the least, was no pacifist. His epitaph on the
First World War is difficult to improve upon:

> The great war through which we have passed differed from all ancient
> wars in the immense power of the combatants and their fearful agen-
> cies of destruction, and from all modern wars in the utter ruthlessness
> with which it was fought. All the horrors of all the ages were brought
> together, and not only armies but whole populations were thrust into
> the midst of them. The mighty educated States involved conceived
> with reason that their very existence was at stake. Germany having
> let Hell loose kept well in the van of terror; but she was followed
> step by step by the desperate and ultimately avenging nations she had
> assailed. Every outrage against humanity or international law was
> repaid by reprisals often on a larger scale and of longer duration. No
> truce or parley mitigated the strife of the armies. The wounded died
> between the lines: the dead mouldered into the soil. Merchant ships
> and neutral ships and hospital ships were sunk on the seas and all on
> board left to their fate, or killed as they swam. Every effort was made
> to starve whole nations into submission without regard to age or sex.
> Cities and monuments were smashed by artillery. Bombs from the
> air were cast down indiscriminately. Poison gas in many forms stifled
> or seared the soldiers. Liquid fire was projected upon their bodies.
> Men fell from the air in flames, or were smothered, often slowly, in the
> dark recesses of the sea. The fighting strength of armies was limited
> only by the manhood of their countries. Europe and large parts of
> Asia and Africa became one vast battlefield on which after years of
> struggle not armies but nations broke and ran. When all was over,
> Torture and Cannibalism were the only two expedients that the

For Notes and References to this chapter, see p. 22 below.

civilised, scientific, Christian States had been able to deny themselves, and these were of doubtful utility.[1]

A second World War, of course, was to surpass even the First in 'utter ruthlessness'. In the First World War 10 million men were killed, 20 million were maimed or seriously wounded; there were 5 million widows, 9 million orphans, and 10 million refugees. The scale of horror in the Second World War was still greater and is impossible to compute exactly: probably the loss of life in Europe and Russia alone directly due to the war came to at least 30 million. The culminating horror of the Second World War was the dropping of atom bombs on Hiroshima and Nagasaki; yet scarcely less horrific were some of the 'conventional' bombing raids of the war, among which the British destruction of Hamburg in 1943 (and, later, of Dresden in 1945) is notorious:

> Its horror is revealed in the howling and ragings of the firestorms, the hellish noise of exploding bombs and the death cries of martyred human beings as well as in the big silence after the raids. Speech is impotent to portray the measure of the horror, which shook the people for ten days and nights and the traces of which were written indelibly on the face of the city and its inhabitants.
> And each of these nights convulsed by flames was followed by a day which displayed the horror in the dim and unreal light of a sky hidden in smoke. Summer heat intensified by the glow of the firestorms to an unbearable degree; dust from the torn earth and the ruins and debris of damaged areas which penetrated everywhere; showers of soot and ashes; more heat and dust; above all a pestilential stench of decaying corpses and smouldering fires weighed continually on the exhausted men.
> And these days were followed by more nights of more horror, yet more smoke and soot, heat and dust and more death and destruction. Men had not time to rest or salvage property according to any plan or to search for their families. The enemy attacked with ceaseless raids until the work of destruction was complete. His hate had its triumph in the firestorms which destroyed mercilessly men and material alike.[2]

Today television brings into every home the sordid reality of war in south-east Asia and elsewhere: the danger now is that familiarity simply numbs the reactions of the sitting-room viewer. This book will be mainly devoted to analysing the social consequences of war; it will be argued that in some cases war has brought beneficial social changes, but such arguments should never be allowed to obscure the central facts of the brutality, horror and waste of war.

## II    The Causes of War

'The story of the human race', wrote Winston Churchill in concluding *The World Crisis*, 'is War.'[3] Certainly, it is difficult for anyone today to sustain the old nineteenth-century liberal belief that wars were an unfortunate interruption in the normal peaceful development of human civilisation. And since the growth of democracy seems also to have been accompanied by bigger and bloodier wars, it is hard also to maintain the view that wars are caused exclusively by the villainies of the rich or the miscalculations of the politicians. It does not seem that either the psychologists or the anthropologists have as yet agreed on a satisfactory theory of the causation of war, but undoubtedly one must look in the first instance at the nature of man himself, and in particular at the problems of man living in society. Much emphasis recently has been given to man's basic aggressive instincts. In the usage of Konrad Lorenz, 'aggression' does not necessarily have bad overtones: to Lorenz and his followers aggression is a necessary part of the human make-up leading to the conquest of physical and other obstacles; without it the human race would not have achieved such progress as it has achieved. The problem is that of the misapplication of aggressive instincts. Lorenz has shown how in the animal kingdom outbreaks of violence between animals of the same kind normally stop short of one animal killing the other. This manifestly is not the case in human society.[4]

Not all psychologists agree that human aggression is instinctive; some have argued that it is environmental, the product of various frustrations. It has been argued that the closed circle of family life engenders aggression in individuals and finally breaks out in the form of hostility to some alien group. This view would put heavy emphasis on early upbringing as a source of violent instincts; the great total wars of the twentieth century have even been attributed to the strict family discipline of the Victorian era. A more obvious environmental source of violence and tension is overcrowding. Study of the animal world shows that when the territory of one animal is threatened by another, or when there is any kind of overcrowding, then violence is likely to ensue. We are all familiar with our own growing feelings of aggression when we are confined too long in a crowded lift. There seems to be a clear link between intensive urbanisation at the end of the nineteenth century and the growing violence apparent in all parts of Europe which flooded over into general war in 1914. Whatever the exact formulation, war manifestly has deep roots in human personality, whether natural or acquired; the political, economic and diplomatic 'causes', which historians have been wont to argue over, stop short of telling the whole story.

This means that in what must be the really crucial issue in any discussion of war and society – how do we prevent future wars? – the resources of psychology, social psychology, anthropology and sociology are probably more vital than those of history. However, until we can be more certain of the common denominators, it is important too to see the way in which different wars have arisen from identifiably different political and economic circumstances. If we are to study the consequences of twentieth-century wars, we have to have some knowledge of their causation beyond a series of generalisations about human aggression. Let us therefore summarise the main points made by historians in discussing the causes of the First and Second World Wars. The basic argument concerns the extent of German responsibility for bringing about both wars. There can be no doubt that at the end of the nineteenth century and at the beginning of the twentieth century the view that war was a noble and necessary activity for any state desirous of demonstrating its power and virtue, though apparent in other countries as well, was most strongly voiced in Germany. It was true too that since Germany had come late to the scramble for overseas possessions, many of her leading politicians and thinkers were happy to argue that Germany's destiny lay in expansion on the continent of Europe itself. It was not altogether Germany's fault that she was the dissatisfied power, but it did mean she was the greatest potential trouble-maker. At the same time, a glance at the map will show the reality of the German fear that she was being encircled, and will give some validity, if not complete justification, to the notion that she might have to fight a defensive war to break out of this encirclement.

With regard to the actual outbreak of war in August 1914 two questions have to be answered. Why was a state of crisis reached? And why, instead of the crisis being resolved peacefully, did it result in a war bigger and more devastating than any previously experienced? A number of elements, apart from the special and difficult question of German responsibility, contributed to the crisis. In the Balkans there was an obvious conflict of interest between the Austro-Hungarian empire, concerned to contain the substantial Slav minorities within her borders, and Russia, who saw herself as the champion of the Slav peoples everywhere. When, following the assassination at Sarajevo of the

Austrian Archduke, Franz Ferdinand, Austria–Hungary declared war on Serbia, she may well have sought no more than limited war designed to prevent her own empire from falling apart; but inevitably she cut across Russian interests and sentiments. A second major conflict of interest existed between Germany and Britain. German industrial expansion and naval expansion were already matters of grave concern to Britain; and to British governments it was settled policy that no single power should be allowed to dominate the continent of Europe. Inflamed national sentiment lay at the roots of the Balkan conflict; but national aspirations and hatreds affected the relations of the great powers as well, particularly those between France, deprived of Alsace–Lorraine in 1871, and Germany, the victor in the Franco-Prussian war of that year. German hatred of Russia was deeply tinged with fear.

The Austrian invasion of Serbia was followed by a Russian declaration of partial mobilisation: to this the Germans reacted with a declaration of war on Russia and on France – German strategic theory was that they must knock France out quickly so as to be free to face up to Russia. 'Knocking out France' involved passing through Belgium: this was made the occasion for the British declaration of war on Germany, though it seems clear that Britain would have felt bound to resist a possible German domination of the continent even had Belgian neutrality not been violated.

Why, instead of being resolved, did the crisis spread so rapidly and so disastrously? The easy answer is to say that there was no international machinery for resolving such a crisis – which, given the present state of the world sixty years later, is really no answer at all. More basically, but scarcely more helpfully, one can point out that all governments accepted without qualification the idea that in certain circumstances their national interests could only be served by going to war. But more important in the 1914 situation is the point that all governments felt that, in the interests of their own national *security*, they dare not stay out of the war. It is here that the military in effect stepped in front of the politicians, arguing that the modern technology of war had made speedy action and the perfect interlocking of alliances essential: thus, once the first moves to war had been made, there could be no turning back.

The Second World War seems more obviously a case of sheer German aggression under the militaristic leadership of Adolf Hitler. There can be no denying the proposition that in the 1930s the National Socialist régime was the greatest single source of international tension in Europe. However, behind this lay the still more important fact of a basic imbalance in the European international situation, which instead of being cured by the First World War, had actually been made worse by it. In appearance Germany was severely defeated in the First World War; but by a curious paradox she actually emerged with her relative position in Europe strengthened, since of the surrounding states, the Austro-Hungarian empire had disintegrated into its separate national components; Russia, in the wake of the Bolshevik revolution, was going through a period of severe internal troubles; and France, with a much smaller population than Germany, had been bled almost to death in achieving the 'victory' of 1918. Despite the creation of the League of Nations there was still in the 1920s and 1930s no effective means for giving reality to the German position and for removing German frustrations; nor, in the end, were the western powers willing to follow the alternative course of keeping Germany a permanently conquered country. But aside from the international political situation we have to appreciate the explosive force and popular appeal of aggressive Nazism. Once again we are brought back to the nature of the human animal, and to the intimate relationship between society and war.

## III     The Consequences of War

Roughly speaking serious historical writing on the social effects of war can be divided into four main categories: 'tory', 'liberal', 'economic' and 'sociological'.[5] The 'tories' (and I should stress that I am using these labels in the particular way described here, not in any wider political sense) are those who continue to insist that the great events in history are the battles and political crises. They oppose what Professor Cyril Falls called the 'fallacious' theory that 'the major, if not the sole object of history should be the study of the artisan, the labourer and the peasant'.[6] Concerned with the strategic and military aspects of war, they realise that modern war necessarily involves the reorganisation of society. At times they come perilously close to justifying war by reference to the social change accompanying it. The first 'tory' accounts of twentieth-century war were in fact part of the patriotic propaganda spawned by the First World War itself. In the summer of 1916 *The Times* (London) published a series of articles on the opportunities for social and political reconstruction provided by the war, subsequently republished with an introduction by that leading social imperialist, Lord Milner, as *The Elements of Reconstruction* (1916). In the last months of the war W. Basil Worsfold, a popular writer on imperial topics, produced a long essay on *The War and Social Reform* (1919). Although the subtitle, *An Endeavour to Trace the Influence of War as a Reforming Agency; with Special Reference to Matters Primarily Affecting the Wage-earning Classes*, was a trifle ambitious, Worsfold did touch on two critical points to which 'sociological' historians have been forced to return: war as a supreme test of existing institutions, forcing reorganisation in the interests of greater efficiency; and war as a revelation of 'the value of the manual worker to the state'.

The outstanding examples of the 'tory' interpretation, concentrating on the problems of politics and strategy, but, almost as a by-product as it were, recognising the necessity for social reorganisation involved in total war, are W. S. Churchill's *The World Crisis* (6 vols, 1923–31) and his *The Second World War* (6 vols, 1948–54). The three-volume *American Democracy and the World War* (1936–48) by Frederick L. Paxson very definitely falls into the 'tory' category in that it is essentially a hymn of praise to the great administrative reorganisation carried through by the U.S. government in order to wage war efficiently; there is no discussion of the effects of war on labour, women or the racial minorities. Other leading British authors in the tory canon are N. H. Gibbs, John Terraine and Correlli Barnett, whose striking phrase 'war is the great auditor of institutions'[7] echoes the first of the points put forward by Worsfold. The tory view has in fact become one of the clichés of everyday conversation. It is wonderfully well expressed in the much-quoted speech which Orson Welles himself wrote into the film *The Third Man*, for Harry Lime:

> . . . you know what the fellow said. . . . In Italy for thirty years under the Borgias they had warfare, terror, murder, bloodshed – they produced Michelangelo, Leonardo da Vinci and the Renaissance. In Switzerland they had brotherly love, five hundred years of democracy and peace, and what did that produce . . .? The cuckoo clock.[8]

Harry Lime was a nasty character, and war is the nastiest and most destructive of all human activities: the 'liberal' historians are in a worthy tradition when they seek either to gloss over the social effects of war, stressing that the antecedents of change lie elsewhere, or else to concentrate upon war's disruptions of traditional civilisation and upon the association between modern war and the growth of totalitarianism. In British historiography the classic 'liberal' account is that of F. W. Hirst, a Gladstonian Liberal and one-time editor of *The Economist*: in *The Consequences of the War to Great Britain* (1934), Hirst lamented that the war had intensified state control, greatly weakened liberalism,

and had fostered 'moral evils' and 'social degeneracy'. Hysteria, un-
truth, propaganda, suppression of civic liberties: these are the products
of war upon which 'liberal' historians have concentrated. The intoler-
ance and suppression of free speech which characterised the United
States rather more obviously than Britain was carefully documented in
Zachariah Chaffee, *Free Speech in the United States* (1921) and H. C.
Peterson and G. C. Fite, *Opponents of War 1917–18* (1957).

The most massive memorial to the liberal view is contained in the 144
published volumes of *The Economic and Social History of the Great
War* sponsored by the Carnegie Endowment for International Peace.
Although different contributors fulfilled their brief in different ways,
many kept very close to the original plans drawn up as early as November 1914. The idea, according to the editorial preface provided for each
volume by Professor J. T. Shotwell, was that 'a study be made of the
displacement caused by the war in processes of civilization, in order that
its full lesson should be brought home to the world which would be
bound to appreciate peace all the more because of the catastrophic
nature of the war. . . .'

One interesting manifestation of the liberal sensibility is the manner
in which many distinguished historians, while clearly appreciating the
significance of war in the social changes of the twentieth century, have
perversely preferred to direct their energies towards studying the years
prior to the war. I am afraid the simple fact is that it is *easier* to write
descriptive 'intellectual' history of the years of peace than to analyse the
turbulent events of war. A major and justly-praised contribution to
twentieth-century American history, Henry F. May's *The End of American Innocence: A Study of the First Years of our Own Time 1912–
1917* (1959) contains the remark that 'everybody knows that at some
point in the twentieth century America went through a cultural revolution'. Arguing that the First World War was 'not entirely the dividing
line', Professor May devotes five pages to 'The War and After' and the
rest of a big book to the pre-war years. Nevertheless his few comments
on the war are extremely shrewd. He notes in true 'liberal' style that in
some ways the conservative reaction against the pre-war intellectual and
progressive revolt was strengthened by the war, but adds that the entire
process of revolt and reaction was changed and distorted by the war.
Later he writes:

> The war and its emotions passed with extraordinary suddenness. To
> see the full meaning of the story that ended in 1917 it is necessary to
> look beyond the complementary savage disillusion of the postwar

years. At some time long after the Armistice whistles had stopped blowing, it became apparent that a profound change had taken place in American civilization, a change that affected all the contenders in the prewar cultural strife. This was the end of American innocence. . . .

This change, on the way for a long time and *precipitated by the war*, is worth looking at very briefly as it affected several segments of the increasingly divided nation. The most obvious aspect of change was the complete disintegration of the old order, the set of ideas which had dominated the American mind so effectively from the mid-nineteenth century till 1912. . . .

The American culture of 1912 fell into pieces not because it was attacked but because attack, *combined with the challenge of events*, brought to light its old inadequacies.[9]

This was well said, but what a wealth of complicated experience, the experience of war, is encapsulated in the two phrases I have italicised. This book will endeavour to analyse that experience, shared in greater or lesser degree by most of the developed and many of the underdeveloped societies of the twentieth century. No one has ever pretended that Britain had an innocence to lose, but an argument remarkably similar to May's was presented by S. H. Hynes in *The Edwardian Turn of Mind* (1966).

The 'economists' are those writers who, both at the end of the First World War, and when their interest was rekindled by the advent of the Second World War, gave special attention to the economic reorganisation necessitated by war. An important study in this style, stressing, as he saw it, the striking development of collectivist economic policies during the war is Samuel J. Hurwitz, *State Intervention in Britain* (1949); none the less his book treads a fairly well beaten path, first pioneered by H. L. Gray's *War-time Control of Industry* (1918). In the last few years a more sophisticated form of economic history has begun to appear: an outstanding example is Alan Milward's *The German Economy at War* (1965) which brings out clearly the inadequacies of National Socialist economic planning exposed by the Second World War (followed up by two further equally brilliant studies, *The New Order and the French Economy*, 1970, and *Fascist Economy in Norway*, 1972).

Into the 'sociological' category, not yet a very extensive one, I place those historians who have looked beyond political and economic reorganisation and have, as appropriate, had recourse to some of the conceptual tools provided by sociology. Actually, the question of the social effects of war has not received a great deal of attention from the social scientists, mainly, I am told, because 'war' is too large and imprecise a term for the fastidious sociologist to handle. Two sociological concepts, however, are of value to the historian: first, the notion that war is in some respects analogous to natural *disaster*, and produces similar effects on the social psychology of the peoples involved in it;[10] and second the idea that class structures are altered by *participation* in the war effort of formerly underprivileged social groups.[11] The broader approach can be seen, implicitly, in my *The Deluge: British Society and the First World War* (1965) and in Gerald Feldman's *Army, Industry and Labor in Germany 1914–1918* (1966); and, more explicitly, in my *Britain in the Century of Total War* (1968).

Histories of the Russian Revolution have not on the whole given as much prominence to the war as might be expected: however George Katkov's *Russia 1917* brings out clearly the importance of the participation element in modern war, particularly as it affected the 'voluntary organisations' of middle-class citizens who had previously played little part in public life; and M. T. Florinsky's *End of the Russian Empire* (1931) very much stresses the way in which the existing régime failed to meet the test of war. In the United States, W. E. Leuchtenberg has analysed the relationship between U.S. experience of the First World War and the ideology of the New Deal,[12] and a limited amount of work has been done on the results of black participation in the war effort.[13] For the Second World War, Henri Michel's many works on the French Resistance have, by implication, stressed the military participation effect; there is a brilliant, but brief paper on the social effects of the war for France, published in 1962 by Stanley Hoffman.[14] While Gordon Wright's *The Ordeal of Total War* (1968) inclines towards the liberal interpretation, it is none the less the first general textbook of modern European history to give serious consideration to the social effects of war. (David Thomson's well-known text-book *Europe Since Napoleon*, 1957, frequently *asserts* the importance of war, but scarcely *analyses* it.)

In general, the problems of assessing and analysing the social consequences of war (as distinct from describing or cataloguing them) have proved so enormous that historians have tended to seek refuge in that supreme non-explanation, the metaphor. Thus, in an unimaginative borrowing from the physical sciences, war is described as a *catalyst*, or, more crudely yet, is said to *accelerate*. Sometimes war is said to *dramatise* existing changes, though what in terms of actual historical processes this theatrical image really implies is impossible to determine. Of France and the Second World War Stanley Hoffman has written, 'what the war did was to bring to a climax a number of trends in the Third Republic'. This is fair enough as far as it goes, but that is not very far. Instead of concrete change in a specific temporal context, we are offered a vision of an almighty orgasm of the trends. Worse still is this effort culled from W. A. Robson: 'war is the midwife of change. But the changes which war brings to birth are those whose seeds have long been germinating in the womb of time.'[15] There is plentiful material, then, for a dissertation on 'Gynaecological Imagery and the Study of War', rather less for the analytical study of war itself.

Here, as a working hypothesis, as a means, I hope, of explaining rather than simply describing the effects of war, I shall present a four-tier 'model' of the inter-relationship between war and society. This may well sound pretentious; or it may seem that I am misusing the somewhat trendy term 'model'. A colleague has suggested that 'four-part analytical framework' would be more accurate. However 'model' is brief and convenient, and I propose to stick to it, though I want it to be understood from the outset that what I am trying to do is extremely simple. I am trying to break up the complicated phenomenon of war into the most meaningful and manageable number of components. Imagine you have to *explain*, as well as describe, the effects of a thunderstorm upon a house and the people living in it. Although a thunderstorm is one phenomenon, it is possible to analyse individually the effects of wind, of rain, of lightning, and perhaps even of the psychological implications, for some human beings, of thunder and lightning. In the same way I break war down into its *destructive* aspects, its *test* aspects, its *participation* aspects, and its *psychological* aspects.

Of course the function of the historian is to find out what happened, not to establish the validity of theoretical models: mine is simply a rough tool, which you are at complete liberty to reject. One of the most important aspects of the study, in any case, will be the examination of the way in which different societies react differently to the impact of war. The comparative approach, with or without my particular methodology, should reveal interesting similarities in social experience; but it should also reveal equally interesting divergencies: and, in the end, the unique and the particular are the real stuff of history.

The first tier of the model is founded upon the basic and simple premise that war is *destructive* and *disruptive*. Loss of life, loss of capital, the razing of houses and factories, may well distort a country's entire social development. However, while such negative effects must always remain in the forefront of our thinking about war, destruction on this scale will often also result – as does a natural disaster such as an earthquake – in rapid reconstruction going beyond the limits of what was originally destroyed. Old patterns of living will be disrupted; different (not necessarily better) ones, willy-nilly, will emerge.

The second tier involves a proposition often noted, though never systematically discussed by other writers: war is the supreme challenge to, and test of, a country's military, social, political and economic institutions. If the institutions are inadequate they will collapse, as in Tsarist Russia. But the *test* of war need not provoke *collapse*: it can, given a determined will to victory, provoke *change* in the direction of greater efficiency. For most countries involved in modern war the experience has resulted in, among other things, the testing of the cruder fallacies of economic liberalism, the testing of human reluctance to exploit the full potential of science and technology, and the testing of the general inadequacy of social provision for the weaker members of the community: looking for the moment only at the broad perspective, one can detect change towards management of the economy, towards a more science-conscious society and towards a welfare state. But it must be firmly stressed here that in talking of the *test* of war, no value judgements are involved. It is not being argued that the 'higher' forms of social organisation (whatever that may mean) 'pass' the test, while the 'lower' forms fail. The word is used in a technical way to represent something which, I believe, actually happens, not as a metaphor representing a process somewhat like a school exam. In some ways 'stress', or 'strain', or even 'challenge', might be better words, though they are not quite right: the *test* I have in mind is in effect a mixture of these. It is also important to note that the 'challenge' aspect, acting in conjunction with the disaster syndrome I have just mentioned, may not come fully into play until a war is over – when indeed a society may react quite amazingly to defeat. In many cases the *test*, in its various forms, may be highly undesirable, diverting social institutions away from their legitimate peacetime development. Apart from collapse (which in itself could be considered highly undesirable) the test of war might well produce dictatorship, secret police, censorship, or, at least, centralisation and secrecy, as well as, or instead of, social reform. Once again, our concern is with change as such, not 'good' change or 'bad' change.

The third tier concerns the element of *participation*. Feudal wars were essentially waged by a small aristocratic minority which alone shared in the spoils, with the peasant masses on both sides suffering from their depredations. In modern war there is greater participation on the part of larger, underprivileged groups in society, who tend correspondingly to benefit, or at least to develop a new self-consciousness. In the past most attention has been concentrated upon *guided* social change, upon the conscious efforts of governments to buy the support of, or to reward, such groups mainly through the processes of legislation. But participation in the war effort also involves, irrespective of direct government action, a strengthened market position, and hence higher material standards, for such groups; it also engenders a new sense of status, usually leading to a dropping of former sectional or class barriers. These are *unguided* social changes.

Finally war is a colossal *psychological* experience. This might be regarded as merely an extension of the idea of war as disaster, and has been so regarded by some sociologists. But war is not just an external phenomenon; it involves many of the psychological responses more properly likened to those of the great revolutions in history. In fact this tier is directly related to each of the other three, but so important is it for a proper assessment of the great changes in the arts, religious beliefs, and intellectual attitudes which accompany modern war, that it must, for analytical purposes, be treated separately.

Throughout this book I shall use this model as my frame of reference in order to explain the effects of war. But to stick rigidly to the model in every chapter would not only do violence to the infinite complexity of the historical process and to the uniqueness of individual events, and relations between events within that process, but would also be very boring. Thus, though I see the model as playing a central organising and explanatory role, I leave the exact shape of each chapter to be determined by the historical reality as I perceive it. The main changes which I wish to discuss can be identified under the following headings (and these, in sum, are what I mean by 'social change' when I talk of 'war and social change'): first, changes in *social geography*, including population, urbanisation and distribution of industry; second, *economic changes*, including changes in theory and attitudes, in activities and structures, and in the exploitation of technology and science; third – a point directly related to the participation tier of my model – changes in *social structure* and changes in and between groups and classes in the community; fourth, changes in *social cohesion*, particularly in regard to racial minorities; fifth, changes in *social ideas and welfare policies*; sixth, changes in *material conditions*; seventh, changes in *customs and behaviour*; eighth – mainly related to the fourth tier of my model – changes in *intellectual and artistic attitudes*; and ninth, changes in *political institutions and ideas*. I make a distinction between economic theory and economic activities, and between social and welfare policies and social conditions and customs, because of the vitally important distinction between guided social change and unguided social change. Many mistakes have been made in assessing the social consequences of war through placing too strong an emphasis on guided change. It is easy to compile a list of social welfare acts coming at the end of a war, and then to point out how little actual effect on social conditions much of this legislation had. But social change is not exclusively dependent upon the will and whims of politicians and social theorists. What I do claim for my model is that it directs attention to the unguided changes which come about irrespective of the good or bad intentions of politicians and theorists.

It may well be that the main social changes which have characterised the twentieth century would have come anyway without the havoc and horror of war. 'Might-have-beens' ('counter-factual conditional concepts' in the pompous language of the econometric historians) can be valuable aids to analysis, but in the end the historian is concerned with the facts as they are: a substantial proportion of the twentieth-century social experience has been consumed by war; and even countries which remained neutral were in practice directly affected by that experience. Certainly there would be no point in studying the effects of war on any society without first grasping firmly the essential features of that society, the processes of change already in motion within that society on the eve of war. So also is it essential to take into account the different intensities with which war impinged on different societies: the devastated defeated power at one end of the scale, the prosperous neutral at the other. Whether a country is technically on the winning or losing side seems to have been of decreasing social relevance in modern total war.

## IV    *Germany, Russia, France, Britain and the United States in 1914*

There are various ways of comparing the 'essential features' of different countries. We may, or we may not, feel it to be possible to talk of differing 'national characteristics'; but we are on safe and sensible ground if we start off with geography.

In 1914, as today, the United States and Russia were the giants. With a total geographical area of about 8·5 million square miles Russia stood out as by far the biggest continuous political unit in the world. She had a population of 130 millions, whereas the United States, covering a total geographical area of just over 3 million square miles had a population of about 82 millions. Outside Russia, France was the largest country in Europe, but even so her total area only came to 213,000 square miles. Germany, with 208,000 square miles, was only slightly smaller, but Great Britain was less than half the size of France with an area of only 88,755 square miles. Population statistics, however, cast a rather different light on the three European countries: Germany had a population of about 66 millions, Britain almost 41 millions, France less than 40 millions; everywhere the rate of increase in population was levelling off, but in France this was already a matter of specially serious concern.

Britain and France were more close-knit and homogeneous countries than any of the others. Britain is an island, 375 miles wide at its maximum extent, and 750 miles long. Though there are no great extremes either of climate or of landscape the country does divide neatly into three regions: the lowland area mainly concentrated in the south, the upland area of the north of England, south Wales, and south Scotland, and the highland area of central Wales and north Scotland. England's earliest prosperity had derived from the agricultural wealth of the lowland south, but the industrial revolution, upon which Britain's wealth still rested in 1914 had taken place in the upland areas. The highland areas had been largely left in a state of neglect. Natural supplies of water and coal had stood Britain in good stead, and she was still a very prosperous nation in 1914, though her industrial position was being steadily challenged by Germany and the United States. With 35 per cent of the world's trade Britain was still the world's greatest trading nation.

France has a coastline 12,925 miles long, and no part of the country is more than 300 miles from the coast. While Britain's island position had isolated her from the worst continental conflicts, France, in the previous century, had twice suffered invasion and defeat. None the less her racially homogeneous population had shown immense resilience and strong national feeling. Physically the country can be divided into two parts: the lowlands, stretching north of a line from Bordeaux to Reims; and the highlands to the south, around the Massif Centrale. Agriculture was still the greatest industry in France, with more than half the population living and working on the land. Indeed France suffered from a lack of the natural resources, particularly coal, needed for industrial development. Her 1913 coal output of 41 million tons compared sadly with Germany's 279 million tons and Britain's 292 million tons, so that France was heavily dependent on coal imports. The continued and growing importance of luxury goods for export, and the tendency of French industry in general to concentrate on the home market, meant that her industries were, on the whole, comparatively small. Such large industries as she had were mainly concentrated in five departments in the north-east, the part of the country most open to invasion from Germany.

Although the German people had a long history, the German State had only existed since 1871; in it Prussia predominated, but there was much evidence of stormy local loyalties to the separate states which made up the German empire. The empire included part of the ancient kingdom of Poland (which had been partitioned between Prussia, Russia and Austria in the eighteenth century) and there was a substantial Danish minority in Schleswig–Holstein. Physically Germany divides into four broad regions: first, the north German lowlands; second, the southern transitional borderlands, which are extremely rich farmland; third, the central uplands; and fourth, the alpine foreland and German Alps. Germany was already an extremely powerful industrial country, but much of her industry was concentrated in the Ruhr area. Large, almost feudal, farming areas existed in the east where ownership was vested in the Prussian 'Junker' gentry; and much of the south still followed a pastoral existence which did not seem to have changed much over the centuries. Of the 5·75 million agricultural properties in Germany on the eve of war, over 4 million were small peasant holdings.

Less than half of the Russian population in 1914 were Great Russians; the remaining half was divided among a large number of different minority groups, including Poles, Finns and Jews. Russia sprawls into Europe and right across Asia. Although she had developed a sophisticated civilisation based on St Petersburg and Moscow, in the eyes of western Europe she seemed, as far as her Asiatic part was concerned at any rate, a semi-barbarous country. Clearly the immense size and range of Russia presented peculiar problems of government and communication. Physically the country can be divided into the great Russian lowlands, the Urals, the west Siberian plain and plateau, and the southern mountains and plateau. Though 27,000 miles of the country's frontiers (two thirds of the total) are provided by the sea, yet Russia is very definitely a land country, since so much of her coastline is permanently frozen-up or otherwise unsuitable for sea-going traffic. The Russian climate is one of bitter extremes, whereas those of the other three European countries are relatively temperate, with southern France and southern Germany enjoying warm, relatively stable summers.

Whatever naval ambitions the two eastern powers might cherish, and whatever hatreds for each other they might nourish, Germany and Russia were brought together as being very definitely land powers. As an off-shore island, with the wider world at her feet, Britain was the most outward-looking of the European countries, though France, too, had shared enthusiastically in colonial ventures. Apart from overseas exploits the European countries had all been involved in internal European squabbles and conflicts, though since 1815 Britain's only European engagement had been against Russia in the Crimean war. Thus far the United States had stood proudly apart from the conflicts of old Europe.

Physically, the United States is roughly divided by the three great mountain ranges. Starting from the east they are the Appalachians, the Rockies, and the Sierra Nevada in the far west. East of the Appalachians are the Atlantic coastlands. Between the Appalachians and the Rockies lies the 'central valley', stretching from the Great Lakes to the gulf of Mexico. The central valley itself is divided and watered by the Mississippi–Missouri rivers and their tributaries. West of the Rockies lies an area of desert, separated from the fertile Pacific coastline by the Sierra Nevada and the Cascade mountains. But this physical division of the United States fails to describe the variety of regions in the country, though undoubtedly it determines the basic composition of these regions. In the extreme north-east lies New England, an area of mountains, lakes, and rocky headlands, with a climate similar to, but more extreme than that of its namesake. Further west are the mid-Atlantic states, New York, Delaware, Pennsylvania, and so on, which are milder in climate than New England. By 1914 these two regions were the industrial heart of the United States. Further west again lie the states of the mid-west and the great plains, the great farming and cattle-raising regions of the United States. To the east these states enjoy a fairly temperate climate, but further west there are great extremes of hot and cold, and the constant threat of drought. The far west consists of mountains, the arid deserts, and also the fertile, warm, fruit-growing Pacific coastlands. The south, an area from Texas to the east coast, from Maryland to Florida, has a climate ranging from Mediterranean to tropical, suitable for the cotton, tobacco, rice, and sugar grown there on small farmsteads. In 1914 the south was one of the most backward areas of the United States, lacking any major industry, poor in transport facilities, and still suffering in the shadow of defeat in the American Civil War, which still cast divisive influences over the whole of American society.

The United States was still a nation of immigrants. In fact the period from 1903 to 1914 saw immigration reach its peak with more than six million people, mainly from Italy, south-eastern Europe and Russia, entering the country annually. And as a historical relic of the institution of slavery the United States had a substantial black population. Though in some respects the most free and democratic of all the nations under review here, the United States was the least homogeneous racially. Russia in 1914 was ruled by a Tsarist autocracy. The few modest experiments in parliamentary institutions had been largely abandoned by 1914. The vast mass of the country were peasants with few political rights; serfdom had only been abolished in 1861. Although positive attempts to speed up industrialisation had been made since the turn of the century there was still not much of a middle class in Russia. Assassination and terror had for centuries formed almost an integral part of Russian politics, and continued to do so into the twentieth century. Military failure in the Russo-Japanese war had, in 1905–6 brought slight modifications in the structure of autocracy. While the old State Council was reorganised to become the upper chamber of the Russian Parliament, a new lower chamber (the Duma) was created, based, however, on a franchise which gave preponderant weight to the big landed interests. The Duma had no say in the selection of the Council of Ministers (or 'cabinet') or of the Prime Minister; opposition to the autocracy was expressed through two upper-middle-class liberal parties, the Octobrists and the Kadets, and through the socialist parties, the Socialist Revolutionaries (most moderate, despite the title), the Mensheviks (strictly 'minority' wing of the Social Democrats – though this was on the basis of one vote at one meeting), and the Bolsheviks ('majority' wing of the Social Democrats, and most militant in their commitment to revolution). The most satisfying outlets for practical political action were to be found in the *Zemstvos* (rural councils) and the Municipal councils.

The German empire had a parliament and universal male suffrage; yet it too shared some of the characteristics of a feudal autocracy. While the entire German people were represented in the *Reichstag* elected by all adult males, there was also a federal council to which the rulers and governments of the twenty-five federated states directly appointed their representatives. The presidency of this council, and the running of government, belonged to the Imperial Chancellor, who was appointed by the Emperor and was not responsible to the *Reichstag*. Prussian predominance was ensured by the provision that all Prussian military legislation must automatically be adopted by the other states; frequently, as we shall see when we look at the course of the First World War, Prussian ministries were more important than the often nebulous imperial ones. The Prussian state parliament (*Landtag*) was based on an electoral system of 'classes', reminiscent of that of the Duma, designed to ensure the supremacy of the Junkers. The officer caste of the army enjoyed a special position of power and prestige. A bustling and self-confident industrial class, aided by the tame and disciplined submission exhibited by the many, spearheaded Germany's rise to industrial power; and German businessmen had shown themselves very willing to exploit the resources of science for industrial gain. There was a strong and highly organised Social Democratic party, but working-class activists were treated almost as aliens in their own land. While a few workers were organised in the 'respectable' Catholic and Hirsch-Duncker (liberal) unions, it was clear by 1914 that the 'free' socialist unions had become the main vehicle of working-class action, though their membership was still well below one million. There was an upper-middle-class liberal party, the Progressives, and a powerful Catholic party, called the Centre, though in fact rather to the right of the political centre; strongly entrenched still further to the right were the National Liberals and the Conservatives. None the less Germany had an enviable tradition of government-sponsored social reform, and had led the world with her social insurance scheme against sickness.

France had universal male suffrage, and, unlike Germany, responsible as well as representative government. The main problem in France was that of a weak executive. According to the constitution as it had developed after 1871, considerable powers rested with the President of the Republic; but in practice these powers were subordinate to those of the French parliament. The position of the Council of Ministers and its President depended upon the will of parliament. But this President of the Council did not have the powers of a British Prime Minister; he was constantly at the mercy of the whims of parliament. Thus French politics before 1914 had presented a picture of a succession of rather weak governments, none in practice differing very strongly from its predecessors. When discussing American or British politics in the First World War it is meaningful to speak of a 'Democratic President', or a 'Liberal Prime Minister'; in France there were all sorts of liberals, 'Radicals', 'Radical Socialists', and so on, all in fact standing for the bourgeois middle, which was flanked on one side by various kinds of 'Socialists' and 'Syndicalists', and on the other by ultra-Catholics and monarchists. Administration in France was highly centralised, and the prefects who headed each department were appointees of the central government. Thus the political reform movement already in being in France before the war, by a curious paradox, aimed on the one hand at strengthening executive government, while on the other it aimed at strengthening the power of local elected bodies at the expense of the centrally appointed prefects.

Britain in 1914 could scarcely be described as a democracy: as was the case everywhere else, save for New Zealand, some of the Scandinavian countries and a few states in America, no women had the vote; but apart from that forty per cent of all adult males did not have the vote either. What Britain did have was a highly developed form of parliamentary government in which government and opposition both played important roles. A strong executive government was able to carry through positive policies; if these policies failed to please, then, after a general election, the government could be replaced by the erstwhile opposition party. Although a monarchy, effective power in Britain rested with the Prime Minister and his ministerial colleagues. The rights of local authorities were still jealously guarded, and there was no system of centralisation as in France.

Unlike Britain or the French Third Republic, the government of the United States was based on one written constitution. Moreover it was a constitution which, with minor amendments, had been continuously in effect since 1789. It certainly had not been written with the conditions of the twentieth century in mind. The Federal Government was divided into three branches: the Executive, in the form of the President; the Legislature, consisting of two houses, the Senate and the House of Representatives; and the Judiciary, the Federal courts, chief of which was the Supreme Court. Government was still strictly by the letter of the Constitution and although the President and the Congress were free to interpret it as they wished, the courts had the last word. Thus the Supreme Court could declare any executive or legislative act unconstitutional. The aim was a balance of power between the various branches of the government; this tended, though not to the same degree as in France, to undermine the powers of the executive.

Although there were strong overtones of feudalism in Russia, and even in Germany, the basic principles of political, economic and social action obtaining in all countries in 1914, were those of individualism and *laissez faire*. However, there was discernible everywhere, and even in Russia, a movement towards ameliorating the worst of the abuses of unrestricted private enterprise. Nowhere had these movements got very far, and they were all conceived within the existing capitalist framework, aiming at no more than piecemeal reform of manifest individual abuses. German social welfare legislation has already been mentioned. France, on account of an older tradition rather than because of recent developments, was more prepared than the other western countries to accept centralised control. In both Britain and France there were similar collectivist measures, culminating in Britain in the intensive legislative programme of the Liberal government in office after 1906; yet even this programme must, I believe, be seen as falling within the context of nineteenth-century individualist ideas. There was a socialist movement as well as a strong middle-class 'Progressive' movement in the United States, and in Britain there had appeared the still very small Labour party advocating socialist policies. There was a strong Socialist party in France, where, however, the conflict between Catholics and anti-clericals tended to divert attention and energies from positive social reform. There was a very strong women's suffrage movement in the United States, which had already made prohibition of alcohol one of its planks. The suffragists and suffragettes were very active in Britain, too, and in Germany; rather less so in France. They were practically non-existent in Russia, though there was a feminist tradition among some upper-class women.

All the major countries shared in certain common trends, particularly the trend towards urbanisation. In 1914 this trend had gone furthest in Britain; it had gone much less far in France; and least far in Russia, though here, crucially from point of view of the link between overcrowding and aggressive behaviour, the *rate* of growth was very high in the last two decades before 1914. The rate of urbanisation was also great in Germany: in 1870 one third of all Germans lived in towns, by 1914 two thirds were living in towns. No wonder German society presented such an aggressive appearance! The United States, too, was rapidly beginning to embark on the process of urbanisation in the last decades before 1914. In 1880 the number of American cities with a population of 100,000 or more was 19; in 1900 it was 36; and in 1910 it was 50. By 1914 more than a third of the total population of the United States had congregated in the urban areas; but in Britain well over half the population had been living in towns and cities since the middle of the nineteenth century.

In many ways Great Britain had the most rigid social hierarchy, with a city-based proletariat, amounting to about eighty per cent of the total population, sharply cut-off from the middle and upper classes. Political, social, and economic power was largely concentrated in the hands of a ruling class made up of the old landed aristocracy and the more successful products of the business and commercial class. In France there was a well defined conflict of interest between the relatively small industrial proletariat and the peasant proprietors, whose economic position might not be very strong. The old aristocratic interests still had considerable influence in the army and in certain other professions; because of the complex revolutionary history through which France had gone politics were probably more open to genuine middle-class influences than they were in Britain. In most respects the United States was a much more open and mobile society than either of these two European countries. In theory at least, there was no traditional aristocracy, though in practice in certain areas local ascendency had certainly been achieved by long-established groups (this was particularly true of the White Anglo-Saxon Protestants – WASPS – in New England and the Planters in the South). Against the undoubted opportunities for social mobility must be set the depressed position of the blacks and of many recent European immigrants; furthermore, sharp conflicts were already apparent between the employing classes and labour.

## Notes and References

1. W. S. Churchill, *The World Crisis*, vol. I (1923) pp. 10–11.
2. Report by Police President of Hamburg on raids of July and August 1943, quoted in Sir Charles Webster and N. Frankland, *The Strategic Air Offensive Against Germany, 1939–1945*, vol. IV (1961) pp. 314–15.
3. *The World Crisis*, vol. VI (1931) p. 451.
4. K. Lorenz, *On Aggression*, trans. M. Latzke (1966).
5. In my article 'The Impact of the First World War on British Society', *Journal of Contemporary History*, III (January 1968), I used the term 'whig', for which Alan Milward, *The Economic Effects of the Two World Wars on Britain* (1970) p. 11, has reasonably substituted 'liberal'.
6. Cyril Falls, *The Place of War in History* (1947) p. 6.
7. Correlli Barnett, *The Swordbearers* (1963) p. 11. Note also J. Terraine, *The Western Front* (1964) pp. 114–15: 'It is largely hypocrisy to discover "virtues" in war; yet it is hypocrisy too to pretend that there are none.'
8. Graham Greene and Carol Reed, *The Third Man* (1968 edn) p. 114n.
9. H. F. May, *The End of American Innocence* (1959) pp. 393–8.
10. An older classic is P. A. Sorokin, *Man and Society in Calamity* (1943). Among many useful recent works are G. W. Baker and D. D. Chapman eds), *Man and Society in Disaster* (1962); A. H. Barton, *Social Organization under Stress* (1963); and F. C. Iklé, *The Social Impact of Bomb Destruction* (1958), Quincy B. Wright's well-known *A Study of War*, 2 vols (1942) I have personally found too general to be of great help in my own studies. In many respects Wright represented the 'liberal' view point, e.g. in his statement on p. 272 of vol. I: 'The preceding survey suggests that in the most recent stage of world-civilization war has made for instability, for disintegration, for despotism, and for unadaptability, rendering the course of civilization less predictable and continued progress towards achievement of its values less probable.'
11. The idea (obvious enough, as the best ideas are) has been put forward in many places, but was first clearly formulated by S. Andreski in his *Military Organization and Society* (1954) pp. 33–8. It appears implicitly in Gaston Boutoul, *La Phénomène – Guerre* (1962) pp. 227–9. See also

Hans Speier, *Social Order and the Risks of War* (1952) especially pp. 252, 261–2. Andreski speaks of a Military Participation Ratio (M.P.R.). I prefer simply to speak of 'participation' or 'wartime participation' since civilian employment in wartime was so often more important than military. For hints of 'M.P.R.' and 'Destruction' ideas, see also A. Pizzorno on 'War and Society' in *A New Europe?* ed. S. R. Graubard (1964) pp. 267–8.

12. W. E. Leuchtenberg, 'The New Deal and the Analogue of War', *Change and Continuity in Twentieth-Century America*, ed. John Braeman, Robert H. Bremner and Everett Walters (1966).

13. However, see the excellent work of Neil Wynn on the Afro-American and the Second World War, particularly his article, 'The Impact of the Second World War on the American Negro', *Journal of Contemporary History*, VI, 2 (April 1971).

14. Stanley Hoffman, 'The Effects of World War II on French Society and Politics', *French Historical Studies*, I (April 1961).

15. W. A. Robson, 'Nationalised Industries in Britain and France', *American Political Science Review*, 44 (June 1950) p. 303. Hoffman's phrase is to to be found in his article, cited above.

# 2. The First World War: Germany and Russia

## I  The Stages of the War

The war began with Germany in alliance with Austria–Hungary against France, Britain and Russia; the United States joined on the side of the western powers in April 1917. Although victory finally went to the west, the first major power to suffer defeat was in fact Russia, which was forced at the end of 1917 to conclude the humiliating truce of Brest-Litovsk with Germany (confirmed in the peace treaty of March 1918). The German plan was to knock France out first, while maintaining a purely defensive posture against Russia; then to turn to Russia. Although the plan failed, a substantial section of French territory, amounting to about ten per cent of the total area, was in fact invaded and became a permanent scene of warfare till the very last months of the war. German territory, on the other hand, remained intact until these final stages. Russia, from the spring of 1915, also suffered from invasion by German and Austro-Hungarian troops. Britain suffered a few air attacks, but like the United States did not suffer from direct invasion. It is the two defeated powers, Russia and Germany (and also, of course, Austria–Hungary) which underwent forms of revolution, while the victors did not. Clearly the effect of invasion and defeat is an important one; yet in many other respects what is most striking is the similarity of the experience which all countries went through – many of the differences in outcome seem to be explicable in terms of the pre-war characteristics of these countries rather than by differences in the military effects of the war.

The division of the war into three separate stages holds up remarkably well for all the European countries. The first one, the period of the outbreak of war and of 'business as usual' lasts until early 1915 (it

For Notes and References to this chapter, see p. 51 below.

ended first in Germany, and last in Russia). The second period is the one in which the realities of total war began to impress themselves on all the belligerents and the first serious signs of the various changes associated with war began to be seen: this period lasts until late 1916. The final period is the period of crisis and revolution, or, particularly in Britain, the period of grim determination to make all necessary reorganisations to ensure a successful conclusion to the war. The United States, entering the war only in the period of crisis and revolution, went through these phases in a telescoped form, though it should also be noted that some of the effects of war were felt very strongly in the United States long before her actual entry into hostilities.

## II  Germany's 'Fortress Truce', August 1914 – November 1917

Germany's declaration of war on Russia and France seems to have been greeted with the same kind of hysterical enthusiasm with which crowds of ordinary people in every country demonstrated that there really was a 'will to war' in pre-1914 Europe: exuberance was not restrained by the news that from midnight (Berlin time) Britain too was involved, though this meant, among other things, that the 'Café Piccadilly' in Berlin had to become 'Café Vaterland'. Yet some contemporary evidence does suggest that below the surface there existed real fears that 'encirclement' might now be more than a nightmare.[1] The immediate emotional impact of war took two forms: hysteria against the 'outsider', and a deep sense of togetherness among the German people themselves.

On 2 August the state of *Burgfrieden* (literally, 'fortress truce') was declared. The expression is a medieval one and implied that just as all personal feuds among the defenders in a beleaguered fortress were suspended till the defeat of the enemy, so now the German employers and trade unions agreed to suspend all labour strife for the duration of the war. The German Social Democrats, as members of the Socialist International, were committed to the policy that, should 'capitalist' war break out, socialists should not take part in it, but should instead turn the occasion to the advantage of socialism and the working class. The government's mobilisation plan called for the arrest of all socialist leaders the moment it went into operation. But, in the event, the Social Democrats gave their support to the war; and the government decided not to arrest the socialist leaders. There was a ban on the sale of socialist literature at military installations and at railway stations, but this was lifted on 2 September.

The German Social Democrats had a very strict code of party discipline; there was a strong minority opposed to the war, but majority opinion prevailed, and, in the Reichstag, the party voted *en bloc* in favour of the granting of war credits to the government. Gradually, however, as the war wore on, a definite split developed between the Majority Social Democrats and the Independent Socialists who took up a positive anti-war stand (in 1916, furthermore, the extreme Marxist group, the Spartacists was formed – though till the end of the war they remained part of the parent Socialist party). But in 1914 the position was as one socialist deputy, who was personally in sympathy with the minority, explained it:

> We stand today before the brutal fact of war, and the terrible threat of enemy invasion. The decision to be made is not whether to take sides for or against the war but rather on the means necessary for the defence of our country. Our heartiest wishes go out to our brethren, irrespective of party affiliations, who are called to the colours. Much if not all would be lost to our people and its future independence in the event of a victory for Russian despotism.[2]

Intellectuals as well as trade unionists and Socialists rallied enthusiastically to the national cause. Max Weber, the sociologist, declared to a friend that 'this war with all its ghastliness is nevertheless grand and wonderful. It is worth experiencing.'[3] There was truth in the Kaiser's emotional utterance of 4 August, 'henceforth I know no parties, only Germans'.

Hatred of the enemy was canalised (not created) by postcards with such slogans as: *Jeder Schuss ein Russ* ('every shot, a Russki'); *Jeder Stoss ein Franzos* ('for every blow a Frenchy'); *Jeder Tritt ein Britt* ('for every step, a Brit'). And by such songs as Ernst Lissauer's 'Hymn of Hate':

> Hate by water and hate by land;
> Hate by heart and hate of the hand;
> We love as one and hate as one;
> We have but one foe alone – England.[4]

Germany proved possibly even more prone to spy scares than any other country (with the possible exception, later, of the United States). As a Danish-speaking deputy from Schleswig–Holstein noted sardonically early in August:

The Gods alone know how many 'spies' have been beaten and imprisoned today! The mobilised reserve officers do not get by unmolested. They have in many instances become fat and round during peace-time and perhaps their bad-looking uniforms account for the mistakes in identity. It is commonly believed that spies go around dressed like Prussian officers.[5]

The social narrative of the war well fits the three-fold division given above – with the final stage culminating in revolution. Germany mobilised her army of 5,250,000 much more efficiently than any other country; none the less, the period to the beginning of 1915 was marked by the same kind of sheer unawareness of the economic and social implications of this mighty war of the nations as we shall find in even greater degree in the other countries.

From the beginning of 1915 to the end of the year we have a middle period in which, as much because of the enforced state of siege as because of any innate German 'efficiency', more effective forms of government control over the national effort were established. In December 1916 there were drastic changes in the German High Command designed to bring more unified control; but 1917 was a year of hardship and political crisis. After the hopeful news of the big German advances on the western front in March 1918 there was a collapse into greater despondency and privation: this is the period of run-up to the German Revolution, which we shall consider in a separate section.

One distinctive feature of the outbreak of war in all countries was the spate of emergency legislation. The *Reichsbank* discontinued redemption of notes in gold on 31 July and special 'Loan Banks' were established to provide credits for business. It became extremely difficult to change large notes as people hoarded the smaller silver coins. General mobilisation was accompanied by the proclamation, in each of the twenty-four army corps' districts into which the empire was divided, of the Prussian Law of Siege (Bavaria, however, was excepted). The proclamation, followed in traditional style by three trumpet blasts, gave sole responsibility for 'public safety' to the Deputy Commanding Generals in each district. The sense of immediate emergency lifted fairly quickly in Germany (as also in Britain) when it became clear that any fears of direct invasion were unfounded. But, as was to be expected, the economy as a whole suffered severe dislocation and general industrial activity dropped by about 30 or 40 per cent. In 1913 unemployment had run at 2·9 per cent; in August 1914 it rose to

22·4 per cent, but thereafter it fell off rapidly to 15·7 per cent in September, 10·9 per cent in October, and 8·2 per cent in November.

Because of her 'encircled' position Germany very quickly found herself facing drastic scarcities. By October all reserves were used up, so that she became completely dependent upon new production; in November both munitions and agricultural production had reached crisis point. From the very beginning the problem had been foreseen by Walter Rathenau, a leading Jewish industrialist: thanks to his persistence and initiative a War Raw Materials Department (K.R.A.), which created government control of procurement of raw materials, was established in August. But when Rathenau also suggested that the War Ministry should control food supply this was turned down as beyond the scope of military authority. But for the mass utilisation by Professor Fritz Haber of his process for fixing nitrogen from the air, agricultural and munitions production might well have failed to survive the first months of war – a good example of war fostering the exploitation of a previous scientific discovery.

The story of the establishment of the War Wheat Corporation (November 1914) shows clearly the conflict of interests which bedevilled the German war effort, and the manner in which collaboration between big business and the Prussian government was to set the pattern for the second phase of the war. As early as September two industrialists, Alfred Hugenberg and Hugo Stinnes, together with some mayors from the Ruhr, sought government aid for the establishment of a corporation to buy up two million tons of wheat in order (the concern was national rather than social) to raise prices, reduce consumption, and save food for the following year. Since the Imperial State Secretary of the Interior, Clemens von Delbrück, rejected the plan, its supporters turned to the Prussian Ministry of Finance (there was no Finance Ministry for the Empire as a whole), where they got a specially warm welcome from the under-secretary Georg Michaelis (a name to remember). When the Corporation was established, Michaelis became its head; business operations were in the hands of officials of two major private companies, North German Lloyd and the Hamburg–America line.[6]

Various restrictions and controls were introduced in 1915. 'War bread', which contained a proportion of 'ersatz' (substitute) material – potato to begin with, later turnips – had been introduced in October 1914: bread cards for rationing appeared in January, followed shortly by cards for fats, milk, meat and butter. In October two meatless days per week were legally imposed. Already German civilians were undergoing conditions which did not reach Britain for another two years. In March beer production was cut to 60 per cent of the pre-war level, and by the end of 1915 to 25 per cent. In a situation of growing labour shortage rival industrialists began to 'raid' each others' factories for workers: thus in January it was decreed that no workman could move without a 'leaving certificate'. However, so strong was the force of *participation* that leaving certificates were not withheld if the worker had *bona fide* been offered a higher wage. Other consequences of wartime participation can also be clearly detected. In November 1914 the socialists and the trade unions mounted a massive campaign against rising prices; early in the following year the imperial government, fearful that the *Burgfrieden* might break down, introduced a system of price controls. At about the same time a youthful labour expert from the Society for Social Reform, Dr Tiburtius, was brought into the Prussian War Ministry where he strongly advocated more equal relations between workers and employers. Labour leaders, too, found themselves welcomed into a kind of tacit partnership with General Groener, chief of the War Ministry.

Even national minorities looked to be making substantial gains, despite the initial attempts of the military authorities to cow their leaders. Soon after the war began one Polish deputy boasted: 'The Foreign Office is soft as prunes these days. It is willing to make large concessions to us. It understands how to estimate our strategic strength.'[7] By December the Centre Party was calling for the abolition of the Exceptional Laws (which imposed disabilities on national minorities): 'We must enter upon a new Germany, a greater Germany – greater in righteousness. We must set a good example to the whole world.'[8] It is a key argument in this book that such emotional utterances must not be dismissed out of hand. But they must yield proper place to the unpremeditated realities of war, recognised, for instance, by another Polish minority leader when he remarked: 'We now have a million Poles under arms, 600,000 in the Prussian and Austrian armies and 400,000 in the Russian army. We are thus a belligerent power and should take advantage of the situation.'[9]

Despite the new restrictions and controls, this middle period of the war began to show very clearly some of the basic weaknesses in Germany's position. Despite the needs of war German agriculture was going into steady decline: vital manpower had been carted off to the front, and there was a desperate shortage of fertilisers; farmers were harried by petty bureaucrats and had their best horses taken by the army; they were forced to slaughter their pigs, and they were not allocated enough fodder for their surviving animals; the entire land was suffering from over-cultivation. The harvest of 1916 fell below expectation by a million tons; requisitions from conquered territories and imports from Austria and from such neutrals as Holland and Denmark could not make good the shortfall. It was just as really terrible shortages of food and fuel, which culminated in the notorious 'Turnip Winter' of 1916–17, began to appear that the new semi-dictatorship of Hindenburg as Chief of the General Staff and Ludendorff as First-Quarter-Master-General was announced (29 August 1916) in place of the discredited military command of Falkenhayn.

At the end of the year the 'Hindenburg programme' of all-out 'war socialism' was promulgated. A law of 5 December 1916 created the 'Patriotic Auxiliary Service' into which every male German citizen between seventeen and sixty, not already on active service, was to be drafted. However, it remained possible for the rich and influential to buy their way out, while, paradoxically, the main long term effect was to intensify the co-operation between government and the official leaders of organised labour. While membership of the free trade unions had declined in the first two years of the war, it now began to rise again, from 967,000 in 1916 to 1,107,000 at the end of 1917. German organisation for war now reached its peak. For the first time there were systematic attempts to exploit the labour-power of women, though women were specifically excluded from the compulsory aspects of the Hindenburg programme. Nothing was done about the flourishing black market, which indeed became almost a systematic organisation in its own right.

As 1917 began, grievances and social tensions broke out into the open. In the Reichstag on 22 March 1917, an Independent Socialist deputy expostulated:

It appears as if neither the House nor the government knows the conditions prevailing in the country. It appears not to be known, or they pretend not to know that workers collapse at their work because of hunger. Although censorship bars much of what happens in the country from publication, it is known well enough. Gentlemen don't try to deny it, but use your efforts to overcome famine as soon as possible.

By April it was obvious to the government that it would have to impose a cut in the bread ration from 200 grams to 170 grams a day. Significantly the government first entered into negotiations with the trade union leaders; official leaders, however, were no longer in control of their embittered rank-and-file. The Kaiser, in his Easter message, promised 'the extension of our political, economic and social life, as soon as the state of war allows'. Then, in a sentence which summarises both the propagandist and the practical implications of wartime parti- cipation, he declared that: 'After the great achievements of the whole people in this terrible struggle, there is no room, in our opinion, for the three-class franchise.' Six days later Bethmann-Hollweg referred to 'the transformation of our political life, which in spite of all opposition must result from the experiences of the war'.[10] The government's ner- vousness was intensified by the feeling that unrestricted submarine warfare, resumed in February in a desperate bid to bring the war to an end, was not producing the desired results; instead, 2 April brought American entry on the side of the western Allies. The bread cuts had to be announced on 15 April: they were followed at once by demon- stration strikes of at least 300,000 workers in Berlin and Leipzig. Accordingly the bread cuts were withdrawn, though the government seemed powerless to handle a situation in which, increasingly, citizens were not able to obtain the ration to which they were officially entitled. In Leipzig the employers agreed to increase wages and to cut the working week to fifty-two hours.

Such formal gains do not, of course, make up for the hardships and risks of war; but they are very important in the long-term history of German labour. Perhaps, in the long view, the *test* to German political institutions did not produce quite such important results. The roots of the political crisis of July 1917 lie in the discontents which broke out in April and again in June, when there were widespread strikes and food riots, and a hunger strike on board the ship *Prince Regent Leo- pold* (treated seriously enough by the government for the ringleaders to be executed). The flaws in the structure of imperial Germany were being cruelly exposed: labour leaders, now often working closely with the creaking bureaucracy, denounced the farmers for hoarding food; the farmers denounced the restrictions and directives issued by the bureaucracy. In a move which has strangely archaic associations, mili- tary commissions were established to take stock of all foodstuffs held by farmers. Two external events provided a further stimulus towards political crisis: the February revolution in Russia; and the interna- tional socialist conference held in Stockholm in June 1917, at which representatives of both groups of German socialists met representatives from the neutral countries (though socialists from the western Allies were prevented by their own governments from attending).

More significant than the attitude of the socialists, who, after Stockholm, were convinced that Germany must seek a negotiated peace, was that of many German Conservatives. On 3 July the *Berliner Tageblatt* published an appeal for reform from leading conservatives who included Professor Hans Delbruck, Professor Friedrich Meinecke, Professor Ernst Troeltsch, Herr Dominicus (the Chief Burgomaster of Berlin) and Count von Monts (former ambassador at Rome). The appeal exemplifies many of the characteristics of the social thinking induced by war:

> The gigantic struggle in which the German people is engaged is not yet ended. The undersigned have hitherto been of the opinion that the promises contained in the Imperial Easter message could be carried out without too hard an internal struggle, in collaboration with the conservative forces in our public life. The resistance, however, from these quarters is so strong that doubts must arise as to the full realization of the Easter message in its present spirit after the conclusion of peace. Such a doubt is today unbearable. To maintain that faith with the German people to which it is today entitled it is necessary to get to work without delay. We therefore do not hesitate publicly to emphasize the demand of the hour, namely, that the German government shall forthwith lay before the Landtag franchise reforms which shall contain provisions for not only a general, direct, and secret, but also an equal franchise, and the Government shall, in addition, give effective and definite expression to the confidence which the German people deserve.[11]

Two days later Matthias Erzberger, a leading figure in the Centre Party, made a significant speech in which, incidentally, he drew attention to the manner in which newspaper advertisements continue to have value as an independent primary source even in time of censorship: 'In the German papers one does not find anything offered as often as one finds "Ersatz" (substitute) for everything. In the columns of the French and English papers one does not find this word. Our enemies still have butter, fats, lard, etc.' The key elements in the speech were a reference to the Russian Revolution, from which Erzberger concluded that 'our Kaiser must come down from his lofty heights', and the support which Erzberger gave to the Socialist demands for a negotiated peace.[12] Discussion of a 'Peace Resolution' formed the background against which there was growing speculation about an imminent change of government. The resolution that 'the Reichstag strives for a peace of understanding and a lasting reconciliation among peoples' was published on 14 July, and passed by 212 votes to 126 on 19 July. Meantime, the Kaiser on 12 July signed an order promising a new suffrage bill in Prussia before the next election; and on that same day Bethmann-Hollweg was forced to resign. His successor was the Michaelis who had proved himself a competent administrator in the Prussian Food Office. The *Frankfurter Zeitung* described him as 'the first Imperial Chancellor to be appointed from the middle classes'; the *Berliner Tageblatt*, rightly, noted that he had, none the less, been nominated from above.[13]

And that really was the crucial point – though the changes were by no means negligible. The transformation of the Social Democrats from being outsiders to being a potential governing party got minor recognition in the appointment of Dr August Müller to the Undersecretaryship at the War Food Office. The Kaiser's Proclamation 'to the German people' of 1 August, promising 'a strong, free Empire in which our children will be able to live in security', showed a clear recognition of the social implications of total war.[14] But in the end a reshuffling of the political pack could not meet the increasing problems of war weariness and discontent. Michaelis had little political skill, and on 1 November he was dismissed, to be replaced by Count von Hertling. With the news of the October Bolshevik Revolution in Russia, Germany entered upon a further period of extreme social and political tension. We shall turn to this in a later section.

## III  Russia: Disruption of War and Growth of 'Voluntary Organisations', August 1914 – March 1917

The very prospect of war brought some sort of unity to the Russian empire, though the actuality of war was from the start to be much more disruptive than it was in any other major belligerent country. On 25 July there was an assembly at Moscow of representatives of the *Zemstvos* (rural councils), which issued a ringing declaration:

> Gone are now the barriers which have divided our citizens; all are united in one common effort . . . who, if not the members of public institutions whose business it is to provide for the needs of the people, who have had many years of practical experience in caring for the sick, and who have organized forces at their command, should undertake the task of uniting isolated efforts in their great work, which demands so immense an organisation.[15]

Five days later the Union of *Zemstvos*, under the leadership of Prince

Lvov was established; it was followed on 8 August by another of the 'Voluntary Organisations' (sometimes translated as 'Unofficial Organisations') which were to play an increasingly important part on the home front, the Union of Municipalities. With ironic prescience, one spokesman from the Municipalities remarked that: 'The success of the war would not depend on the strength and the organisation of the army alone; it would depend directly upon the efficient organisation of the public forces, on the organisation of the community.'[16] Meantime the opening of hostilities had been greeted with the usual enthusiasm. In the *Duma* opposition was voiced only by the handful of left-wing deputies; the Mensheviks, the Bolsheviks and the Trudoviks. At the end of the year the five Bolshevik deputies, who remained obdurate in their opposition, were arrested and exiled to Siberia. For the moment, despite all the harshness and inequity of the Tsarist régime, patriotic enthusiasm was triumphant – one mother reported that her small son told her he was building gallows 'to hang the Germans.' Another small boy wrote to a soldier at the front: 'Rip them up! Rip them up like dogs!'[17]

Of the 5,115,000 men who were mobilised in the first days of war, 4,092,000 were peasants. Agricultural production need not have suffered greatly since agricultural labour in the past had been chronically underemployed. But in fact there was a deliberate cutback, based on such prognostications as that delivered by Prince Shakhovskoy to the influential Moscow Agricultural Society in August: 'Wheat will for some time lose all its value for its holder because there will be no purchaser for it on the domestic market.'[18] Following the same false logic manufacturers cut their own production by anything from a quarter to a half. Russia had not been in the van of European social progress; now the Ministry of Education announced that:

In view of war conditions, no grants or subsidies, except those already authorised, shall be issued for building purposes to the primary schools. Such institutions as have received only part of their grants must arrange for the completion of their buildings on that basis, without counting on any additional sums, whether in the current year or in 1915. Those towns and *Zemstvos* whose petitions have not, as yet, been granted, must regard them as refused. In the coming year, 1915, the local bodies must not count on receiving new grants for the purpose of universal education.[19]

Education and housing problems were made worse by the inflow of refugees from the territories invaded by the Germans. By the end of the year there were serious housing shortages in the towns, while the general price index had risen by 40 per cent.

Though Russia lagged behind other European countries in almost all other respects, she did give the lead in one sphere: liquor control. Total prohibition of liquor sales was imposed at the end of July as a temporary measure to cover the period of mobilisation, when, it was rightly felt, the temptation to down copious draughts of crude vodka would be more than usually strong. Mystical zealotry and the ingrained autocratic instinct towards social regulation reinforced the desire for military efficiency. By the imperial *Ukase* of 22 August prohibition was extended for the entire duration of the war. The results were ironic. Since the sale of liquor had been an extremely profitable state monopoly the government was denying itself about one-third of its normal revenue. The peasants meantime turned cheerfully to manufacturing their own home brew, so that they now had money in hand with which to buy up scarce food supplies. A university professor summed up the situation after two years of war:

> Drunkenness continues, the illicit sale of liquor proceeds undisturbed in the private rooms of luxurious restaurants. The distilleries are unable to satisfy the demand for liquor. Dealers make incredible profits. Chemistry is reported to be in the home to rectify methylated spirit, varnish and eau-de-cologne! Consumption of alcoholic liquor flourishes, especially among the wealthier classes. The State has merely renounced the taxation of alcohol and has not succeeded in suppressing its consumption.[20]

While the relatively sophisticated economies of the other European countries were fairly successfully modified to meet the *test* of war, Russia was never able to recover from the initial cutbacks. Partly, of course, this was because for her the military war was uniquely unsuccessful; but more critically it was due to the inadequacies and inconsistencies of the economic system as it had developed before 1914. By 1917 Russia had mobilised fifteen million men: the economy was weakened, yet when the men reached the front they often found that there were no rifles, no uniforms, no boots and little food. In the summer of 1915 the massive German advances in Galicia, Poland, and Russia proper brought the total of Russian casualties to nearly three-and-a-half million. Instead of new factories being opened to meet the needs of war, factories steadily closed down. Iron and steel production slumped; fuel was desperately short; transport, by the beginning of 1916, was in a state of complete paralysis. Agricultural production continued to fall.

Yet through the confusion, disruption, and inadequate administrative responses which shortly gave rise to a revolutionary situation, hints of some of the longer-term social effects can be discerned. Peasant communities, which for centuries had known nothing of the outside world, were suddenly jerked into an awareness of great events proceeding beyond their limited horizons. Newspapers began to reach districts where their existence had hitherto hardly been known, and letters from men on service brought families and friends into vivid contact with the wide world of violence and change. Still more significant was the development of the middle-class 'voluntary organisations', a striking and unique form of *participation*. The two Unions already mentioned were joined in June 1915 by the central War Industries Committee, headed by A. I. Guchkov of the Octobrist party, and a series of local War Industries Committees. These bodies formed the main forum for middle-class action and aspiration. Towards the end of 1916 certain trade-union leaders began to join the War Industries Committees, and were denounced by the Bolsheviks for so doing. Russian students played an important part in hospital and refugee work, preparing them too for a role in the February Revolution, and, in the longer view, adding strength to the movement for the founding of new universities.

The first crisis point in Russia's domestic war history came in June 1915. Action, and this continued to be a characteristic of events in Russia, took place on two different social levels. Among the industrial workers there appeared the first serious outbreak of strikes since the beginning of the war; at the same time middle-class leaders of trade and industry held a conference of their own in Petrograd (the German-sounding St Petersburg had gone the way of Berlin's Café Piccadilly). The basic middle-class demand was for a reconvening of the *Duma*, which had met only at the outbreak of the war and again in February to approve the budget. Middle-class demands brought piecemeal changes in the Council of Ministers: over two-and-a-half years of war, four Prime Ministers, six Ministers of Internal Affairs, three War Ministers, and three Foreign Ministers lost office, though it could not be claimed that any really significant gains had been made for liberal middle-class sentiment; indeed the influence of the disreputable imperial favourite, Rasputin, seemed to be increasing. The *Duma* was summoned on 1 August, and a further advance in the political coherence of the middle-class groups was made with the formation three weeks later of a 'Progressive Bloc' in the *Duma*: 236 of the 442 deputies joined the Bloc, leaving only the extreme right wing, and the Bolsheviks and Mensheviks outside; although the Socialist Revolutionaries did not formally join, they gave general support to the Bloc. But in face of this significant new development, the Tsar very shortly dissolved the *Duma* again.

1916 opened with more and bigger strikes than ever before: since 1914 wages had gone up by about 100 per cent, but prices of food and other goods had gone up by anything from three to five times as much. There was something of a lull in the middle of the year as the Russian armies achieved their only true successes of the war against the Austrians. But in the autumn it was clear that the entire economic and social structure was on the point of collapse. During 1916 strikes involved more than a million workers – twice as many as in 1915; and the pace appeared to be hotting up all the time: certainly, clearly-stated demands for political change were taking over from simple claims for economic satisfactions. In this wider context the murder of Rasputin was hardly of great significance: it was indeed a 'profoundly monarchist act' designed to save the monarchy in the 'old Russian way'. Much more significant was the fact that by January Prince Lvov was telling the Progressive Bloc that victory against the Germans could not be achieved under the existing régime: it could only be achieved through revolution.

## IV    Revolutions in Russia and Germany, 1917–19

Argument may still rage over the precise reasons for the overthrowal of the Tsarist régime in March 1917 (February according to the 'old-style' calendar). But the part played by the war is perfectly clear. The war was a *test* which the existing régime could not surmount: it lost battles, and thus alienated the patriotic middle-class activists, and it failed to protect workers and peasants from the scarcities and privations brought on by unsuccessful war. The new cohesion achieved among middle-class activists through their *participation* in the voluntary organisations enabled them to offer an alternative 'provisional government' in place of Tsarism. The upheavals and *disruptions* of war gave a new self-consciousness and new knowledge to workers, and even to peasants. The hot-house growth of war industry created a concentration of nearly half-a-million workers in Petrograd. Enormous armies, suffering enormous losses, could not preserve intact their old aristocratic officer class: by February 1917 sections of the army, for long the devoted defenders of Tsarism, were ready to identify themselves with the grievances of citizens. Of course the long tradition of revolutionary political activity played its part; no doubt German secret service activity did too.

On 20 January Rodzyanko, chairman of the Duma, warned the Tsar that very serious outbreaks of protest were likely. The Tsar's only re-action was to place Petrograd under military command. On 23 February Rodzyanko warned that revolution was possible. On 8 March 90,000 Petrograd workers came out onto the streets, basically in protest against the breakdown in food supplies. The inept attempt of the régime to use troops simply widened the strike in numbers and in aims: protests against the war and against the autocracy were added to the demands for bread. By the third day, Saturday 10 March, Petrograd was at a standstill, with 250,000 men out on strike. It was in the following days that the attitude of a section of the army had a decisive effect: almost the whole of the Petrograd garrison went over to the workers, who them-selves seized the arsenal and its 40,000 rifles.

In face of further reports from Rodzyanko on the seriousness of the situation, the Tsar simply dissolved the Duma again. But this time the members of the Duma decided to remain in informal session, and on 12 March they elected a 'provisional committee', which aside from the Progressive Bloc, contained a Menshevik, and a Socialist Revolutionary, Alexander Kerensky. Since the central government had in fact collapsed, this committee, de facto, became one of the centres of power in the country. But it had a rival. On the very same day the Petrograd Soviet (Council) of Workers' and Soldiers' Deputies had come into being to represent the elements whose co-operation had produced the final crisis. On 15 March Nicholas II abdicated; since the Grand Duke Michael refused the succession, the monarchy was at an end.

That was the first, and, in some ways, crucial revolution; certainly the one which clearly demonstrates the *destructive* and the *test* aspects of war. In what happened next the special circumstances of Russian society and Russian political ideology share in significance with the con-tinued pressures of war. The war had created the revolutionary situation, but the continuance of the war rendered the solution thrown up by that situation ultimately untenable. To begin with, the Provisional Govern-ment and the Soviets (formed in Moscow and other towns, as well as in Petrograd) seemed to manage to work together reasonably well. But the division represented a real split deep in Russian society. This was the split between the small, educated middle class, sensitive, but, for all the experience engendered in the Voluntary Organisations, largely out of touch with the realities of humble life in Russia, and the rest of the population, urban workers and peasants. The peasants, in fact, now moved into the act as separate agents in their own right. In March they began direct action, simply taking over the large estates. Seventeen were taken over in that month, 87 more were taken over in April, 55 more in May, 18 in June, and a further 545 in July. The *disruption* of war had provided the opportunity; the actual political events of March, together with the pronouncements of the left-wing politicians who came to the fore during these events, provided the incentive. Final power would go to the group which could canalise this elemental movement of the peasants.

Meantime the continuing test of war exposed the inadequacies and ill-preparation of the middle-class government, and the fundamental differences between it and the Soviets. It must always be remembered that the mainspring of middle-class action, encouraged by the western Allies, came from a desire to turn a military shambles into successful war. The Provisional Government too readily assumed that the Soviets shared this desire. In fact, from their point of view the war could not end soon enough. In certain social circumstances the coming together in war of middle-class protest and working-class protest – however divided in certain basic respects – can have long-lasting constructive effects. We shall see this in regard to Britain in the Second World War, where middle-class activists, enthusiastic about the war against Hitler, combined with a working-class whose major sentiment was often deep distrust of the existing government. In the context of Russia in 1917 the split emerged irreconcilably when the Provisional Government made clear its intention of continuing to prosecute the war in the Allied cause.

Once again we have the paradox that the war thrust forward the Provisional Government, but that the continuance of the same war made it impossible for that government to go on ruling. First Prince Lvov gave way as Prime Minister to Alexander Kerensky, a voluble lawyer. Kerensky went ahead with an offensive in Galicia, which once again turned into military disaster. Open demonstrations against the government followed. However, still no clear pattern emerged out of dislocation and chaos. At the beginning of April the Bolshevik leader, Lenin, who, since September 1914, had been in exile in Switzerland had arrived back in Russia with a group of close followers. Against some opposition, Lenin promulgated the policy of 'All power to the Soviets', and total opposition to the Provisional Government. The demonstrations which followed the disastrous Galicia campaign gave Kerensky an excuse to act against the Bolsheviks, and Lenin fled to Finland. However, Kerensky was shortly under attack from the Right, when General Kornilov attempted to raise a military insurrection. Direct action by the peasants continued. Soldiers and citizens who had participated in the war effort, and in the revolutionary events since February, now knew their own power; together they sabotaged Kornilov's adventure. Now too came the opportunity for the Bolsheviks. Particularly through the tactical brilliance and will to power of Lenin, they had the inestimable advantage of really *believing* that the time was ripe for socialist revolution. Partly it was that, despite the frequent inconsistency of their utterances, they had been most successful in adapting Marxist ideology to Russian conditions; partly, too, there was the *psychological* factor that the war which many had envisaged as the possible harbinger of revolution, had in fact occurred, and had now brought total collapse of the old system in Russia. 'History', said Lenin, as he moved back towards the Russian frontier, 'will not forgive us if we do not seize power.' The final ingredient, the ultimate expression of wartime participation, was that the Bolsheviks had at their disposal something like 25,000 trained soldiers. (This was the situation which Lloyd George and other political leaders feared might develop in Britain at the end of the war; it never did – which is why there was never any real danger of revolution in Britain in the 1920s). The well-planned, and bloodless, Bolshevik coup took place on the night of 6–7 November 1917. The first task of the new régime was to end the war against Germany and Austria which had unleashed the discontents which, finally, had brought this régime to power. The second was to recognise the expropriation of the land by the peasants which was already a *fait accompli*; whether the régime could have done anything else at this stage is a moot point, but at least this, for the time being, secured to it the invaluable support of a peasantry now self-confident enough to take action in its own interests.

Peace negotiations began with the Central Powers at Brest-Litovsk on 20 December. Russia's ramshackle multi-racial empire was already falling apart, and the Poles, the Finns, the Estonians, the inhabitants of the North Caucasus, and the Ukrainians had already established autonomous régimes. But the Germans demanded a further dismemberment, and backed up their demands by an offensive which took them within a hundred miles of Petrograd; so, under the pressures of war, Russian government was moved back to its historic home in Moscow. On 3 March 1918 the Treaty of Brest-Litovsk was concluded. The immediate direct losses to Russia were enormous: one-quarter of her European territory, two-fifths of her population, three-quarters of her iron and coal.

But the 'October Revolution' (old calendar) had acted as a tremendous encouragement to left-wing elements in Germany. News of the terms which the German High Command was demanding of Russia produced, in January, the most massive strikes yet, involving a million workers. However, in face of strong action on the part of the German government the strikes were called off in February. In the Reichstag only the Independent Socialists voted against the government. In the same month Germany launched her powerful offensives in the west which suggested that the war might yet be won. A number of shifts had taken place within the structure of German government and society, particularly in the form of the recognition granted to the official leaders of labour, but as yet there was no sign of any really serious challenge to the régime. As we shall see several times in the course of this study, it is social and economic institutions which respond first to the test of war; only where these fail, or where the political structure is particularly weak, or where the impact of war is direct and disastrous (all of which happened in Russia) do political institutions, as it were, move into the front line. But it is certainly arguable that the imperfections and inadequacies of imperial Germany were now being forced by the war into open stress and breakdown, to a far greater degree say than similar strains were being exposed in France. Even had Germany somehow managed to escape defeat, it is impossible to believe that the pre-war shape of society could have survived intact, or have been restored in its entirety.

One of the most striking (and most quoted) single pieces of testimony to general breakdown is the memorandum sent by the Municipal Council of Neukölln (a suburb of Berlin) to the War Food Department. The memorandum begins by describing how the large firms are buying up food to supply direct to their own work-people. The Municipal Council, therefore, had to join in the free-for-all and buy food on behalf of the smaller firms. In turn the big firms were intensifying their efforts to get a corner in food supplies. Thus, continued the memorandum, the towns were 'confronted with an insoluble problem as regards their future supply of food. To this position we have been brought in consequence of the complete collapse of the economic system of the government departments.' The extent to which anarchic private bargaining had gone was brought out by instances cited in the memorandum of certain Rhineland towns which were monopolising potato supplies by offering coal in return. Other similar instances, involving towns and big firms, are detailed, before the memorandum concludes by talking of the existence of 'shortages and famine' and predicting 'catastrophe'.[21]

Now, such a document must be faced with some caution. Obviously it had its part to play in Neukölln's battle to secure supplies for itself; but none the less the overall picture of economic anarchy and social breakdown (substantiated in other sources) is unmistakable. Yet till early

August it was far from clear that the German armies could not win. The collapse then of Germany's allies convinced Ludendorff that an armistice must be sought if Germany's armies were not to be destroyed in the field; at the same time (27 September) he reported that a change of government was necessary. Prince Max of Baden thus formed a government which for the first time in German history included a substantial number of Social Democrats. Abruptly, in response to the demands of the Social Democrats, the constitution was altered so that the Reichstag became a genuine parliament to which Chancellor and government were to be responsible.

When it became clear that Germany would not receive as favourable terms as the pronouncements of the American President, Wilson, had suggested, there was a movement in Germany to continue the fighting. On 28 October orders were issued to the German fleet, which since its one inconclusive encounter at Jutland in 1916 had endured the demoralising experience of being cooped up in its harbours, to put to sea for one last mission. Mutinies began at Kiel and Wilhelmshaven. Soldiers sent in against the mutineers joined them (the same participation effect that we saw in Russia – there soldiers, after all, were but workers in arms).

Prince Max wisely handled matters with restraint, and one of the main negotiators sent to meet the sailors was the Social Democrat, Noske, whom the sailors themselves unanimously elected governor of Kiel. But the mutiny spread, till in Hamburg it emerged in much more political form under the leadership of Independent Socialists and Spartacists. Much more surprisingly, revolution, led by Kurt Eisner, appeared in Catholic, conservative Munich. Eisner was a good example of a man who, believing the war to have revealed the utter inadequacy of his former moderate socialism, had moved quite far to the left. He was able to profit from the utter war-weariness of the Bavarians and their complete disenchantment with Prussian policies. To some extent, too, he was pushing on an open door, in the sense that the King of Bavaria had already followed Prince Max in introducing parliamentary government. Finally, in actually taking over power, Eisner, like so many other revolutionaries at this time, had the indispensable assistance of the soldiers themselves. Similar events took place in other leading towns with 'Workers'' or 'Workers' and Soldiers'' Councils being established everywhere without resistance.

Meantime, at the centre of imperial government, the Social Democrats were insisting that the Kaiser must abdicate. This William was immensely reluctant to do, and it was only the replication on a mass scale of a crucial fact with which we have now become very familiar –

the fact that the ranks of the army could not be relied on to support him – that forced his abdication (9 November). The Social Democrat, Ebert, replaced Prince Max as Chancellor. In Berlin the movement towards the establishment of Workers' and Soldiers' Councils came to a climax, and by the evening of 10 November Ebert found he held office by virtue of a dual qualification: he was both quasi-constitutional Chancellor under the remnants of the old dispensation, and the choice of the Berlin Workers' and Soldiers' Council. Under the guidance of Ebert and his fellow Social Democrats, the stress was entirely on parliamentary institutions and under their aegis the Weimar Republic came into being.

The Weimar Republic has not had a good press. It maintained the power of the military and of the old civil service. It became increasingly conservative. Finally it yielded place to Nazism. The German revolution has usually been thought of as a revolution that failed. It is true that the Workers' and Soldiers' Councils never came to anything, but in any case they largely represented Majority Socialist feeling. Ebert as Chancellor, together with Noske, acted closely with General Groener, and used the army to suppress extreme leftist movements. Official sanction was even given to the Freikorps – paramilitary organisations of out-of-work officers and roughnecks, *participation* showing itself in other colours – which played an important role in crushing the attempted Spartacist rising of January 1919, and in destroying Eisner's Bavarian Republic in the civil war which broke out there in February. On 13 January the Spartacist leaders, Karl Liebknecht and Rosa Luxemburg, were murdered. Four days later elections were held for the constituent assembly which was to become the parliament of the Weimar Republic. The Social Democrats and the Independent Socialists between them polled 185 (only 22 for the Independent Socialists), the Centre 89, and the bourgeois liberal party, the Progressives (formerly the Democrats) 74: these parties together formed a centre–left coalition government under the chancellorship of the Social Democrat Scheidemann (Ebert became first President of the new Republic); in opposition were the Nationalist People's Party (formerly the Conservatives) with 42 seats, and the People's Party (formerly the National Liberals) with 22.

The 'non-revolution' in Germany is sometimes compared with the very real Bolshevik revolution in Russia, where, despite the bloodlessness of the November coup there followed years of civil war and bloodshed, greatly aggravated by western intervention on behalf of 'White' counter-revolutionary forces. On one level the differences certainly are very great and can be explained in three obvious ways. These are: first, the greater complexity, sophistication and cohesion of German government and society in 1914; second, the greater and more destructive impact of the war on Russia (Germany twice came near to victory, Russia seldom looked set for anything other than defeat – this, of course, is itself related to the first point) and, above all the continuance (thanks to the Allied attempt first to keep Russia in the war, and, second, to defeat the Bolsheviks) of a war situation there until 1920; and third, the absence in Germany of an effective revolutionary party (again the existence of such a party and such a tradition in Russia is related to the first point).

Of these points the second is the most complex (and debatable). War and revolution became closely bound up together. Without the specifically Bolshevik seizure of power probably there would have been no intervention; on the other hand the war against Germany would have continued: at all events armed conflict and chaos were certainly on the cards. For Russia, there was, in a sense, just one massive discontinuity whose essential characteristic – resort to extreme violence – was the essential characteristic of war. Beginning as international war, it ended as revolution and civil war, just as in France, over a century earlier, the great violent discontinuity had begun in 1789 as revolution and continued as both civil and international war. Conscious, 'guided' revolution, as such, is of less significance than the great range of reactions touched off as revolution escalates into, or merges into, general war. Men make their own history, as Marx said; but, as he also added, they do not know they are making it.

The revolutionary thrust in Russia, I have suggested, was intensified by the psychological impact of war. In Germany, if anything, it was blunted. The Majority Social Democrats, as the Independent Socialist Bernstein pointed out, were 'prisoners of August 4th': swept up then in patriotic emotion, they could never, after October 1918, free themselves from their ties with the old system, and above all, from their faith in the military command who seemed to have fought so bravely for Germany. The Social Democrats, too, were woefully unpractised in the real arts of power: the Bolsheviks, at least, had their sense of conviction and destiny to carry them through.

Turning for a moment to the checklist of social change which I suggested in Chapter 1,[22] it is in the area of my final point, change in political institutions and ideas, that the contrast between Germany and Russia seems sharpest. How to characterise the régime in Russia which emerged from crisis and war in 1921 inevitably depends partly on the point of view. Certainly, it was something completely *new* in the European scene. Its theoretical commitment to the well-being of workers and peasants was more explicit than that of any other country; at the same time the dictatorship exercised by the Communist Party was more total even than that of the old autocracy. After the October *coup*, Kerensky's tentative plans for the election of a constituent assembly went ahead. That there was to be a complete break with the past was made clear the day after the first meeting on 18 January 1918 of this assembly; being in a complete minority (175 out of 707 seats) the Bolsheviks simply used the force at their disposal to ensure that the assembly did not meet again. Civil war, famine, intervention from without, and fear of subvention from within, intensified the movement to dictatorship, backed, ultimately by terror. Centralisation meant the end of real power, not just for the *Zemstvos*, but also for Soviets and Workers' Committees. The point here is not to establish the character of the régime (surely a mixture of high motivations, never entirely submerged, and the corruption and brutality which, in the real world, so readily afflict closed systems of government), but to set it up as a frame of reference against which to judge developments in Germany. And in this connection the most significant fact is the destruction of all the old political élites, and the creation, in the Communist Party, of a new one.

In Germany there was no dictatorship (not till the 1930s, anyway – that train of thought will be explored at the end of the next chapter); old élites, in particular the officer caste, the civil service, and the judiciary, retained much of their power; but there was a strong movement in what had also been an empire of several states subject to strong centrifugal forces, towards centralisation; and, above all, the political ideals of the new régime were almost as firmly orientated towards alleged mass interests as those of the Russian Communist régime. Every historian quickly learns to distinguish between paper constitutions (and paper welfare states) and the realities of political (and social) life. Still, it is worth paying some attention to the actual terms of the German constitution which came into effect on 14 August 1919. This constitution was the outcome of much argument, discussion and amendment among the various interest groups which were to the fore at the end of the war, and can therefore be taken as genuinely representative of the state of German political thought as it was when the war ended. The fast hold of tradition can be seen in the continued description of the new state as a Reich ('empire', though the German word does not necessarily have all the same connotations as the English). But this was a Reich based on the sovereignty of the German people, not on the gift of a Kaiser. Hence the preamble:

The German people, united in all their branches, inspired by the determination to renew and strengthen its Reich in liberty and justice, to preserve peace both at home and abroad, and to foster social progress, have adopted the following constitution.

And the first article: 'The German Reich is a republic. Political authority derives from the people.' The Reichstag was now in reality the supreme legislative authority, upon whose support the Chancellor and his government depended; it was elected by universal suffrage, with proportional representation and secret ballot. The President, whose powers were more those of the contemporary French, rather than American, presidency, was to be elected separately by popular vote.

The first draft of the constitution had sought to establish a centralised, unified state, but pressure from some of the individual states forced modifications. None the less the central government was no longer to be financially dependent on the states, but would raise its own finances directly, and was to control its own military forces. The individual states, furthermore had to conform to the republican form of the Reich. The second chamber, the Reichsrat, wherein they had direct representation, was clearly subordinate to the Reichstag. Gone were Prussia's special rights (and special 'wrongs' – including the three-class franchise), though she continued to hold more than half of the population. The decision to hold the first meetings of the Assembly and Reichstag in Goethe's town of Weimar were, in part, meant to represent a turning away from Prussian influence.

If the new régime moved steadily to the Right, it also managed to defeat the right-wing Kapp putsch of March 1920 – partly because the civil service in fact remained loyal to the lawful government, mainly because the trade unions had the self-confidence to paralyse Kapp's attempt with a general strike.

In broad outline the geographical changes springing from war and post-war settlements seem similar. If the Saar (whose main revenues went to France while administration was in the hands of the League of Nations, pending a plebiscite after ten years) is included, Germany's territorial loss as a result of the Versailles Peace Settlement amounted to 13·1 per cent, her population loss to 10 per cent; she lost 14·6 per cent of her arable land, 74·5 per cent of her iron ore, 68·1 per cent of her zinc ore, and 26 per cent of her coal production. She also lost the Alsace textile industry, and she suffered considerable disruption of her communications system. Russia's losses, partly because of the terms exacted from her at Brest-Litovsk, partly because of civil war and then the war against Poland, were even greater. Deaths from war and its aftermath were high in both countries: over three million in Russia; half that in Germany. Although Germany continued to be in a better situation than France, loss of man-power and a low birth rate were national preoccupations throughout the inter-war years. The amount of personal distress (shared by all of Europe) can easily be guessed, though the broader social consequences can scarcely be computed. For Russia added complications were the mass return, during the Civil War period, of workers from the towns to the land, and the outflow of 1·5 million refugees from the Bolshevik régime. Germany, on the other hand, had an influx of almost a million former citizens from the territories which had been taken away from her.[23] If we look for a broad comparison of the economic significance of these developments, we are driven back again to consider the different nature of the two societies, and the different degree to which the war and post-war crisis impinged on them.

Although the economic disruptions of war brought apparent chaos and a spectacular inflation to Germany, there seems also to have been a release of energies, or, at least, a revival of the spirit of hard work of pre-war days. The big inflation of 1923 was overcome with remarkable ease, and German industry – generously supplied with American capital – embarked on a period of expansion: the phrase 'German Economic Miracle' was first coined in the 1920s. American management methods became very fashionable too; and the faith in technology, apparent in German industry since the previous century, had been greatly strengthened by the experience of war. In Russia the disruption, the demoralisation, the losses of war and civil war had gone almost too far; it took all the energy and all the ruthlessness of the régime to get the economy moving at all in the 1920s.

In economic theory and policy after the war, Russia seems a vastly different country from Germany – here, it can be said, there was a 'real' revolution. Yet it is remarkable how, in the early stages, the Bolsheviks scarcely looked further than the kind of managed economy which all of the belligerents had been forced to develop from 1916 onwards; Lenin, in fact, was greatly impressed by some of the German wartime experiments.[24] It was the dire necessity of the civil war period, together with the almost total collapse of traditional forms of economic management, as much as ideology, which produced the period of full-blooded 'War Communism'. After 1921 this was in fact followed by the New Economic Policy which, by restoring some scope for private initiative, was intended to do something to win back the support of the peasants. However, whatever the shifts induced by the crushing exigencies of the times, and however incompetent in practice, Russia undoubtedly did have a new, 'non-capitalist' system, directed from the top. Germany, on the other hand, remained a capitalist country. In fact Ebert, Scheidemann, and his successor Bauer, made little attempt to follow strong socialist policies. Yet, if the Social Democrats had not progressed much, the Conservatives (now the National People's Party) had: in 1919 they agreed to the 'socialization of the big industries if productive capacity would not suffer thereby'.[25] State interference in industry had gone further in Germany in 1914 than in any other country. From the very first stages of the war, it went very much further. As early as 1915 Friedrich Naumann, former Lutheran Pastor and premature (though relatively liberal) national socialist, had written:

> In the war our self-knowledge is this: that we Germans have slipped into this state-socialism or folk-economic activity in the strict sense of the word. When we emerge from the war we shall no longer be the same economic beings as before. Past, then, is the period of fundamental individualism, the period of imitation of the English economic system, which was already more or less in decline; but at the same time past also is the period of an internationalism which boldly vaulted beyond the present-day state. Upon the basis of wartime experiences we demand a regulated economy; *regulation of production* from the point of view of the necessity of the state.[26]

Naumann's observations were coloured by his own beliefs, yet German policy after the war, retaining many developments of the war, and assisted by the dominant position in the banking system which the new Reich now also assumed, moved much further towards a mixed economy of private and state management of industry than did any western country. When labour policy, to be discussed in a moment, is taken into account it can be said that the economic system of the Weimar Republic showed strong 'Socialist elements'.[27]

In Russia the social structure was drastically altered, in its upper reaches at any rate. Whatever the reality of life after a protracted period of revolution and civil war, the status of workers and peasants as full members of the community was undoubtedly improved. No such striking changes took place in Germany; none the less the full legal recognition in the Weimar constitution of the rights of labour must be accounted a real break with the traditions of the Kaiser's Germany. The new constitution placed labour 'under the special protection of the Reich'. The eight-hour day was guaranteed. Trade unions were given legal recognition as the spokesmen of the workers, and collective bargains established by the unions were to have primacy over all other agreements. The Shop Council Act of 1920 ratified a development of the war whereby the workers had gained shop-floor representation. Germany remained a class society with sharp, and often bitter, divisions, but the working class had at last come definitely within the pale. In both countries women gained full political equality. Oddly enough this was only partly due to the participation effect coming into play. Basically it was connected with the collapse, under the test of war, of the old political systems, thus giving the opportunity, within the relatively limited area of franchise reform, to do something completely new. Votes for women in both countries was as much a product of Social Democratic or revolutionary ideology, operating, certainly, in a situation created by the war, as it was a direct outcome of women's wartime participation. In other respects certain social tensions in Germany were made worse by the disruptions and heightened feelings of war: in a rather obvious parallel with what happened in America at the same time with regard to racial minorities, there was at the end of the war a virulent outburst of anti-semitism made manifest in leaflets and in slogans chalked on walls. The emergence of the Freikorps as the violent defenders of the threatened upper and middle classes, too, shows clearly the class strains intensified by war.

There was extreme privation and starvation in Russia till well into the 1920s at least, partly caused by the direct destruction of war, partly caused by the upheavals of the civil war, and partly caused by Bolshevik policy. In the most comprehensive study of social change in Russia published in English it has been argued that war and revolution did not significantly affect the material condition of the mass of the people for the better, since they also had the effect of interrupting the moderate reform movement already in being before the war.[28] This is a difficult one to settle. Probably it would be fair to say that the negative effects of the war on material standards were so great as to cancel out any positive gains springing from the changes of the revolution. In Germany too the aftermath of war continued much of the privation which had been suffered during the war; however by 1928 average real wages of the working classes were 6 per cent higher than in 1913 – not a magnificent gain over this timespan. Again it is a case of the negative effects of war, particularly the economic disruptions which culminated in the great inflation of 1923, cancelling out the positive gains such as the formal recognition of labour's bargaining position.

In both countries there were major developments in social welfare provision, though in many cases these simply served to mitigate existing hardship rather than to secure a real improvement over pre-war conditions. In Russia the break with the past was very sharp. Social Assistance was introduced for the first time in November 1917, and the People's Commissariat for Social Assistance was set up in April 1918. The Labour Code of November 1922 included a complete social insurance system and holidays with pay. From 1918 the intention was the establishment of a universal educational system, but in civil war conditions even the first aim of elementary education for all was difficult to achieve. Social provision in Russia undoubtedly went much further than in any other country – thanks more to Bolshevik ideology than to the impact of the war.

All historical study, dominated as it is by the imperfections of historical evidence, deals with uncertainties. Matters of social customs, life styles, and patterns of behaviour are often held to be the most uncertain area of all. Yet, taking Russia and Germany together, it seems to me to be in this very area that change can be seen to be most striking as between, say, 1910 and the 1920s. It is in this area that archive film material comes into its own as a central, rather than an ancillary source material, backed up in turn by a wealth of evidence in newspapers, and works of fiction.[29] The end of autocracy really did mean the end of a whole set of social customs. The great working class has come out from the shadows, and has joined the modern crowd, wherein gradations of class are not immediately apparent. The urban environment in Russia as well as Germany (and the West) moves towards Art Deco and brutalism. Talk of sexual freedom is shortlived in Russia; its surface exaggerations are notorious in Germany: but everywhere it is clear that right down into society older canons have been given a great shake-up, that the grammar of sex relations has changed. I believe that all of this can be seen; though it is certainly hard to substantiate in the form of a few bare footnotes – better for the reader too to look at the films, read the novels. But that does not solve the central problem. Change has taken place – but can we attribute it to the war? For that sort of analysis of cause and effect, the sources are less satisfactory. Here I can only invoke my 'model' to suggest the *likely* interconnections: the disruption of war creating new social situations and making inevitable new patterns of social behaviour; the psychological impact of war ratifying and making acceptable such upheavals. The whole related question of changes in intellectual attitudes is so big, and so much a European and North American phenomenon, not easily treated country by country, that I propose to leave it to the next chapter.

*Notes and References*

1. See, for example, H. P. Hanssen, *Diary of a Dying Empire (Fra Krigstiden)* trans. O. U. Winther (1955) pp. 7–33.
2. Hugo Haase, the Socialist spokesman in the Reichstag, quoted in K. S. Pinson, *Modern Germany* (1954) p. 314.
3. Quoted by Pinson, p. 313.
4. Ibid. p. 315.
5. Hanssen, p. 23.
6. Here and elsewhere I have leaned heavily on that excellent book mentioned in Chapter 1, *Army Industry and Labor in Germany* by Gerald Feldman (1966).
7. Hanssen, pp. 28–9.
8. Hanssen, p. 86.
9. Prince Lubornirsky, quoted by Hanssen, p. 49.
10. These documents are all quoted in R. L. Lutz (ed.), *Fall of the German Empire: Documents of the German Revolution*, vol. II (1930).
11. Ibid. p. 261.
12. Quoted ibid. pp. 262–6.
13. The relevant documents are printed in Lutz, pp. 266–82.
14. Lutz, pp. 298–9.
15. Quoted in T. J. Polner *et al.*, *Russian Local Government during the War and the Union of Zemstvos* (1930) p. 55.
16. Quoted in N. J. Astrov, *The War and Russian Government* (1929) p. 171.
17. Quoted in P. N. Ignatiev, *Russian Schools and Universities in the World War* (1929) p. 60.
18. Quoted in M. T. Florinsky, *The End of the Russian Empire* (1931, 1961 edn) p. 48.
19. Quoted by Ignatiev, p. 67.
20. Professor Ozerov, quoted by Florinsky, p. 44.
21. Quoted by Lutz, pp. 177–86
22. See above, p. 13.
23. E. Kulischer, *Populations on the Move* (1949) p. 39.
24. See Alec Nove, *An Economic History of the U.S.S.R.* (1969) pp. 43 ff.
25. Quoted by Pinson, p. 393.
26. *Mitteleuropa* (1915), quoted in Rohan Butler, *The Roots of National Socialism* (1941) p. 208.
27. Gustav Stolper, *The German Economy 1870–1940* (1946) p. 202.
28. C. E. Black (ed.) *Social Change in Russia 1860–1960* (1961) p. 677.
29. See, for example, Open University War and Society Archive Film Compilation, *Russia and Germany in World War I*.

# 3. The First World War: France, Britain and the United States

## I  Destruction and Disruption

### France

Of all the major western countries affected by the First World War France was the first to feel its direct impact, since the German Schlieffen plan involved a rapid German invasion of north-eastern France. The Germans did not in fact succeed in making their quick break for Paris; but for almost the whole of the rest of the war the north-east corner of France was a battle zone whose economic and social potential was completely lost to her. The invaded territory amounted to 6 per cent of France's geographical area: it had contained almost 10 per cent of the total population and, because of the heavy concentration of industry there, 14 per cent of the industrial population. In addition to the area actually invaded, a further stretch of marcher land was given over to the needs of war, so that it was effectively lost to industrial use. Altogether, French economists calculated, there was a loss equivalent to 22 per cent of the industrial labour force.

Although the extent and duration of this loss was not foreseen at the beginning of the war, none the less the very fact of the nearness of the German invaders had a profound effect on the main centres of French life. When war was declared all theatres were closed, restaurants stopped serving at half past eight, and all local transport systems were put on emergency schedules. The Germans were able to use their advanced positions to mount air attacks over Paris and (in the first stages of the war) this brought a general blackout of the city.

During the first two weeks of August general mobilisation took 2,877,000 reservists from their homes. In the country areas a feverish

For Notes and References to this chapter, see p. 96 below.

effort was mounted to secure the harvesting of the crops before all the available able-bodied men disappeared into the army. There was considerable immediate unemployment in industry – amounting to 600,000 in Paris and the Seine department alone. Frequently the mobilisation of one manager, or of a few specialist workmen, might result in an entire workshop being thrown out of work. By the end of the first week of August only about half of all the workshops and factories in France were still in operation, and unemployment may have reached as high as 60 per cent.

For the first few days railways were almost completely closed to commercial traffic; and normal running was never restored. The authorities requisitioned most of the other means of transport, such as horses, waggons, lorries and even taxis. Overseas and coastwise trade suffered similar interruptions. A dearth of basic commodities quickly began to make itself felt, particularly in the case of goods produced by the invaded areas: coal, wool, thread, needles. Imports from Germany naturally dried up; and many other commodities were available only to the army.

The French parliament began in heroic mood. René Viviani, the Algerian-born Republican Socialist Prime Minister, read to the Chamber of Deputies Poincaré's rousing war message:

> France will be heroically defended by all of her sons, whose *sacred union* in the face of the enemy nothing will break, and who are today fraternally assembled in a common indignation against the aggressor and in a common patriotic faith.

But, however heroic, parliament did not feel itself adequate to the demands of war and on 4 August it adjourned itself indefinitely. Certainly the expectation was of a short war; but the result, for the time being, was to replace parliamentary government with a military dictatorship headed by General Joffre.

When, at the end of August, the capture of Paris seemed imminent, Joffre himself encouraged the idea that the deputies and the government should move to the safety of Bordeaux. This was done on 2 September, to the accompaniment of the chorus of witticisms about '*francs fileurs*' and a cutting parody of the *Marseillaise*,

> Aux gares, citoyens
> Montez dans les trains.[1]

However, by the end of the year, when the first battle of the Marne had put a permanent stop to the German attempt to advance into France, the deputies refound their courage. The government returned to Paris on 8 December and a special session of parliament was called for 22 December. The Comédie Française gave its welcome to the politicians by opening its doors again two days before their return. Regular sessions of parliament were resumed on 12 January 1915, and the first stage of unchallenged military dictatorship was effectively over, though Joffre retained his ascendancy against the increasingly assertive parliamentarians.

However, the return of the politicians did not prevent France from running into her first major industrial crisis at the beginning of July 1915. Agricultural productivity had been steadily declining since the beginning of the war (by 1917 production of oats was down by 37 per cent, of wheat by 60 per cent, of sugar beet by 67 per cent); and industry, lacking any positive guidance or assistance from the government, was beginning to suffer seriously from the various disruptions and losses mentioned at the beginning of the section. Unemployment was still running at a level of over 30 per cent. Industrial crisis was followed by political crisis. Endeavouring to find a way round the deadlock on the western front, France and Britain had together landed troops in Salonika; but this venture proved a complete fiasco. The political repercussions were such that on 25 October 1915 Viviani was forced to resign as Prime Minister; he was succeeded on 29 October by Aristide Briand. Briand slowly but steadily tried to increase the authority of the politicians against the generals. When in the summer of 1916 France suffered heavy losses at Verdun, the way was open for parliament to oust the military. In December 1916 Joffre was forced to resign; he was succeeded by General Nivelle.

Although France never suffered quite the same privation as was felt in central and eastern Europe, 1917 was undoubtedly a great year of austerity. While unemployment was steadily falling as industry expanded to meet the demands of war, the cost of living had reached unprecedented heights: in 1917 it was 80 per cent up on 1914. Paris had endeavoured to recapture something of the gaiety of pre-war life: the Opéra had reopened in January 1916; and there was an almost frenetic quality about the social round of dances and visits to nightclubs with which the more properous citizens sealed themselves off from the worst horrors of the war. Yet, one commentator sadly reported, 'Paris seems no longer to be Paris'.[2] Provincial towns too, suffered seriously from various kinds of shortages, particularly of coal. Cartoons of the time depict the coalman as a person of power, to be cajoled at all costs: 'the silly idiot has been fighting the coalman's son', says a mother holding the ear of her erring son.

1917 was a year of considerable labour unrest, provoked by the rising cost of living and the steady attrition of the original patriotic enthusiasm. In the course of the year there were 696 strikes, involving 293,810 strikers (in 1915 there had only been 98 strikes, involving 9344 strikers). 1917 was also a year of political disruption and scandal. Briand resigned in March to be succeeded by Ribot. In May Nivelle, who had proved more optimistic than Joffre but not more competent, was eased out, to be succeeded by Pétain, whose avowed policy was one of avoiding further French losses. This was the period of 'mutinies' when, in the aftermath of the dreadful bleeding at Verdun, French soldiers in the front line simply refused to take part in any further action against the Germans. There was little direct contact between the 'mutineers' and the strikers; but altogether the very survival of existing French society seemed in grave jeopardy. Certain politicians began openly to argue for an immediate accommodation with the Germans; and the entire situation was pointed up by a series of scandals, involving such colourful names as Bolo and Mata Hari, which in peacetime would have been merely juicy, but which in war spoke of danger and decay. The upshot was the resignation of Ribot and the emergence for the first time of a really strong political leader, the 76-year old Clemenceau. After November 1917 Clemenceau established what was almost a civilian dictatorship[3] in which control of all aspects of the war effort was considerably tightened up. This was just as well since at the beginning of 1918 the Germans carried out some devastating aerial bomb attacks. France had come near to total collapse, but, perhaps because of the personal ingredient provided by the character and leadership of Clemenceau, she just managed to survive. In the following year the British and the Americans, together with the French, were at last able to open up a war of movement and force the Germans back into Germany; had the military position not taken this turn the personal leadership factor would have counted for little.

France paid a very heavy toll indeed for the destructions of war. Altogether 8 million men were mobilised (20 per cent of France's population); of these 5 million were killed or seriously wounded. The death toll amounted to a full 10 per cent of France's active male population. For a country already suffering from a declining population, this loss was doubly serious. So too was the direct economic cost of the destruction of her northern industrial areas: a survey conducted in 1919 estimated the losses, expressed as percentages of pre-war productive capacity at: for coal, 74 per cent; for pig iron, 81 per cent; for steel, 63 per cent. Little attempt was made to finance the war out of current taxation so that huge internal and external debts were created. Indeed, it must be reckoned another item in the negative account arising from the war that the long overdue introduction of income tax in France which was scheduled to go into practice on the eve of the war was now completely shelved.

There is no very obvious evidence in France of a release of new energies brought about by the disaster effect of war: the increase in social solidarity, for which there is much evidence in 1914 and 1915, was subjected to severe strain in 1917, though partially consolidated again in the hour of victory. Certainly the destruction of the northern industrial areas necessitated the development of new industrial centres in other parts of the country. But this and other developments may more properly be treated as being related to other aspects of my model. For the moment it is perhaps more important to note that in a very real sense France did suffer direct loss from war. The most severe disruption to normal patterns of social life, naturally, was felt among the two million or so French citizens cut off by the German invasion. The remainder of France had to accommodate about a million refugees. Thus overcrowding became a feature of many French towns, to combine with what commentators described as 'la vie chère' and 'la vie difficile'. Petty functionaries on fixed salaries felt the squeeze keenly; but for the self-employed and for small businessmen there was ample opportunity for amassing considerable fortunes. Butchers tended to do well; bakers and owners of pâtisseries, subject to price control and restrictions, fell on evil days. Skilled workers, as we shall see in more detail later, rose to new levels of income and prestige. Because of the lack of any adequate taxation policy the tendency at the very top of society was for wealth to be yet more concentrated in the hands of a few mighty families.

Physically, then, there were considerable movements of population. Socially and economically there were movements within and between social classes, not all in the direction of greater equality. In the realm of morals, Paris entered upon a new phase of hedonistic living: interruptions in normal family life; the billeting of vast numbers of soldiers, French and foreign, in rural areas; conditions of privation and of heightened emotion: all these factors understandably had a direct effect on standards of moral behaviour. The evidence has to be sought as much indirectly in the literary sources as directly in the few relevant statistics; which, for example, tell us that the number of illegitimate births per thousand rose from forty-six in 1914 to seventy-three in 1918.

*Britain*

Being invaded, France had no choice but to fight. To the very last there was some doubt as to whether Britain would in the end involve herself in the war. However, apart altogether from the question of the German violation of Belgian neutrality which was made the occasion of the war, the British Liberal government was clear that Britain could not stand aside and allow possible German domination of western Europe. An ultimatum, due to expire at 11 p.m. on 4 August (midnight in Berlin), was given to the Germans calling upon them to withdraw from Belgium. As the time limit approached, people gathered in Trafalgar Square and Whitehall, singing and waving flags. When the British declaration of war upon Germany was issued at the Foreign Office, it was greeted with round after round of cheers.

Britain had no citizen army of trained reserves, but she had prepared a small expeditionary force for European service. The first British expeditionary force, numbering less than 100,000 men, was shipped across the channel as quickly as possible to join up with the French left wing. But from the start Lord Kitchener, the government's last minute secondment to the office of War Secretary, knew that Britain must make military efforts on an altogether new scale. His first call to arms appeared on 7 August, offering general service for a period of three years, or till the conclusion of the war. Kitchener, however, was almost alone in foreseeing a long war.

It was the battle of Neuve Chapelle (10–13 March 1915) which brought home to the British people that this was a war on an altogether different scale. Already by mid-September 1914 half-a-million new recruits had enlisted, and the recruitment of a further half million was well under way. In November 1914 an increase in the army of a further million was authorised and by the end of 1915 a third and then a fourth million. Neuve Chapelle was one of the last battles fought by the old professional army. Slowly the new men of Kitchener's armies began to move in, glad at first to be quit of their overcrowded camps where training facilities were often totally inadequate, and so far unaware of the squalid horror ahead of them.

The effects of trench life on the more articulate can be traced in the many collections of soldiers' letters. 'I hope this bloody war is going to end soon – of course there is no chance, but the sooner the better', wrote one in August 1915. 'Any faith in religion I ever had is most frightfully shaken by things I have seen', wrote another in March 1916.[4] There were heavy British losses in the latter part of 1915; and the first British

Commander-in-Chief, Sir John French, was removed. Thus the British troops in France – still less than a million of them in January 1916 – began the new year under a new Commander-in-Chief, Sir Douglas Haig. After initial reservations, Haig plunged enthusiastically into preparations for the great Anglo-French push to take place on the Somme in midsummer. The volunteer army was now at its peak; conscription had been in force since the spring and a new breed of soldiers was in training. For the first time the British took over the major role, since the long agony of Verdun had gravely weakened the French. The Somme brought the second phase of the military war to an end, destroying the volunteer armies just as early battles of 1915 had destroyed the old professional army. On the first day of July 1916, the first day of the battle of the Somme, nearly 20,000 British soldiers were killed.

The Somme push failed. The early months of 1917 went badly for the allies. In the summer, therefore, Haig again sought a breakthrough in the campaign which will always be remembered as Passchendaele. Passchendaele was fought over low-lying ground whose normal trench system had been destroyed by constant shelling, so that it had become a vast swamp in which death by drowning was added to the hazards of high explosives. The gains were negligible; the casualties between June and November 1917 were a quarter-of-a-million.

Not till the late summer of 1918 did the tunnel war at last break out into a war of movement. 745,000 of the country's younger men, about 9 per cent of all men under 45, had been killed. 1·6 million had been wounded, many of them very seriously. It is impossible to measure in exact terms the effects of this loss on British society: economically the effects were probably not very significant; and overall the losses were nothing like as drastic for Britain as the French losses were for France. None the less the agony was real; and Britain, in common with the other countries of Europe, exhibited in the inter-war years all the signs of having suffered a deep mental wound, or *trauma*.

The actual destruction of capital assets was probably not of great economic significance either. On the other hand the economic cost of the war did have to be met somehow. Though the first stages of the war were financed, as in France, by the traditional method of borrowing, gradually from September 1915 onwards, when an excess profits duty was introduced, super tax on incomes above £8000 per annum was increased, and income tax was raised by 40 per cent, the possibilities of direct taxation began to be exploited. For the upper classes the incidence of death duties, the level of which was steeply increased after the fighting was over in 1919, was rendered more severe by the high casualty rate among young infantry officers of which this class provided a high proportion. The trend then, though of course it should not be exaggerated, was towards a levelling of disposable incomes. The extension of income tax to working men earning more than £2 10s a week, while adding to their immediate grievances, was a subtle blow at one of the rigid lines of demarcation between the Edwardian classes and masses. A further development in this new financial democracy was the introduction early in 1916 of War Savings, aimed specifically at the humbler members of the community.

The war undoubtedly caused gross dislocation to Britain's world trading position. Cut off from Britain during the war, underdeveloped countries, which had hitherto been fine markets for British products, were forced to build up their own industrial potential or find other sources of supply; by the end of the war they had ceased to be markets. Before the war Britain had functioned as the world's banker on remarkably narrow reserves. The costs of the war drastically curtailed these reserves; and the disruption of the war destroyed for ever the international confidence on which Britain's banking position was based. The scene was set both for economic depression and unemployment, and for the situation in which Britain would find it desperately difficult to retain confidence as a world banking centre.

There were direct interruptions to social progress. Large increases in the education grants were announced by the government in March 1913 and February 1914; but these were suspended by the outbreak of war. Teachers were withdrawn from schools; so too were children, allegedly to participate in work for the national interest. During the first three years of war 600,000 children, to the certain knowledge of the Board of Education, had gone 'prematurely' to work; there were hundreds of others of whom the Board had no official knowledge. At the same time the school medical services were severely curtailed, with a 28 per cent cut after 1916 in the number of children medically examined.[5]

Housing conditions were bad enough before the war. With the cessation of ordinary house building and the congregation of hoards of people in the munitions centres, they became infinitely worse. Reports multiplied of nightshift workers sleeping by day in beds occupied by night by dayshift workers. Short of 120,000 houses in 1913 the country needed 600,000 in 1918. But now we come to the paradox of war as 'disaster'. So great was the problem of housing, so great also the problem of the educational and social neglect of young children, that politicians were forced to contemplate action on a scale beyond anything they would have tolerated in Edwardian times. Hence both the great

Education Act of 1918 and the Housing Acts of 1919, which we shall look at in more detail at the end of the chapter.

The outbreak of war, as everywhere throughout Europe, sent a spasm of excitement through the country, with jubilation, spy scares, and various forms of anti-German hostility. But otherwise the disruptive action of war was slower to take effect on the ordinary patterns of daily life. Led by W. H. Smith & Son, owners of the country's biggest chain of booksellers and newsagents, and by Harrods, the top department store of Edwardian England, the businessmen and shopkeepers adopted the phrase 'business as usual'. True, distress and unemployment were expected, and within a few days of the outbreak of war 40 per cent of the women employed in the luxury trades were thrown out of work or on to short time; and two national relief funds were launched. But soon 'business as usual' became a cover for an unwillingness to come to grips with the real needs of war, and by the middle of November 1915 the government had abandoned its own endorsement of the slogan.

'No cricket, no boat race, no racing', R. D. Blumenfeld, editor of the *Daily Express*, sadly confided to his diary after twelve months of war. Eighteen months later a working man in Lancashire, harrassed by the increasing stringency of British liquor control was heard to mutter as news filtered in from Russia : 'Russia was never troubled by revolution till she went teetotal'. By the end of the war, another commentator noted, the country had become so 'accustomed to restricions of every sort . . . that we found it difficult to jump back in our minds to the pre-war world in which we lived in July 1914'.[6] Austerity did not in fact become severe in Britain until 1917, when shortages of sugar, margarine, and many other commodities, were serious enough to bring a new phenomenon upon the civic scene – the queue. Private and local rationing schemes eventually gave way in April 1918 to a nationwide rationing system. Yet there was certainly at no time widespread privation in Britain and the effect of shortages and rationing was rather to level the standards of nutrition among social classes than to deprive the poor. With government control of the purchase and distribution of meat, for instance, prime joints would frequently find their way to East End shops, while scraggy cuts, equally, might make a first appearance on the shelves of high-class West End butchers.

Bomb attacks, obviously, were one of the most direct manifestations of the destructiveness of this total war. And even before bombing became serious there was the attack by a German cruiser force on a number of English east coast towns on 10 December 1914 which resulted in 137 civilians being killed and 592 injured. Two harmless aeroplane attacks at Christmas 1914 were followed by a year of airship raids which occurred roughly every fortnight. Uncoordinated and not always very effective blackout schemes followed. After a slight lull in 1916 there came, on 13 July 1917, the worst raid of the whole war, when 162 citizens of London were killed and 432 injured: in the autumn that followed many Londoners took to sheltering in the tubes. Altogether between January 1915 and April 1918 there were 51 Zeppelin raids causing nearly 2000 casualties, and between December 1914 and June 1918 there were 57 aeroplane raids, causing nearly 3000 casualties. Yet again the 'disaster' syndrome appeared to come into play. At any rate the Cabinet, which often entertained exaggerated views about the effects on civilian morale of pacifist and 'pro-German' agitation, was clear that these bomb attacks had simply had the effect of fortifying civilian morale.[7]

The leisure pursuits of both rich and poor were seriously interrupted by the war, but since the various sporting activities were resumed practically unchanged after the armistice, the long-term effects on British society of these various minor disruptions can be discounted. On the other hand the new tensions and excitements of war undoubtedly gave rise to new leisure patterns in which dancing and night clubs played a prominent part, paving the way for the characteristics usually associated with the 1920s. Profound social significance does attach to the introduction in 1916 of military conscription. Conscription meant that first-hand experience of war was brought, not just to a couple of million volunteers and professionals, but, whether they wanted it or not, to twice as many ordinary unadventurous citizens – one in three of the adult male population.

### The United States

The United States felt the effects of war well before her actual formal entry into it. Very quickly, whether the federal government desired it or not, U.S. industry became closely implicated in supplying the war needs of the western Allies. Thus the United States was forced to develop a new industrial potential. And well before May 1917 one of the most significant new patterns established by the war was already becoming apparent, the migration of black Americans northwards in search of more remunerative work in the expanding war industries.

Once the United States did enter the war in May 1917 she proceeded very quickly to national mobilisation: the Selective Service Bill received President Wilson's signature on 18 May 1917. First registration took place on 5 June 1917 when 9·5 million men between the ages of 21 and

31 were registered for military service. At the end of August 1918 Congress lowered the age limit to 18 and at the other end of the scale raised it to 45. Altogether by the end of the war 24·25 million men were registered for military service; nearly 6·5 million were found to be fit or available for service; and rather less than 3 million were actually inducted into the armed services. If volunteers are added the total number of men and women under arms when the war ended comes to 4,800,000.

Direct American losses from the war were very small compared with those of France or Britain: altogether 112,432 men were killed. Financing of the war was met in the first instance by war loan acts, of which the first is dated 23 April 1917. War revenue acts of October 1917 and September 1918 imposed relatively high progressive taxation, but do not seem to have been a significant factor in levelling incomes: there was, in fact, a good deal of profiteering.

In Britain the war on the whole fostered national unity; in France the strains were severe, but in the end she too pulled through. The United States, however, was a much less homogeneous society; and it is not surprising that, although in some respects the sense of national identity was strengthened, in other respects a gross divisiveness appeared in many sectors of American society. Anti-German hysteria was much stronger, and much more serious, in the United States where of course a considerable proportion of the population was of German origin. Spy scares were constant, possibly assisted by the government's Espionage Act of 15 June 1917. Anti-German hysteria became directed towards anyone who had reservations about the rightness of the war. American life was riddled by many unsavoury occurrences in which neighbours spied on each other and even, in some cases, children spied on their parents. On the other hand support for the anti-war cause was more obvious in the United States than in any other country. Socialist, anti-war, mayoral candidates in 1917 polled quite remarkable votes in certain areas: 22 per cent in New York City; 34 per cent in Chicago; 44 per cent in Dayton, Ohio; and 25 per cent in Buffalo.[8]

The most obvious alteration to traditional patterns of behaviour fostered by the war came in the realm of drinking habits. The first Conscription Act, very reasonably, ruled that no liquor should be on sale near military bases. Then, to conserve grain, manufacture of all alcohol was in practice banned later in 1917. Prohibition became increasingly associated with patriotism; by the time the war ended the country was effectively dry anyway, and many Americans seemed to accept this state of affairs as a necessary part of the war effort. A magnificent opportunity lay open to the minority of dedicated activists, many of them women, who had always campaigned for prohibition; their cause, too, was greatly strengthened by the recognition at the end of the war of women's rights. When these activists succeeded in securing the fifteenth amendment which made prohibition permanent throughout the United States, there was for the time being remarkably little opposition; this, after all, was a ratification of the new wartime *status quo*, not a sudden innovation.

The boot-legging and gang warfare associated in the 1920s with America's unfortunate experiment in prohibition form only one of the delayed consequences of the disruptive effects of the war. Another, more obvious, one was the 'red scare' which afflicted the United States in virulent form in the first post-war years. This too was directly related to wartime disruption and the sense that American society was endangered, not just by Germans, but by other recent immigrants, and, of course, Bolsheviks, real or imagined.

The negative total piled up by the war is completed by a study of the war's effects on 'progressivism' – the broad political movement towards social amelioration which had been one of the characteristics of the pre-war American scene. We shall see in a moment that there were indeed many positive results from the point of view of American social welfare; but there can be no doubt that the war, because it posed so many complicated problems of individual conscience, took much of the steam out of the American liberal intellectual movement. Most American liberal intellectuals were pacifist on the eve of the war. They then swung round very enthusiastically behind the war effort, leading in the chant which presented the war as a Holy Crusade. For many this induced a personal crisis which in the end diminished their own faith in liberal progress; it in any case diminished their credibility as sincere, consistent reformers. Only conservatism on the one hand, or a more pragmatic approach to social problems on the other, could succeed.

## II The Test of War

### France and Britain

Partly because of the example of Germany, all three of the western countries by 1914 had moved some distance away from the pure doctrines of private enterprise and *laissez-faire*: none the less on the eve of the war it would still be basically true to say that these doctrines of economic orthodoxy still reigned supreme, although Britain was the only country to practise the doctrines of free trade. These doctrines eventually proved inadequate to the *test* of war: slowly the pressures of necessity forced their modification in the direction of much greater state management and control. Although there are considerable, and illuminating, differences in detail, France and Britain followed a remarkably similar course in this respect. In the first phase of excitement and emergency there was immediate state interference for certain limited purposes, which no one saw as directly challenging the basic economic orthodoxies. There followed a second phase, beginning in both countries in the spring or early summer of 1915, when it became clear that a total breakdown of the war effort would result if much more positive state action were not taken to direct and control the economy. The attempts in this second phase were often blundering, half-hearted and ineffective. It was only in late 1916 that really wholehearted efforts were made to come to grips with the economic problem in Britain; France actually took a few more months to come to similar conclusions – though perhaps her middle phase had shown more determination and efficiency than had Britain's.

The biggest step taken in both countries on the outbreak of war was government control of the railways; however, there was nothing very surprising about this since such action had been provided for in Britain by an act of 1871, and in France by a law of 1873. Other immediate emergency actions concerned control of telegraphy, shipping, suspension of stock exchange dealing, printing of more paper money, and so on. In France customs duties on food imports were suspended, while exports of food and other vital commodities were prohibited: in both countries the governments entered directly into the business of purchasing grain abroad. But this was all done in a most unsystematic manner, and while the government was endeavouring to act in some areas, in others it allowed private traders to take part in chaotic bidding for scarce imports; particularly was this true in the munitions industries. Because the immediate disruption was more serious in France, France was forced in November 1914 to establish the Office Centrale de Placement des Chaumiers et des Refugées, which directed the unemployed and the refugees to sectors of the economy where there were labour shortages.

In examining the expansion of policies of state control in economic affairs we can see the effects of the sense of crisis which affected both countries in the early summer of 1915; but we can also see that in some cases, once the first fumbling measures of state intervention had taken place, an internal logic asserted itself by which further control had to follow. This can be seen in France where from March 1915 the railways, which had simply been run on a purely temporary basis to meet immediate military needs, were now systematically reorganised in order to give the most efficient service to the community as a whole. This was also the case with the Office Centrale, which gradually took on the tasks of directing all labour in the national interest. For all that a very definite change can be detected in the first part of 1915. In Britain this was made manifest in the 'munitions crisis' of May 1915, and in the formation of the first coalition government (though Asquith remained Prime Minister). These were the surface signs of a much deeper crisis in which it was clear that the Liberal government had failed to respond adequately to the challenge of war.

In France the symbolic event was the decree of 15 July 1915, which aimed at nothing short of complete industrial mobilisation. The most significant feature of this decree was that substantial government subsidies were made available to the basic war industries. Logic again demanded that once the government had a stake in these industries, it would proceed to demand the right of supervision and control over them. Many similar actions were taken at this same point in time. For instance it was in July 1915 that skilled workers were first brought back from the trenches to work in the factories; this implied programme of labour control was made explicit in a law of 17 August 1915. At the end of August Regional Consultative Economic Committees were established in an effort to exploit to the full the economic and agricultural resources of the localities; this act was paralleled in Britain by the setting up of local War Agricultural Committees. In October 1915 the French government took powers to requisition crops for the feeding of the civilian population. In both countries, but in France more obviously than in Britain, there was now a proliferation of various government departments, bureaus and committees. Many simply provided more jobs and more paperwork, and in fact contributed little to national efficiency. There remained strong resistance in both France and Britain from private vested interests; and politicians in both countries continued to be reluctant to adopt full-scale collectivism – Asquith in particular stands out as an old-style liberal who was only with the greatest reluctance pushed towards any sort of economic intervention.

The autumn of 1916, the time of the resumption of unrestricted German submarine attacks, was the time when informed opinion in both countries began to coalesce in support of much more determined economic management. France, with a total shipping tonnage of just under 2·5 million tons in July 1914, actually lost something over one million tons during the war. Yet, thanks to the vigorous actions of the French government, especially after the establishment at the end of 1916 of the Undersecretariat for Transport, French trade kept afloat remarkably well. State credit and state insurance were made available to ship owners, while at the same time the Undersecretariat went out to secure purchases of shipping overseas. And at the end of the war France had a total shipping tonnage of over 2·25 millions, only 200,000 less than the total at the beginning of the war.

In Britain disquiet with Asquith's policies finally brought his fall (and replacement by Lloyd George) in December 1916. There was no magical transformation: Lloyd George was not so much an initiator of change, as Asquith had been an obstacle to it. In the last stages of the war there came rationing of civilian foodstuffs and government control of almost every sector of the economy. France, as we have seen, was in a state of social and economic crisis in 1917. It was in fact on 8 September 1917 that the Minister of Public Works, Claveille, drew up an important memorandum which set out the theoretical basis on which France waged the last year of war: he described what was in effect a mixed economy – government direction and control, but in co-operation with private businessmen. On 10 February 1918 Clemenceau obtained the right to legislate by decree in the whole domain of the country's economic life; and now the theories outlined by Claveille were very firmly put into practice.

Even the more full-blooded measures were seen as being designed to meet the war emergency; yet there were also plenty of commentators to remark that this reorganisation to meet the needs of war ought to become a permanent part of national life in facing the different hazards of peace. Some of the wartime experiments were in fact retained. More crucial than this an example had been set, which would again be appealed to amidst the economic difficulties of the inter-war years. The shuffle towards a mixed economy was given some permanence in France by the establishment in 1919 of a system of Federations of Chambers of Commerce, while the Mining Law of 9 September 1919 established a permanent role for the government in mining concessions; a similar system for hydro-electric power was established by the law of 26 October 1919. Although full nationalisation was not retained for the French railways, the law of 29 October 1921 laid down that all the individual lines should have a common board of directors and that they should be under the guidance of the government-sponsored Railway Council.[9] A remarkably similar situation was established in Britain where the historic companies formed in the railway booms of the nineteenth century were amalgamated into the 'Big Four', over which the government exercised a loose supervisory capacity. There were other minor, yet significant, examples of state enterprise in Britain: for example the establishment of the Forestry Commission.

## The United States

For the United States the time sequence does not quite correspond with that to be observed in the European countries. The period of emergency actually came before she entered into the war. Once she had entered she embarked with some determination on an intermediate period of government intervention. The period of crisis did not come till late 1917, to be followed by the final full-blooded phase of economic direction and control. Two examples of state action in the pre-war period are illuminating: the organisation, under the auspices of Herbert Hoover, of Belgian Relief Funds; and the United States Shipping Board Act of 1916, which created the organisation needed to replace the ships already being destroyed at the rate of half-a-million tons monthly by German submarines.

The test of war affected the United States in a more indirect way than it did France and Britain, but it was none the less real for all that. Indeed in some ways the test was greater, since the United States' fundamental task was to supply and support the Allies, a task which involved phenomenal transport problems both across the enormous girth of the United States, and more crucially, across the Atlantic. From the time of U.S. involvement Congress conferred extensive powers upon President Wilson, permitting him to commandeer essential industries, to requisition supplies, to fix prices, and to control transportation and distribution. As in France, rather too many boards charged with carrying out these tasks were set up, though they were placed under the overall supervision of the Council for National Defense. In the summer of 1917 this Council established the War Industries' Board, whose objective was total industrial mobilisation. But although all of these moves involved an unprecedented degree of governmental interference and management, they were not universally successful. For example the Emergency Fleet Corporation (established in April 1917 as a subsidiary of the Shipping Board) only managed to build one ship, and even then it was not delivered until after the war was over.[10]

The first sign of the new urgency in face of widespread economic breakdown was the government take-over of the railroads in December 1917, so that they could be run as a unified system under the direction of the Secretary of the Treasury, William G. McAdoo. As in Britain, generous compensation was guaranteed to the railroad owners. Given the title of Director General of the Railroads, McAdoo embarked on an ambitious programme of investment in new equipment (to the tune of five million dollars), and of standardisation, rationalisation, and consolidation of rail terminals and of freight traffic. In March 1918 Wilson responded to the evident failings of the War Industries Board by putting it in the charge of a Wall Street broker, Bernard M. Baruch. The Board now assumed direct powers of initiative in all spheres of production and supply. It took over control of all existing war industries and established new ones. It gave detailed lists of priorities of production and delivery, it fixed prices, it laid down and enforced standards of productive efficiency, and it controlled all war purchases not only for the United States but for the Allies as well. Under Herbert Hoover, the Food Administration accomplished similar tasks with regard to the country's food supply. As in other countries, the main weapons were bulk purchase and price control. Wheatless Mondays, meatless Tuesdays, porkless Thursdays were imposed. The United States might be far from the battlefront, but her commitment to the Allied cause was total: in 1918 the United States was exporting almost three times as much wheat, meat and sugar as she had in pre-war years. Many other agencies of federal economic control were established. Few of them survived the war; but again an experiment had been made, lessons had been learned. It was to these experiments that Roosevelt was to turn in his New Deal policies of the 1930s.

### The United States, France and Britain

War tests a nation's readiness to exploit the resources of science. Since science, by its very nature, is even more international than the development of economic theory, the results for all three countries were essentially similar. Before the war France and the United States had been ahead of Britain in their peacetime exploitation of the latest advances of science and technology: thus the test was the greater for Britain, and had the greater effect in encouraging her to make more use of the resources of science. In all three countries governments undertook the direct sponsorship of research, provided of course it bore some relationship to immediate war needs. In the long run such emphasis on immediate needs is undoubtedly detrimental to the progress of pure science, but as a matter of observed fact, science as a social institution gained enormously in prestige, and there were a number of significant advances in the realm of applied sciences and technology.

At least six major areas may be distinguished: the electric power industry, chemicals, the exploitation of the internal combustion engine, the development of wireless components, medicine, and psychoanalysis. With regard to the first of these there was an expansion of capacity everywhere because of the basic need to maximise power sources. With regard to the second it was very much a case of Britain having forcibly to catch up on other nations, her heavy dependence on the German industry being dangerously exposed by the war. In the motor car industry Henry Ford had already developed his mass production methods in the years before the war, while the British industry remained on a very modest scale. During the war this industry was greatly expanded to meet the various needs of army transport and ambulance services, and was ripe for speedy adaptation to civilian needs at the end of the war. Mass production methods not only spread to the motor industries in all three countries, but were adapted for many other industries as well. More than this, the internal combustion engine was enlarged and modified in order to meet the new opportunities for air transport. Little more than a toy before the war, the aeroplane – used both for reconnaissance and for aerial bombing – had arrived as the most efficient method of long distance transport by 1918; at the time of the Armistice three Handley Page bombers were standing ready for the long flight to bomb Berlin. Both on the ground, and more important between ground and air, radio communication turned out to be a necessity. Hence there was an enormous expansion in the production of radio valves, creating a new capacity which at the end of the war could only be used for civilian broadcasting services. In medicine valuable advances were made in the development of new antiseptics, and in the treatment of dysentery, typhoid, and cerebral spinal fever. The incidence at the front of what was at first called 'shell shock' gave a stimulus towards serious study of psychiatry and psychoanalysis. The pioneering works of Sigmund Freud were scarcely known in any of the three countries before the war. In a rather popularised and debased form they were to become widely current in the 1920s; but there was a genuine advance in the serious study of diseases of the mind.[11]

In the realm of social custom we have already noted the interruption brought by the war to the consumption of alcoholic liquor in the United States. Certainly there was a case to be made that the cause of national efficiency was not served by inebriated or hung-over workmen – though exaggerations of this case rightly incensed teetotal British trade union militants. In both France and Britain severe restrictions on liquor production and consumption were introduced. These did not prove to be permanent in France, but Britain was left with the controlled licensing system which has lasted for nearly sixty years. The test of war also revealed the prodigal waste of daylight involved in adhering to standard time throughout the summer: all countries introduced measures of daylight saving, which were also to be extended into the years of peace.

Inadequacies in social welfare provision were revealed by the new emergencies of war, though to begin with change was not always in the direction of better conditions. In August 1914 French labour inspectors were instructed to interpret existing factory regulations less stringently in order that production might be increased. But as it became clear that employers, under the plea of national interest, were grossly abusing their employees, overworking them and evading safety regulations, it became necessary for the government to take much stronger action. New regulations, which gave French employees greater protection than ever before, were introduced in 1915 and 1916. Furthermore, the problem of unemployment in the early days, together with the influx of refugees, forced the government to hand out much more in the way of pensions than had ever been the case previously. In both France and Britain the entry of women into various types of employment meant that there was a significant raising in the standard of factory welfare: a situation from which male workers were to benefit as well as female. Employers everywhere were encouraged to realise that factory welfare and fringe benefits could often be a means towards promoting productivity. This was a line to which many employers in the United States responded readily. Large-scale population movements, founding of new factories, and the growth of federal initiatives and control, brought social insurance from being, as one historian has put it, a 'peripheral idea' to a 'primary' and 'immediate' one at the end of the war.[12] At the outbreak of war, war pensions in Britain were still raised by voluntary subscription. The clear obligation of the government towards the dependants of those killed or seriously injured in battle brought it into the centre of the pensions business. By the end of the war the obligation had been extended to cover death and injury in civilian war work, and the principle of 'out-of-work' pensions for returning soldiers had been accepted. The way was being cleared for the extensive changes in social insurance policy which marked the first years of peace.

In the three major western countries the economic and social changes were considerable: but in none of them was there political change or collapse on anything like the scale of what happened in Germany and Russia. Where social and economic institutions are successfully adapted to meet the needs of war, this serves to protect the existing political structure; or, alternatively, invasion and defeat are needed to bring about substantial political change. In the United States there was a re-ordering of the balance between the federal government and individual states, and between governments and private individuals. This trend could not be reversed, but there was no structural alteration in American politics. Where there is a critical change is in the position of American Progressivism. The somewhat vague, high-minded ideals of this move-ment were severely tested by the war. In the face of what was happening in Europe, and in the face of the increasingly total control exercised by the government in the United States, it was extremely difficult to main-tain the liberal tenets of Progressivism. On the one hand there was a consolidation of the conservative Right, and on the other the develop-ment of a more reasoned approach to the practicalities of social reform, involving the sort of federal action which liberal Progressives had for-merly been reluctant to support. In Britain the wartime political experi-ments did not prove permanent either, save for the introduction of a permanent Cabinet Secretariat and the institution, for the first time, of a system of regularly minuted cabinet decisions. In the realm of party politics the challenge of war affected many British Liberals as it affected American Progressives, exposing the helplessness of much liberal thinking in face of the realities of the twentieth-century world. Again there was a consolidation on the side of conservatism; but on the other side the socialist cause benefited from the triumphs, as they were held to be, of the wartime controlled economy.

The weaknesses of the French political structure were more deeply probed by the war; it may be that had victory not come, these political structures would have collapsed or been radically changed. Failure to resolve the perennial problem of how to create a strong executive within the frame of existing parliamentary practices led first to the situation where there was a virtual military dictatorship; but then, in what amounts to a strong refutation of the usual banal argument that total war leads to totalitarianism, military dictatorship had to be abandoned in favour of restored parliamentary rule; only thus could civilian morale and civilian co-operation be maintained. Various expedients were tried, such as the greater use of ministers without portfolio, or later rather feeble imitations of Lloyd George's innovations, but the one really important and enduring innovation was the development of the wide use of parliamentary committees. One former minister wrote in 1917: 'I was aware that the machinery of government was ill designed and ill constituted, but it required a war – and such a war as this – to bring home to me the dangers of this faulty working and this inadequacy of output.'[13] But in the end the joys of victory were sufficient to lead

Frenchmen to believe, not altogether without reason, that their political system had in fact proved adequate to the greatest challenge it could possibly be called upon to face. As we shall see later, there is a remarkable parallel between the attitude of informed Frenchmen in 1918 and the attitude of informed Britons in 1945 : they too had muddled through, so why change the system? The distinguished French historian, Pierre Renouvin, remarked at the time that the first impression of French politics and administration during the war was 'complexity and confusion' but that 'none the less . . . the work effected by the public services was immense, and in many respects remarkable'.[14] France therefore would cheerfully carry on, politically, as before. If we are to attempt a value judgement here, it might well be said that the war had an adverse effect on France in so far as it directed attention away from the need to reform French political institutions.

Let us finally turn to the way in which the war tested the existing style of international relations, well described as one of 'international anarchy'. The Allies were forced to evolve means and methods of co-operation among themselves to a remarkable degree. After the Bank of France had provided massive support for the franc in the first months of the war, a French devaluation seemed imminent early in 1915. At this point Britain and France entered into co-operation to maintain the international parity of their respective currencies – a first, if small, step towards international monetary control. Problems of trade and of feeding civilian populations became increasingly severe during 1915, and in August the Commission Internationale de Ravitaillement was established as a co-operative agency between Britain and France. Italy joined a month later. These three countries were also participants in the Inter-Allied Wheat Executive established in November 1916, and in the Meats and Fats Executive established in August 1917. Transatlantic co-operation became manifest in November 1917 when the United States joined with these three countries in forming the War Purchase and Finance Council, and (of greater significance) the Allied Maritime Transport Council, which became the dominant organisation for economic co-operation between the western Allies. In 1918 seventy-five per cent of all French overseas commerce was being carried in the ships of her allies. Although there was an attempt to prolong this almost nuptial state through the setting up of the Supreme Economic Council in February 1919, the speedy revival of former jealousies and rivalries meant that by the end of 1919 economic co-operation had broken down almost completely. But not quite completely : as the economic difficulties of the inter-war years began to multiply, nations found that they had again to return to the ideas of economic co-operation fostered during the war. For co-operation at the highest political level there was, of course, the League of Nations established in 1919. The League was not in the end to prove a successful venture in international government. None the less it is testimony to the way in which the war had demonstrated the full implications of a state of international anarchy, and to the way in which out of the discussions and experiments of the war period some new remedy was attempted.

## III  Participation

Different social groups in the different countries benefited in different degree from their participation in the war effort; but all were affected in one way or another. The main under-privileged groups which concern us here are: the industrial working class in all three countries; the peasants in France and the agricultural workers in the other two countries; women in all three countries; and the Afro-Americans.

The manner in which their increasing participation in the war effort affected these groups can be easily analysed. In the first place there is the simple question of strengthened market position. Men were required, first of all, to fill the vast armies in the front line. But beyond that, men were required to man factories upon which the entire war effort depended. As men were sucked into the trenches they had to be replaced by up-grading unskilled labour, by bringing women into jobs which women had never done before, and (in the United States) by giving employment to black Americans. Because there was a demand for labour, all of these groups were able to exact higher wages. It simply was not worth while for governments to tolerate strikes; better to offer the war bonuses demanded than to permit a country's entire war effort to founder. That labour was in fact willing to use its strengthened bargaining position is clearly seen from the large number of strikes which took place in all three countries, particularly in the year 1917. It is true that in all countries the cost of living tended to rise faster than actual wage rates. But in general family earnings in all countries kept rather ahead of rises in the cost of living, because of the increased number of wage earners per family, and because of the longer hours of work available to anyone willing to put them in. Overall there was a very clear gain to the working class: they had the chance to purchase goods previously denied to them. And this taste for new standards of affluence was to remain with them as a continuing spur towards demanding further rises in their standard of living. (Even life in the army meant, for most Frenchmen, a rise in levels of consumption: campaign rations of meat were 300 to 500 grams a day, whereas before the war average daily consumption in the towns was 175 grams and, in the rural areas, only 66 grams.[15])

Labour's improved market position can also be seen in the growing strength of the organised trade union movements in all three countries. This was most striking in Britain where the trade union movement anyway had developed furthest in pre-war years. Total membership of British trade unions increased from 4 million in 1914 to 8 million in 1920. In the United States membership of the American Federation of Labour increased from just over 2 million in 1916 to over 3·25 million in 1920. In France the increase in membership from pre-war to post-war was also from around 2 million to over 3 million. More critical in France, perhaps, was the development of a militant and self-conscious upper proletariat, based on the new metal industries centred in Paris and central France. Stronger trade unions meant that everywhere working hours were reduced at the end of the war. In the United States the average number of hours worked per week in 1914 was 53·5; in 1920 this figure had dropped to 50·4. In France the working class had on the whole managed to establish the eight-hour day as a general practice by the end of the war. In Britain, similarly, average weekly hours dropped from 50 at the beginning of the war to 48 in the early 1920s. True, the economic depression was to eat away at some of the gains made by the working classes. The widespread labour troubles of the early 1920s represent the struggle of the workers, successful on the whole, to maintain the gains which they had made during the war against attempts to return them to pre-war conditions.

A second way in which the wartime situation could be turned to the advantage of labour was through direct participation of the representatives of the working class in government. Again this went furthest in Great Britain where as well as a strong trade union movement, there was an organised political wing in the form of the Labour Party. When the coalition government was formed in May 1915, a post was allotted to the Secretary of the Labour Party, Arthur Henderson, whose general brief was to watch over the interests of labour and to maintain Labour support for the government. When the small War Cabinet was formed in December 1916 Henderson joined the select few, while a number of other Labour men were given important posts. These representatives of labour, then, were able to pressure governments into giving special attention to the social issues which were of particular interest to the working class. In the long term, the fact that Labour men were in government and were seen to work efficiently in government, gave a tremendous boost to the claims of the Labour Party eventually to be accepted as a possible governing party.

In the United States Samuel Gompers, the great American trade union leader, was welcomed and accepted by the politicians, so that he was able to influence social policies in a direction favourable to American labour: in return for its support of the war effort, in face of strong pacifist sentiment in the trade unions, organised labour in September 1917 demanded protection against any cuts in standards, the right of collective bargaining, equal pay for equal work, and representation on all agencies concerned with the war effort; finally a War Labor Administration, whose fundamental rationale was the conciliation of labour, was established in January 1918 under William B. Wilson. Similar developments took place in France, where, as we saw, socialist members were welcomed into the government at the very beginning of the war. Léon Jouhaux, brightest of the younger trade union leaders, was given administrative responsibility as a 'delegate of the nation': he used his experience to build up a new conception of trade-union leadership, prepared to co-operate with governments, but determined at the same time to extract maximum concessions on behalf of labour.

Too much is sometimes made of the point (which is, none the less, extremely important) that governments felt it necessary, as it were, to *buy* the support of labour: that they deliberately sought, through social welfare measures, to maintain working-class morale and support for the war effort. Governments, too, were not completely immune to the feeling that the working classes *deserved* a certain reward for their important part in the national effort. We can see something of this, as also of the other influences we have identified, in France, where in January 1917 minimum wage rates were established in all industries with which the government had made direct contracts. Also in January 1917 permanent arbitration and conciliation commissions were set up to resolve industrial disputes. The twin notions of boosting morale and of conceding rewards to the working class are a very important element behind the major social reforms which took place in all countries at the end of the war, and which we shall examine in detail in the final section of this chapter.

These influences affected all industrial workers. In France it was probably the skilled worker who benefited most: in the later stages of the war the French government was forced to release skilled men from the armed forces in order that domestic industry could be maintained (neither in Britain, nor in France, revealingly, was there any attempt to confine soldiers thus released to army rates of pay). In Britain un-skilled workers made considerable gains through the opening of employment opportunities previously closed to them. For the French peasantry benefits were less directly obvious. They bore the brunt of the war, and considerable jealousy of the industrial workers was aroused thereby. At first glance, therefore, it might appear that the French peasant suf-fered nothing but loss through his participation in the war. Yet there can be no doubt that he came out of the war a changed animal, pre-pared now to stand up for himself and unwilling ever again to be treated as cannon fodder[16] – French policy at Munich twenty years later was justified by the then Prime Minister, Daladier, on the grounds that France must not 'sacrifice another million or two million peasants'.[17] In France, as in Britain and the United States, incomes directly derived from work on the land showed a marked rise due to the high wartime demand for agricultural produce: rents, where payable, did not rise to the same degree. Participation, of itself, then, brought definite economic and moral gains. But in any final reckoning the enormous disruption in the marketing of agricultural products, which took a serious toll in the post-war years, must also be taken into account: in this respect the American farmer, who had been furthest from the firing line, suffered most; the French peasant, who had been closest, suffered least.

The women's success story in the first World War is well known: in Britain women over the age of thirty, who were themselves house-holders, or whose husbands were householders, were given the vote in 1918, and the various states of the Union granted votes for women throughout that, and the two following years; in each country including France, there was a spate of legislation affecting the social position of women. It is important to be clear first of all how much these successes depended on the participation in the war effort, not of women, but of men. It was this, obviously, which provided the first employment oppor-tunities for women; and, in the end, it was because a drastic reform in the franchise for men was being contemplated in Britain, so that those men who had never had the vote, or who had actually lost their resi-dence qualification by going out to fight, might be rewarded for their part in the war effort, that the question of women's suffrage also became a pressing issue. Although voting rights for women in France were widely predicted as early as 1915, French women did not get the vote at the end of the war. Partly this was because traditional attitudes about the roles of the sexes were stronger in rural, Catholic France. But two other factors, particularly significant with regard to this question of *participation*, are also relevant: *all* French *men* already had the vote, so in this case there could be no question of men's efforts helping to open the door for women; and, secondly, the French labour movement, being weaker than the British, was less able to push anyway. A third point brings the United States into the comparisons and contrast: it was in the United States first, then in Britain, that the Women's Rights movements were strongest before the war. Due weight must be given to the unguided forces of change: yet in history, as elsewhere, those are helped who help themselves.

But once all differences are stated, the process by which women's participation in the war effort brought considerable social, economic and political gains can be traced in a very straightforward manner. The first issues to stress this time are again strengthened market position and the desire of governments to offer rewards for services rendered. But two further changes are also critical: the increased sense of their own capacity and increased self-confidence on the part of women themselves; and, on the other side, the total destruction of all the old arguments about women's proper place in the community, which both men and women had previously raised against any moves towards political and social equality for women (in France both changes appear only in a much weaker form). In the political story what is most striking in Britain and the United States is the way in which one after another all the old leading opponents of the idea of votes for women recant, and declare that since women have played such a vital part in the national effort, of course they must be allowed to share in the politics of their country. However, political rights are only one side of the story. Women also gained a measure of economic independence. And, whatever the intentions of law-makers, they had gained a new self reliance and new social freedoms.

The story of black participation in the U.S. war effort is a complicated one. The Wilson administration, despite hopes which it had aroused in 1912, showed itself to be very strongly anti-Negro in policy. Lynchings and other atrocities against black Americans continued throughout the entire war period, as did the most determined efforts to maintain segregation within the armed forces and other ancillary national services. Such gains as the Afro-American did make were very largely in spite of, rather than because of, national policy. Whether the government liked it or not, the war brought certain basic issues to the fore. The key point again is that the government had no wish to dispense with the potential resources, military and civilian, of the black population. Enlistment of blacks in the armed forces, accordingly, raised a controversy over the whole question of segregation within the army, and over the commissioning of black officers. Likewise there was a blaze of publicity over the employment of Afro-Americans in the Red Cross and other related services. Secondly, there was the effect of the government's own propaganda. Allegedly this was a war on behalf of democracy against a vicious German autocracy. Afro-American leaders could not fail to point out the contrast between these highflown aims and the realities of the racist society in which they lived. Whether or not black leaders made much headway against white opposition, they were certainly very successful in arousing the enthusiasm of black Americans who had formerly been apathetic in their own cause.

If it would be wrong to say that the U.S. government wished positively to buy or reward black support, their thinking certainly included a wish to buy off black opposition. A government Intelligence Report of 1918 noted: 'the cooperation of this large element of our population in all civil and military activities is of vital importance; the alienation, or worse, of eleven million people would be a serious menace to the successful prosecution of the war.'[18] An earlier sign of the wish to appease black sentiment was the appointment in October 1917 of the black American, Emmett Scott, as Special Assistant to the Government.

The war opened job opportunities to the Afro-American, and created a substantial migration of black Americans from the south to the north. Conditions were far from ideal in the northern states. But at least the black man escaped from the worst forms of Jim Crow rule. And he had higher wages and a greater measure of economic independence than ever before. Thus his entire scale of values was changed. He no longer lived in an environment in which his 'natural' inferiority to the white man was constantly thrust upon him; and he acquired a taste for some of the basic ingredients of affluent American civilisation. To all this we can add the experiences of Afro-Americans who served in France, and found there a country which did not automatically regard black men as inferior to white, a country where it was readily accepted that black men could associate with white girls (something which the U.S. Army did everything it could to prevent).

If we try to add up gains to the black American resulting from guided political action we will find that they are very few. But if we look at economic gains, changed frames of reference, and the new sense of self-confidence, then we can see that participation in war had had positive consequences. One problem was that increased self-consciousness, increased militance and aggressiveness, ran headlong into the entrenched white position, and provoked further bloodshed and atrocity against the

Negro. An educated leader among the Afro-Americans, writing in December 1918, declared of the war that it had created 'new aspirations for higher standards of living' and a desire 'for some of the real, substantial things of American democracy'. He added that: 'Negroes . . . seek this as part of the democracy for which they have shared their possessions, their labor and their blood. . . . They are coming to believe in themselves as men and women to whom the blessings of the world are to come, and by whom the enjoyment of these blessings are to be shared.'[19] But the American Justice Department in 1919 put matters slightly differently, when it referred to the 'dangerous spirit of defiance and vengeance at work among the Negro leaders, and, to an ever increasing extent, among their followers'.[20]

Together these two very different comments sum up both what the black American had achieved, and what the unpleasant implications of that achievement were to be in a still predominantly racist society. The reality is to be seen in the rapid expansion which the Afro-American press underwent at the end of the war, and in the newly found vigour with which this press was prepared to denounce injustice, and to advocate Negro self-defence in face of white racism. At another level it can be seen in the great Afro-American literary movement of the early 1920s known as the Harlem Renaissance.


## IV    Psychological Implications

In examining the implications of the fourth tier of the model there is much to be learned from the disaster studies of the social scientists. However, war is itself a human activity, and any war, particularly a long war, brings into play a highly complex range of responses. Psychiatric evidence – useful for studying reactions to the Second World War – is non-existent for the First World War and Wilfred Trotter's pioneer work of social psychology, *Instincts of the Herd in Peace and War*, published in 1919, is mostly of interest for the amount of anti-German propaganda it manages to squeeze into an allegedly scientific work. In this section I propose to take together all the major belligerent countries that we have already looked at, and to look at the psychological effects of war under the following crude headings: first, strengthening of 'in-group' feelings, and of hostility to 'out-groups'; second, reactions to the excitement, emotional intensity, and sense of change, engendered by war; and third, reactions to the horror and destruction of war. To conclude I shall look at the relationship between war and the arts, where, up to a point, one can also discern these three types of reaction coming into play.

Traditionally, what I have termed 'tory' accounts of the effects of war have talked of the growing spirit of national unity fostered by war; it has been easy, by pointing to the sharp class and community conflicts apparent in all countries, particularly towards the end of the war and immediately after it, and by contrasting promises of social reform with the actual lot of both workers and national minorities during and after the war, to pour scorn on such accounts. In fact, strengthening of in-group feelings does take place, but it takes place in two distinct, and, in some respects, contradictory ways. It is true that most of the contemporary testimony to a sense of national unity is to be found in the pronouncements of the better-heeled members of society: for all that it is not necessarily totally unfounded or insincere. We have already noted some of the expressions of national unity dating from the early days in Russia and Germany. From Britain F. S. Oliver, a right-wing businessman and not unacute observer, wrote to his brother in Canada that the nation in the first month of war had been 'born again'.[21] A leading American Progressive reported on the effect of 'this bloody sacrifice' on France: 'It has united all classes, swept aside the trivial and the base, revealed the nation to itself . . . a new, a larger, a more vital life has already begun for invaded and unconquered France.'[22] Similar sentiments were expressed by British tory politicians at the time, and have been expressed by level-headed American commentators since: during the war, wrote John M. Clark ten years after, America moved from being 'a nation of self-confident people' to being a 'self-confident nation'.[23] Evidence that those lower down the social scale felt a similar sense of united nationhood is less prevalent, but by no means nonexistent. Among labour leaders we have the testimony of Jouhaux in France, Gompers in the United States, and the official pronouncements on the war of the British Labour Party and Trades Union Congress. Much more impressive, though, are such statements as this one, buried in the Report of the Commission of Enquiry into Industrial Unrest in Yorkshire and the East Midlands in 1917: 'The relations of employers towards their men, on the whole, appear in many districts changed for the better, and there is evidenced a like improvement in the men's attitude.'[24] A sentence such as this is all the more striking since the bulk of the report is taken up with the very legitimate grievances which the workers had against employers and government.

However, an intensified sense of solidarity across the nation could coexist with a heightened sense of solidarity within classes and groups, accompanied by intensified feelings of hostility towards other groups within the same nation. The demonstrable existence of this tendency has been used to refute all arguments associating the war with the spread of social equality. How can one talk of advances for the Afro-American when in 1917 there were at least 38 lynchings, in 1918 at least 58, and in 1919 at least 70? [25] How can one talk of national solidarity and the spirit of social welfare when strikes and industrial unrest were prevalent everywhere in 1917? How can one speak of the emancipation of women when many wives were struggling desperately to exist on inadequate allowances, and when Sylvia Pankhurst was successfully organising a militant working woman's movement in the East End of London? [26] The two currents were real, and opposite: coming together they did not cancel each other out, but engendered a swiftly rising swell for change. Militant agitation from below might not always have been enough, but when combined with a feeling in high places that a new-found national unity must be given the recognition of positive social reforms, then the result was the social legislation which we shall study in the next section.

The most exaggerated expression of in-group feelings comes in the form of national propaganda. In my view historians have tended to pay too much attention to propaganda as if it were an independent variable whereby 'they' manipulate 'us'. [27] Actually there were amateur hate merchants and atrocity mongers enough in the first stage of the war to render government initiatives almost unnecessary. Only as war weariness and unrest spread in 1917 did governments have to step up their efforts, though from the start they did have to concern themselves with establishing such domestic goals as recruitment, food economy and national savings, and with winning the support of neutral opinion. The long-term consequences were various. As the many wartime lies were exposed, liberal disenchantment increased. Rulers of totalitarian régimes, on the other hand, happily seized upon the lessons of wartime mobilisation of opinion. One important incidental result was that film gained an enormous prestige as an instrument of national purpose: from this time onwards the middle classes joined with the workers in flocking to the cinema, where many of the social attitudes for the ensuing decades were to be established.

A potent force often affecting those same people who spoke so freely of national unity, was the sense that the war was such a mighty event that it *must* be the herald of change. Here is Mrs I. P. Lampson of the American Federation of Teachers addressing the American Women's Trade Union League Convention in 1919: 'The war has not destroyed man's faith; it has renewed our faith in mankind – renewed it, strengthened it, justified it . . . the spirit of man has been transformed, society has been reorganized, and the world reconstructed.' [28] Friedrich Naumann said that he had deliberately sat down to write *Mitteleuropa* in time of war because 'it is only in war that minds are prepared to entertain transforming thoughts'.[29] During the war a British journalist remarked that the war had 'turned the whole world topsy turvy' later adding exultantly, 'that horrible ogre, Tradition, lies in the dust'; another writer explained that 'days and weeks have the fulness and significance of years and decades'; and a top civil servant saw the war as a time of 'gestation of a new social ideal'.[30] Politicians, faced with the need to justify the ever mounting destruction and slaughter, made the same kind of pronouncement. Yet again, just because some politicians were cynical and calculating that is not sufficient reason for dismissing the wealth of evidence that many did feel that the war must inevitably be a time of great transformations. The very excitement of war conditioned a wider majority to expect and accept change. Again, then, there is a twofold effect: the activist, influential, minority drew up plans for specific changes; meantime the wider majority became receptive to such plans. (One sphere in which this process stands out very clearly is that of British working-class attitudes to education: over the war period Labour Party Conferences and Trades Union Congresses reveal a steady diminution in the previous hostility to the raising of the school leaving age.)

In his autobiography the Oxford historian E. L. Woodward spoke of the 'scorching' effect of the war on European liberal intellectuals.[31] The image is a good one. Labour leaders could support the war and believe, or insist, that it should bring social reform. Conservatives could speak of a nation united, and often mean it. Many Liberals were strongly opposed to the war till the thirteenth hour. When, finally, they swung round, they enthusiastically adopted the theory that the war would bring a better world. As it became clearer and clearer that the war was simply destroying the best of the old European civilisation, the shock was a powerful one. Thus, in addition to the militant demands for reform, the upper-class acquiescence in reform in the name of national solidarity, and the belief in change, we have, at the end of the war to reckon also with another force: bitterness, disillusionment and a rejection of politics. This force was intensified by two other developments: the sharp alienation of the men who fought and suffered at the front from those who stayed at home; and the feeling of loathing aroused in the minds of more sensitive spirits as they began to contemplate the debauch of patriotic hysteria and propaganda in which, in every case, their own country had indulged.

## War and the Arts

Literature and the arts can be used as evidence for these various, and sometimes contradictory, reactions. The 'disenchantment' of the war poets is much cited by historians: and reference can readily be made to the bitter irony in such paintings as Paul Nash's rendering of the havoc and desolation of war, entitled 'We are making a New World'. The mood of social upheaval and change is plain enough in plenty of novels, particularly lesser novels. The strengthening of national loyalties can be seen in official patronage of the arts, and in the growing interest in the home-bred arts, apparent, though unevenly, in all the belligerent countries. All countries wished to demonstrate that they were fighting for culture against its deadliest enemies. Isolated instances of the solidarity and developing sense of identity of particular groups within the wider national communities can be seen in the products of the Harlem Renaissance and, indeed, in the products of the coeval 'Scottish Renaissance'. The sense of the group solidarity of a squad of fighting men forms the underlying motif of Henri Barbusse's great novel of 1915, *Le Feu* (*Under Fire*).

Nash's commitment, as well as his bitterness, comes through in a letter from the front line to his wife, written in 1917: 'I am no longer an artist interested and curious, I am a messenger who will bring back word from the men who are fighting to those who want the war to go on for ever. Feeble, inarticulate will be my message, but it will have a bitter truth, and may it burn their lousy souls'.[32]

Historians often, and legitimately, use art itself, the statements of writers and artists, and the manner in which art is organised as a social institution, in order to illustrate reactions and tendencies they believe to be prevalent in the wider society. At a more profound, though potentially riskier, level, the historian can also attempt to use the artist's insights into social behaviour in formulating his own interpretations of historical situations. Thus there is much to be gleaned on the whole nature of war from creative writers. Naturally, the very fact of the war – especially on this horrific scale – stimulated imaginative thought on all the greater issues involved. Or did it? That question must be taken with another, still bigger one.

Leaving aside the nature of war, did the nature of the arts change because of the war? The notion of artistic styles, and of the possibility of chopping these styles up into chronological periods, is well established. To come straight to the point: did the war bring to an end one period in the arts, replacing it by another one, which could be called the period of 'modernism'? A brief glance at artistic trends since the late nineteenth century would immediately show this not to be so: Stravinsky, Joyce, the Post-Impressionists, were all carrying through their major innovations in the years before the war. Yet the notion of the war as some sort of dividing line is not a totally erroneous one for two reasons. The horrific experience of war gave a new validity to the discords and extreme percussive effects (as they seemed to many contemporaries) of Stravinsky and the new generation of musicians, and to the new modes of literary and artistic expression. Wilfred Owen, as is often said, was no great technical innovator, yet he created for himself a jagged personal style to deal with the pity, and the ghastliness, of war:

> For of my glee might many men have laughed,
> And of my weeping something had been left,
> Which must die now. I mean the truth untold,
> The pity of war, the pity war distilled.[33]

The English art critic, P. G. Konody expressed, better than I can, the relationship between the war and the new techniques of the artist:

> It is fairly obvious that the ordinary representational manner of painting is wholly inadequate for the interpretation of this tremendous conflict in which all the forces of nature have to be conquered and pressed into service against the opposing enemy. A more synthetic method is needed to express the essential character of this cataclysmic war, in which the very earth is disembowelled and rocky mountain summits are blown sky-high to bury all life under the falling debris. How could even a faint echo of such things find its way into that species of enlarged and coloured newspaper illustration that continues to represent the art of the battle painter on the walls of the Royal Academy?[34]

It is not in the nature of war to create new ideas or new modes of expression. But the very situation of war itself was a new situation, in which the calamitous novelty was unprecedented in scale and impact. Just as this new situation brought new economic and social organisations into being, so too artists wishing to cope with the reality of war had to stretch to the limit every available new technique.

But the audience was affected as well as the artist. There was a new receptivity to new styles and techniques. We must get our numbers right, of course. Only a tiny minority before the war had any kind of view on the arts, whether modernist or traditionalist. But within that tiny circle one can see that up to 1914 the innovators continued to be met by hostility and outrage. Stravinsky's *Rite of Spring* roused the first-night Paris audience in May 1913 to violence; characteristically it only aroused the British to contempt: 'such stuff should be played on primeval instruments – or, better, not played at all.'[35] When Roger Fry attempted to mount Post-Impressionist exhibitions in London in 1910 and 1912 they were greeted with derision. The tiny minority widened slightly over the war period,[36] and more important, within that minority there was a swing towards accepting that the traditional representational modes could not begin to express the truth about the war.

These are the broad and, I think, important matters, concerning change in the arts as a whole rather than changes in the arts studied only as a reflection of the war experience or as conveying a message about the nature of war. There is much that is interesting and informative to be gleaned from a study directed simply towards war paintings, war novels and war poetry as such. It says something about the different impact of the war on different countries, and about the different reactions to war, that the greatest number of direct statements in paint about the war emanated from Britain, and the least from Germany. But even that has to be balanced by the fact that the most powerful retrospective literary statement was Erich Maria Remarque's *Im Westen Nichts Neues* (*All Quiet on the Western Front*, first published in 1929). But rather than detail the various works that speak directly of war, and the differences in treatment, it is more important for the historian of society to note the manner in which the experience of war hangs broodingly over so many of the works of the twenties and thirties whose overt subject is not war. This, I am sure, is true of the great artists of the Weimar republic – Kandinsky, Klee, Beckmann – who in so many ways gave a lead to artistic developments throughout Europe. It is true of Hemingway, and it is true of Scott Fitzgerald.

In the end one has to return to an obvious point I made earlier, and a question I coupled with it. It was difficult for anyone – least of all someone with the sensibility of a creative artist – to live through the First World War and not be affected by it. Total war had entered the artist's 'agenda'. Dozens of novels and poems of minor literary interest make this clear enough. But is it worth dragging in Thomas Mann, Franz Kafka, James Joyce and T. S. Eliot? In their works there is nothing remotely approaching a one-to-one relationship with the war. From great writers we learn, if anything, something of the nature of man himself, and the relationships he has created. From the great writers of the twentieth century we learn as much or more about the humanity which let the war happen than about the humanity which emerged from the war. We learn about twentieth-century man in his various aspects, rather than about one twentieth-century war. Thomas Mann's *The Magic Mountain* (1924) can be taken as showing allegorically the nature of the Europe which went to war in 1914. But what an inadequate comment that would be.

The single-minded message that does come through in all the overt treatments of war from the watershed marked by the publication of Barbusse's *Under Fire* onwards is that war is no longer something to be glorified retrospectively nor to be imagined enthusiastically in the future. Thirty years before it became a cliché for the man in the street living in the atomic era, the insistent theme was being developed: any future war will destroy mankind. In 1921, in the capital of the newly established state of Czechoslovakia, Karel Capek staged the play *R.U.R.* (*Rossum's Universal Robots*). But the indictment again was not just of war, but of industrial civilisation itself, which had already produced one catastrophic war and which, if not controlled, would easily produce another, even more catastrophic.

## V  General Consequences of the War

### Geographical

The political geography of Europe was drastically altered by the war. The diligent student need go no further than the Treaty of Versailles itself, and the elaborate maps which accompany it,[37] aided of course by any good text book of international history – for, as an official document, the Treaty contains traps for the unwary (not everything that the Treaty said should be done was actually carried out in practice) as well as a wealth of uses for the perceptive, which go far beyond the dry-as-dust of diplomatic history and lead into many of the issues directly or indirectly related to social change. The obvious political facts are there. Russia is ignored. Germany, though (all things considered) treated not unfairly, is to be kept in the position of a defeated power, as various clauses scattered throughout the document make clear. The reconstitution of Poland had implications for the territories and populations of both Russia and Germany, as, of course, had many of the other territorial readjustments. Something of the human reality behind these strokes of the political pen comes through in the detailed clauses of the Treaty.

Eupen and Malmédy were to be ceded by Germany to Belgium: the clauses of Section I reveal some of the implications. Thus a special commission had to be appointed to settle the exact frontier, 'taking into account the economic factors and means of communication'. Former German nationals were to become Belgian save that those who became resident after 1 August 1914 would require a permit from the Belgian government; however, special registers were to be opened to enable former German nationals to opt for German nationality, in which case they would have to move to Germany, freely taking their movables with them, and retaining their rights in their immovable property. The German government was to hand over all documents, registers, and so on to the Belgian government (this was a vital provision, given the complexities of modern government, and was repeated every time the treaty dealt with transfers of territory).

It was in the area of Germany's frontiers with the reconstituted Polish state that the human problems were most complex. The details of the plebiscite to be held in Upper Silesia were spelled out, together with the provisions for temporary administration by an Allied Commission; so too were the necessary provisions for opting between Polish and German nationality and for place of residence. Most important of all was Article 93, designed to safeguard German minority rights in Poland. Such safeguards recurred throughout the Treaty, pointing up the problems associated with racial, linguistic and religious minorities which were intensified, rather than solved, by the war. The settlement of Germany's boundaries in the east created a 'Polish Corridor' separating East Prussia from the rest of Germany. Article 89 guaranteed free communication between the two parts of Germany. The issue of nationality came up again in regard to Memel (Section X of the Treaty); and the setting up of the Free City of Danzig also created special problems. Danzig was, in fact, predominantly German, so there had to be special provision against 'any discrimination . . . to the detriment of citizens of Poland and other persons of Polish origin or speech' (Article 104 (5)).

### Economic

Substantial sections of the Treaty were devoted to economic matters. In such matters as the levying of reparations from Germany, the transfers of public debt, the complicated arrangements for land–water transport across disputed territories, and the plans to give France the economic fruits of the Saar, we can, with hindsight, see pointers to the economic dislocation which was to affect Europe in the post-war years. However, many other factors have to be taken into the account, all explicable in terms of our basic model.

Cumulatively, the destruction of capital, loss of production, and disruption and destruction of populations had a serious effect on international commerce. Old economic units had been broken up, and the delicate mechanism which up till 1914 had held together all the trading nations of the world was shattered. Cut off from European supplies, overseas countries had developed their own productive resources and thus ceased to be outlets for European industries. Germany was stripped of her colonial possessions, and France lost her heavy investments in Russia. Britain's losses were relatively not so high, but they had a special importance in that, in pre-war days, London had been the acknowledged banker to the world. Now, in an atmosphere of general distrust and widespread economic nationalism (the psychological aspect of this question), her reserves were dangerously threadbare for the continuance of her banker's role. A point which deserves special attention – and which must be balanced against the process whereby the test of war produced beneficial industrial change – is the deleterious result of the distorted growth in certain sectors provoked by the war. The most significant, and most tragic instances were to be found in the shipbuilding, coalmining, and heavy metallurgic industries. The immediate needs of war provoked a temporary expansion, together with a false sense of optimism, in these industries. The let-down at the end of the war was all the greater. Miners, in particular, having in any case been among the aristocrats of labour in pre-war years, could not understand how, having played an apparently indispensable role in the war effort, they were now pinned to the fortunes of a declining industry. The international economic organisation which had worked quite effectively in pre-war days, of course, had no universal validity: the very manner in which it depended upon a certain favourable aggregation of circumstances was made disastrously apparent in the test of war, and in this case, because guided political action was called for, no new system was put in its place.

## Social Structure and Social Attitudes

The Versailles Treaty tells us nothing directly about changes in the social structures of the European countries, yet it does give many insights into the way in which social attitudes had changed. The Treaty, it could be said, enthroned the principle of the plebiscite, the very notion of which would have staggered many pre-war European governments. More than this, wherever pebiscites are to be held, it is clearly spelled out that women, equally with men, are to have the vote. The exact limits upon what the participation and psychological effects of war had brought in the way of female emancipation are nicely defined by the way in which, throughout the Treaty, it is made clear that whenever it is a question of choosing nationality, wives are bound by the decisions of their husbands. (Note that the Treaty, also, called for equal pay for women – a dead letter.) As an international document the Treaty was unique in that an entire Part (XIII) was given over to the welfare of labour and the setting up of an International Labour Office. The pre-amble to this Part declared that 'universal peace' was dependent on 'social justice', and called among other things for a maximum working week, prevention of unemployment, a living wage, protection against sickness, protection of children, young people and women, and provision for old age and injury. In this key twentieth-century document, then, we have a fair index of the wartime changes in social attitudes and of the degree of recognition accorded to the claims of the working classes and of women.

## Social Legislation and Social Conditions

However, we must obviously look elsewhere if we are to find evidence to support the view that the interaction between war and society, which has been discussed analytically in the earlier sections of this chapter, did indeed issue in concrete changes in social conditions. Let us then turn to the main 'paper' changes in the western countries, asking our-selves how far they arose from war's fourfold interaction with society, how far they were simply a continuation of pre-war developments, and how far they arose from particular post-war needs which had little or nothing to do with the war. Wartime changes in attitudes towards wel-fare legislation proved least enduring in the United States. Partly this was because the length and scale of American involvement in the war was less than that of Britain and France; partly it was because *laissez-faire* sentiments in the United States were even stronger than they were in Britain, and because, uniquely in the American situation, states' rights were so firmly entrenched against Federal intervention: and partly it was because America prospered throughout the first post-war decade. Three types of social security, introduced within the individual states, incon-trovertibly have their origins within the war period, and, pretty certainly, arose from the war experience: Mother's Aid (allowances for dependent children, subject to means test) which had been introduced into thirty-nine states by 1919; Workmen's Compensation (but this was not compulsory); and private pension schemes, which suddenly blossomed in the period 1916–20. For striking developments in social legislation we have to wait till the period of the New Deal, and then, certainly, the legislators made explicit reference to the example set by wartime legislation. But more will be said on that shortly.

When the war ended turmoil broke out in French industry, as activists sought to turn the dislocations of war in the direction of revolution, and the majority sought to consolidate their wartime gains: the workers' one major achievement in 1919, unguided product of workers' war participation, was the eight-hour day. The participation effect can also be seen at work in the Housing Act of 1922 (based, however, on a parent Act of 1894) which provided cheap government loans and, in special cases, subsidies, for working-class, pensioners' and (here is the key) war victims' housing. The destruction syndrome can be seen coming into play in the establishment in 1918 of the first Equalisation Funds whereby employers could help each other to finance Family Allowance schemes, and, even more obviously, in the Act of 1923 whereby the state tried to encourage large families through providing cash allowances for all children beyond the first two. It should be noted that the French labour movement was hostile to these schemes, seeing them as devices for keeping down wages. The Unemployment Fund, which, as we saw, had been set up shortly after the outbreak of war, was made permanent at the end of the war. But compared with unemployment provision in Britain the scheme remained a very modest one, which in itself tells us something of the relative importance of post-war circumstances *vis-à-vis* the pressures of war: France did not suffer from mass unemployment in the way Britain did (the point is strongly reinforced by the fact that while Unemployment Insurance provision in Britain was greatly extended, Health Insurance fell far behind – sickness being a less pressing issue).

The paper achievement appears greatest in Britain. Agreed that it was the problem of post-war unemployment itself which produced the massive extensions to the unemployment insurance scheme of 1911, which were enacted in 1920 and 1921; for all that it was the experience and the developments of the war that made possible such affronts to Edwardian economic orthodoxy as 'extended benefit', 'uncovenanted benefit' and 'transitional benefit' (benefits not covered by previous insurance contributions). Even more important, the scheme was extended to the entire working class. There is the further point that unemployment was itself a product of the disruptions of the war and indeed (this is the critical point linking theory to the actual thoughts and deeds of politicians) was *expected* by politicians – in legislating for it they were doing their duty by working-class heroes. The 'Fisher' Education Act was actually passed before the war ended. In explaining his bill to the House of Commons, H. A. L. Fisher had referred to the disruptive influence of the war, which had caused 'intellectual wastage' and had 'raised the industrial pressure upon the child life of this country to alarming proportions', to the manner in which 'deficiencies' had been 'revealed by the war' and to the way in which the participation of the working classes in the war had created an 'increased feeling of social solidarity' so that 'the same logic which leads us to desire an extension of the franchise points also to an extension of education'.[38]

Strong vested interests delayed the passing of the Ministry of Health Act till 1919, though discussion of this project had begun in 1916. As finally passed, the Act left much power in the hands of the individual local authorities. None the less by abolishing the old Local Government Board, a focal point of reactionary civil service opinion, and centralising in one ministry functions which had previously been scattered among several competing departments, the Act established the necessary minimum requirements for a co-ordinated attack upon the nation's health problems, and for a national attack upon the scandalous housing situation. The very fact that these measures met with such determined resistance brings out clearly how much their successful enactment owed to the war situation – in other words they were clearly not simply the logical culmination of a peace-time trend. The Housing and Town Planning Act of 1919, more than any other single piece of legislation, symbolises the extent of the revolutionary influence of war on social policy. House-building had practically ceased during the war, creating a gap so wide that a mighty dynamo was required to get a spark across it. Commissions of investigation, provoked by the need to appease working-class grievances, had brought out the iniquity of existing housing conditions. The government stood committed to building 'Homes fit for Heroes'. Heroes, and others, in a time of galloping inflation, had become used to the idea of controlled rents. That private enterprise could provide the necessary 600,000 houses was dubious; that it could provide them at the sort of rents people expected to pay was out of the question. Now it was clear that the only solution was a massive state initiative in house-building with subsidies from the central government (pre-war public housing schemes had depended entirely on support from local taxation). Public direction and control of other areas of the economy in time of war had accustomed the public to the notion of such action, and, for the time being, had silenced the upholders of the older orthodoxy.

Education, health, and housing all suffered drastically in the economy campaign mounted by the British government in response to the onset of depression in the early 1920s. To say that 'the principle had been established' or 'the groundwork laid' or (tiredest phrase of all) that 'a step forward had been taken', while true enough, does not take us very far. What did have real effect was the determination of certain local authorities (and Labour made sweeping gains in the 1919 local elections) to hold as near as possible to the strict letter of the Acts, whatever the government's own attitude; and Cabinet debates make clear how reluctant in fact the government was to impose cuts on education.[39]

If we were to judge the war's effects on social change, then, purely on the record of social legislation alone, and the practical results of that legislation, our conclusions might not be too impressive (though we would be wrong, I think, to speak of 'The Failure of Social Reform'[40]). Even if we turn to the apparently 'hard facts' of wage rates and living standards the answers are still rather messy ones. In the United States real wages rose by as much as 30 per cent over the war period, and continued to rise till the Wall Street crash of 1929; in Britain real wages were 20 per cent up on pre-war and held that level throughout the 1920s – for those in employment. But unemployment ran at 10 per cent from 1921 onwards. In France real wages in 1920 were down on pre-war, and they advanced only slowly during the decade; but there was no mass unemployment. What can be said, I think, is that the war, along with all its negative effects, did provide the working man everywhere with a unique possibility, which would not have come about otherwise, of bettering his lot. How far he was in practice able to do this depended on a large number of other circumstances.

*Social Customs*

When it comes to social customs, life styles, patterns of behaviour, appeal must be made, as in the previous chapter, to novels, newspapers and films. The break is not as sharp as in Russia and Germany because the western societies were less obviously autocratic in 1914. 'The jazz age' and 'the Roaring Twenties' are well known cliché phrases: they describe, if at all, life in the upper reaches of society. Yet, in a way which had never ever been true in history before they are not – because of the growth of film, the rapid spread of broadcasting, the building of dog-tracks and dance halls, and the margin of time and money for leisure gained in the war by most workers – totally inapplicable to the whole society. The U.S. 'withdrawal' from Europe at the end of the war is much stressed; but the decision of April 1917 had brought not just American military support, but the canons of American popular culture to Europe: no decision of Congress could end that traffic.

It is always fun to read, and write, about changes in sexual morality, and the historian has the sanction of the great Macaulay's declaration that 'the mutual relations between the two sexes seem to us to be at least as important as the mutual relations of any two governments in the world'. Seen in the perspective of the first seventy years of the twentieth century the changes of the First-World-War period do not seem too staggering; seen, indeed, in the light of the one major fact of true historical and sociological significance, that after seventy years marriage and the family stood almost unchanged as fundamental social institutions (though the disruptions of war played a part in trend away from the 'extended' to the 'nuclear' family), none of the changes across the century seem too cataclysmic. Among the controls governing human sexual behaviour are the following: social and religious sanctions; accepted standards of what is 'normal' and 'proper' (differing between different groups, and, usually, between the sexes; what is thought 'normal' may at the same time be thought 'improper', which may add to its appeal); personal inhibitions and complexes; physical fears (of, for example, pregnancy or venereal diseases); lack of opportunity. Directly or indirectly the war involved adjustments to each of these controls, though once the war was over there were many adjustments back again. When, in war, life itself seemed so cheap, older restraints often seemed scarcely worth maintaining. Authority in general, and religious authority in particular, was severely dented – 'whatever your pastors and masters tell you had best be assumed to be just a bellyful of east wind.' [41] In pre-war days a few blithe spirits had argued the merits of sex dissociated from marriage, but it is in the post-war years that sex begins its progress towards becoming a central topic of public discussion – the pace being set in Berlin by the newly established Institute for Sexual Science and in Hollywood by Cecil B. de Mille who, as has been said (I cannot remember by whom), 'devoted his earlier works to showing people in great detail and at great length what they ought not to do'. Obviously Freud, or rather Freud traduced and popularised, was a more potent force than the war; still the war situation had made possible, indeed necessary, the franker discussion of such matters as venereal diseases and 'war babies'. Though in face of much hostility, it became possible to argue again (as had been freely accepted until the nineteenth century) that sex was for women to enjoy as well as men. A lot of talk, not so much action, would seem to be a fair reflection on the 1920s (women in Britain complained to social investigators that their husbands 'used' them so many times a week[42]); yet it is through reading and discussion and through the precept, apparent or real, of others that the individual begins a revaluation of his own standards. Prophylactics were distributed to the troops during the war (prophylaxis against venereal disease, not pregnancy). The subject of contraception remained on the borders of taboo throughout the inter-war period, but at least the knowledge was being spread around that there were mechanical ways of intervening between the sin and divine retribution. Above all else, the disruptions of war created opportunity: and the destruction of old close-knit communities, the sudden creation of new urban areas, and increased mobility were permanent facts.

Where there were changes, the war played a distinctive part. For the student of history, though, it is, as suggested above, probably more important to be clear about the definite limits upon these changes. The single most illuminating source I know is a film made by the celebrated (and in her own day infamous) advocate of birth control, Marie Stopes. Originally the film was to have had the same title as her most famous polemical work, *Married Love*, but such was the notoriety attaching to that title that the film had to be released as *Maisie's Marriage*. It tells the story of Maisie, daughter of an overcrowded slum family, who refuses to marry the suitor she loves because she fears being borne down by childbirth as her mother has been. She makes a bravely defiant speech on behalf of independent womanhood to the super-chauvinist male pig of a magistrate who sends her to prison for running away from home and attempting suicide. She is taken into service by a rich family (little evidence here of any departure from Edwardian class attitudes, it must be admitted). In an incredible sequence in which we see roses being pruned with a pair of secateurs, her mistress allegedly explains to Maisie the secrets of birth control. The delicate obscurity of the whole thing is a telling comment on what little progress sexual liberation had made by the 1920s: whether men thereafter went in holy dread of encountering young ladies armed with secateurs is not known, but without doubt large sections of the British public must have remained very mixed up in their ideas about sex.

However we must turn from such fascinating matters to the more serious debate over the nature, and the relationship to the war, of longer-term intellectual and political changes. The picture is well known –

dictatorship in Russia of apparently growing brutality and irrationality; an uneasy Republic in Germany, which provided Europe and North America with intellectual and cultural leadership, but a leadership which seemed totally destructive of all old values, collapsing in 1933 into Nazi dictatorship, the most vicious régime the world had ever seen; in France the Third Republic staggering onwards towards the disaster of 1940, its labour movement split between Socialists and Communists, seriously menaced in its later years by movements of right-wing extremism; in Britain a General Strike, hunger marches, fascist demonstrations, but democratic politics remaining intact and even contriving a few unspectacular social reforms in the thirties; in the United States prosperity at first keeping company with violent 'Red scares' and witch hunts, then a severe depression, followed by slow recovery with the New Deal policies which involved unprecedented federal initiatives. It would be inaccurate to speak of a universal tide of violence and glorification of the irrational, yet if we are to single out one distinctive general motif in the post-war world it would have to be that: certainly fascism and nazism were no more isolated phenomena dependent on the crazy whims of a handful of bloodthirsty maniacs, than they were the inevitable products of a certain level of capitalist development.

Loss of faith in classical liberalism, the cult of violence and irrationality, the roots of fascism and the roots of totalitarianism, were apparent in Europe long before 1914. So too were ideas of democracy and collectivist social reform. The significance of the war (and here I must refer again to the psychological tier of the model) is that for two decades it bulked large in everyone's minds as the inescapable *universal analogue*. The war provided both precept and practice. In the midst of the war, Friedrich Naumann exulted that

> only we central Europeans will have learnt and experienced something positive, something particular . . . for we have experienced the 'closed commercial state', the bold dream of the German philosopher Fichte, which thanks to fate and folk tendency realized itself with us in war. The enemy thought to do us evil, but God, the God which Fichte believed in and taught, thought to do us good.[43]

But it was not only Nazi autarky which was based on the analogue of war. As W. E. Leuchtenberg has shown in his brilliant article, President Roosevelt and his advisers constantly turned to the example set by American wartime policies in devising the New Deal; so too the advocates of collectivist policies in Britain in the 1930s also harked back to the war. Leuchtenberg thinks it unfortunate that Roosevelt was obsessed by military analogies when he ought to have been devising the exact policies needed to win the peace. And it certainly is worth reflecting on the fact that the country which apparently found the best solution to the economic unheavals of the inter-war years had no war experience to conjure up, that is Sweden. However, human affairs being what they are, it was probably better that western politicians had some example, however inexact, to refer to. For fascism and totalitarianism, as well as later western collectivism, the war provided, not the precondition, but a potent exemplar.

## Notes and References

1. Quoted by Denis Brogan, *The Development of Modern France* (1967 edn) p. 512.
2. 'Paris semble n'être plus Paris', Marcel Poëte, in H. Sellier, A. Bruggeman and M. Poëte, *Paris pendant la Guerre* (Carnegie series, 1926) p. 71.
3. Gordon Wright, *France in Modern Times* (1962) p. 205.
4. See A. Marwick, *The Deluge: British Society and the First World War* (1965, 1967 edn) pp. 234–5.
5. Ibid. pp. 124–5.
6. Ibid. pp. 156, 71, 274.
7. Cabinet Minutes, Public Record Office, London: CAB 23/3, 154(3) (5 June 1917). See A. Marwick, *Britain in the Century of Total War* (1968) p. 68.
8. A. S. Link and W. B. Catton, *American Epoch*, 2nd edn (1963) p. 215.
9. My summary of economic developments in France is drawn mainly from two volumes in the Carnegie series: Arthur Fontaine, *French Industry during the War* (1926) and Charles Gide, *Effects of the War on French Economic Life* (1927); from the more specialised studies in the same series; and from Shepherd B. Clough, *France: A History of National Economics* (1939).
10. This account of American developments depends heavily upon chapter 6 of S. E. Morison, H. S. Commager and W. E. Leuchtenberg, *The Growth of the American Republic*, vol. II (1969 edn), and Link and Catton, *American Epoch*.
11. L. S. Hearnshaw, *A Short History of British Psychology* (1964) p. 245.
12. Clarke A. Chambers, *Seedtime of Reform: American Social Service and Social Action 1918–1933* (1963) p. 23.
13. Quoted by P. Renouvin, *The Forms of War Government in France* (Carnegie Series, 1927) p. 145.
14. Renouvin, p. 97.
15. P. Pinot, *Le Contrôl du Ravitaillement* (Paris, 1923) p. 36, and M. Augé-Laribé, *L'Agriculture pendant La Guerre* (Paris, 1923) p. 123.
16. M. Augé-Laribé, *La Revolution Agricole* (Paris, 1955) p. 308.
17. Quoted by G. Wright, *Rural Revolution in France* (1964) p. 28.

18. Quoted by J. L. and H. N. Scheiber, 'The Wilson Administration and the Wartime Mobilization of Black Americans', *Labor History*, x, 3 (1969) p. 440.
19. Quoted by the Scheibers, p. 458.
20. Ibid. p. 458.
21. S. Gwynn (ed.), *The Anvil of War: Letters from F. S. Oliver to his Brother* (1936) p. 42 (6 Sep. 1914).
22. Robert Herrick, 'Recantation of a Pacifist', *New Republic* (30 October 1915).
23. J. M. Clark, *The Costs of the War to the American People* (Carnegie Series, 1931) p. 286.
24. *Parliamentary Papers* (1917) vol. xii, Cd 8664, 'Yorkshire and East Midlands Area', para. 13.
25. J. H. Franklin, *From Slavery to Freedom: A History of the American Negroes*, 2nd edn (1956) p. 464.
26. For interesting film evidence on this point see Richard Dunn's E.M.I.– Pathé compilation film, *The Emancipation of Women*.
27. See the fascinating, but in the end unsatisfying film, *The First Casualty* made by John Terraine and Peter Morley for Thames Television.
28. Quoted by Chambers, *Seedtime of Reform*, p. 2.
29. Quoted in Rohan Butler, *Roots of National Socialism* (1941) p. 201.
30. See A. Marwick, *The Deluge* (1967 edn) p. 144.
31. E. L. Woodward, *Short Journey* (1940) p. 122.
32. P. Nash, *Outline, an Autobiography and other Writings* (1949) p. 211.
33. Wilfred Owen, 'Strange Meeting'.
34. P. G. Konody, introduction to *Modern War: Paintings by C. R. W. Nevinson* (1917).
35. British reviewer, quoted in E. W. White, *Stravinsky: A Critical Survey* (1947) pp. 44–5.
36. For the British evidence see Marwick, *The Deluge*, pp. 155–6.
37. The treaty is printed in vol. liii of the *Parliamentary Papers* for 1919, and as *Senate Document 49*, of the first Session of the 66th Congress of the United States.
38. *House of Commons Debates*, 10 August 1917.
39. See e.g. Cabinet Minutes, Public Record Office, CAB 23/29, 13(22)(3a) (24 February 1922).
40. P. Abrams, 'The Failure of Social Reform 1918–1920', *Past and Present*, no. 24 (Apr 1963).
41. C. E. Montague, *Disenchantment* (1922) p. 24.
42. A. J. P. Taylor, *English History 1914–1945* (1965) p. 166.
43. Quoted by Butler, *Roots of National Socialism*, pp. 207–8.

# 4. The Second World War: Germany and Russia

## I Totalitarianism and Democracy on the Eve of the War

The divide between east and west had seemed pretty obvious in 1914: autocracy, or near autocracy in Russia and Germany, parliamentary democracy or near democracy in France, the United States and Britain. In 1939 there seemed to be just as sharp a divide between the totalitarianism of Communist Russia and National Socialist Germany, and the parliamentary democracies of the west. Yet that is only part of the distinction: it is very important, especially if we are to be able to assess the consequences of the war, to grasp that both Russia and Germany were revolutionary countries – while France, Britain and the United States seemed firmly set in the traditional political forms as they had emerged from the previous war. Those in Britain and France in the 1930s who were disappointed with their own country's failure to deal with the pressing social and economic problems of the time pointed to the contrast between their stagnant societies and what they thought of as the dynamism of Germany, Russia, and, also, of the United States of the New Deal; many Americans were more conscious of the inadequacies of the New Deal in face of continuing unemployment than of its successes.

Short of invasion or defeat, I have argued, political structures are the last to change in face of the test of war. In terms of voting rights, Britain by the 1930s had become a full political democracy, though many anachronisms remained, particularly in the administration of the civil service, of local government, and of the law. The two-party parliamentary system seemed almost to have fallen into abeyance since the Conservative-dominated 'National Government' had achieved a crushing parlia-

For Notes and References to this chapter, see p. 149 below.

mentary supremacy in the aftermath of the 1931 financial and political crisis. In France the multi-party system and the constitutional weakness of the executive had provoked a condition verging on political disintegration. On 6 February 1934 a massive right-wing demonstration took place against the Socialist-supported Radical government of the day. Fourteen rioters were killed, and over 600 were injured. During the period of high tension which followed, the then Prime Minister, Daladier, gave a nice demonstration of parliamentary weakness in face of pressure from outside, by first securing a vote of confidence from parliament, then promptly resigning. His successor, just to drive the point home, was an ageing former President recruited from outside parliament, who preferred to govern by executive decree rather than through parliament. In 1936 a new alliance of left-wing parties, including the Communists, was formed, and this did sufficiently well in the general election of that year for Leon Blum to head a 'Popular Front' government and became the first Socialist to assume the office of Prime Minister. This victory was hailed by an exuberant outburst of strikes, leading in turn to further action on the part of the extreme right-wing and fascist organisations (the Croix de Feu, the Cagoulards, and the Parti Populaire Français), whose strength was growing all the time. Anti-semitism (Blum was a Jew) reappeared as a disruptive feature of French public life. Because he had to act in co-operation with the conservative-minded Radicals and because he lacked the executive power to overcome entrenched resistance to financial reforms, Blum fell from power after little more than a year. The old round of shifting coalitions pursuing compromising policies was resumed, against an ominous background of mounting fascist and anti-democratic sentiment within France.

In the United States the election to the presidency of Franklin D. Roosevelt (he took office on 4 March 1933) and his re-election in 1936 seemed to suggest that the country had moved into a new era of strong federal initiatives to combat the evils of the depression. However, the United States' 'balanced constitution' stood unchanged, and the Supreme Court was able in 1935 and 1936 to declare unconstitutional two important products of Roosevelt's New Deal – the National Recovery Administration, and the Agricultural Adjustment Act – as well as many other pieces of legislation. Throughout 1936 the lower federal courts granted hundreds of injunctions against the National Labor Relations Act. But when the President attempted to carry through a reorganisation of the judiciary he was unable to carry Congress with him. Nevertheless the threat of enforced reorganisation did bring a slight change of heart in the Supreme Court, and in 1937 it upheld both the Labor Relations Act and America's first Social Security Act.

The single salient characteristic of the three western countries was the persistence right through the 1930s of low levels of industrial production and high levels of unemployment. Well over seven million were out of work in the United States at the end of the decade; over a million in Britain. In France the crisis of 1929–31 had not struck so sharply as in the United States and Britain, but there was on the other hand, even less sign of 'recovery' and unemployment persisted at around half-a-million. If we are to arrive at a clear picture of the relative effects of the Second World War on eastern and western countries we must be careful not to parody the condition of the democracies in 1939. There is much to be said for the view which sees the social policies of the New Deal, the Popular Front and the National Government in Britain, as laying down some of the basic framework of the social policies of the forties, fifties and sixties. No one has cast doubt on the essential resilience of the American entrepreneur in the thirties; economic historians now stress the very real character of British economic recovery in the thirties; and Stanley Hoffman, while describing France in the thirties as a 'stalemate society', has noted that already in the thirties this same stalemate was being challenged.[1] For those in employment real earnings were moving up slowly in all three countries, but everywhere, as social surveys made clear, there were pockets of dire poverty – old age, unemployment, and having, or belonging to, a large family, being three of the commonest preconditions for this. Public medical provision was probably best in Britain, yet even here there were serious weaknesses inherent in the distinction made between 'panel patients' covered by the health insurance scheme, and private fee-paying patients, and, in the divide between private 'voluntary' hospitals and local authority hospitals.

On one level the increasing homogeneity between social classes, already noted as one of the consequences of the previous war, continued; but on another the existence of a very sharp class commitment and bitterness must be noted as an outstanding characteristic of thirties' society in the west. In the formal, political, sense, these societies were certainly democratic, though the existence of unemployment, poverty, unequal educational provision, and strong class and community prejudices formed important qualifications upon any claims they might have made towards also being economic and social democracies. Radio and sound film had joined newspapers as means of communication and of influencing opinion. In none of the three countries were the media directly controlled by the government, but without doubt they served to perpetuate and to standardise attitudes which were very much those of the powerful, wealthy minority.[2]

## Russia

That revolutionary Russia was to be a totalitarian society became apparent in 1921 and 1922, when any lingering faith in Marx's notion that the revolutionary state would wither away in order to leave full self-government was clearly abandoned. All parties other than the Communist party were outlawed, 'opposition' groups within the Communist party were suppressed, political activity which might help the 'international bourgeoisie' was banned, and, to ensure the enforcement of these policies, still more power was given to the secret police (the *Cheka*, established in 1917, became the G.P.U. in 1922 and the O.G.P.U. in 1923, and in 1934 was integrated into the N.K.V.D., the People's Commissariat of International Affairs). The forms of the All-Russian Congress of Soviets, elected by the whole population, and the Central Committee, elected by the Congress, remained, but power was effectively concentrated in the ten-member Council of People's Commissars, and, in greater degree, in the five-man Politburo of the Communist party. As the party expanded in size from being, as Lenin had envisaged it, a small, distinct élite, Stalin was able to use the Party Secretariat as a base from which to build himself up to the position of Lenin's undisputed heir. In 1928 Stalin launched what is often referred to as the 'second revolution', the period of rapid industrialisation achieved through combining maximum production with minimum consumption (which in effect meant the waging of a ruthless 'second civil war' against the richer peasants), designed to make Russia a first-class modern power. In 1939 this 'revolution' was still in process, though already Russian industrial production had – at enormous social cost – not only recovered completely from the war and post-war disruptions, but was at least three times as high as in 1913; and this at a time when production was practically static in the west.

In any summary of the state of Russian society on the eve of the Second World War certain features stand out. At a time of rapid industrialisation and massive population movements, life in general was pretty grim. Soviet statistics are not always completely helpful; in calculating real wage levels, furthermore, account has to be taken of the large discrepancy between official prices and free-market prices for the same goods. The broad picture agreed on by relatively sympathetic western commentators is of a sharp overall drop in standards from

1928 when the second revolution began, followed, after a period of serious privation and shortages of goods and services, by quite a sharp rise in real wages from around 1936 onwards. At best, real wages in 1937 were back to about 85 per cent of the 1928 figures.[3] But it also has to be appreciated that the Stalinist industrialisation policies involved a definite emphasis on incentives and wage inequalities. While on the one hand the average was brought down by the influx into the towns of unskilled former peasants, who could still only command low wages, on the other hand many workers had seized the opportunities open to them to earn considerably more in 1937 than they had in 1928. As a consequence of rapid industrialisation and population movement, housing conditions were appalling, and were not improved by the concentration of state policies on the construction of such prestige projects as the Moscow Underground. In 1935 40 per cent of all 'families' (the term includes single persons subsisting alone, as well as full family units) inhabiting the 'old', that is the major, part of Moscow, lived in one room, 23·6 per cent had less than a room, 25 per cent lived in kitchens or corridors, 25 per cent lived in dormitories, while a lucky 6 per cent had more than one room.[4] In other aspects of social welfare Russia was genuinely moving ahead of anything else in the world (and, indeed, the Moscow Underground could be regarded as a specially luxurious kind of social service). The system of paid holidays, henceforth an integral part of Soviet social policy, began in the 1930s. There were at the same time great developments in health provision, with the institution of general sickness benefits and of the system of polyclinics. On the eve of the war Russia had more doctors per thousand of the population than Germany, France, Britain or the United States.

The theory of Russian political life was embodied in the new Soviet Constitution of 1936, which, within a social and economic framework determined by collective farming and state ownership of industry, guaranteed democratic rights and individual liberties to all citizens. The reality lay in the wave of terror, involving arrests, show trials and no trials, executions, and exile to Siberian labour camps, by which Stalin rid himself of any possible threat, however remote, to his own supreme power, and which, ironically, was just getting under way as the new Constitution was published. All the remaining 'old Bolsheviks' of 1917, including all of Lenin's Politburo (apart from Stalin himself), Marshal Tukhachevsky, Chief of the Red Army, Admiral Orlov, Commander-in-Chief of the Red Navy, and most of the top military and naval leadership, ambassadors, leading figures in all Soviet institutions, party workers, and thousands of ordinary people, perished.

Two aspects of the purges have to be stressed. First, they represent the extreme of arbitrary totalitarian power, and suggest in an awesome way the limits on political freedom possessed by the ordinary Russian. Second, they are part and parcel of a continuing revolutionary situation in which the entire social and political leadership as established in the early 1920s was replaced by a new leadership which had grown up with post-1929 policies. This social revolution was intensified by the manner in which, from being a separate political élite, the Communist party had taken over leadership in all walks of society; no longer could the non-party expert expect to wield any influence. In one area Russian society was quite consciously, as it were, counter-revolutionary. The older family virtues, from which there had been some 'liberation' in the twenties, were re-emphasised: 'a bad family man cannot be a good citizen and social worker', said *Pravda*; [5] divorce was again made difficult, abortions made illegal, the ideal of virginity once again promoted.

## Germany

The inhumanity and suffering which characterised much of Russian life in the 1930s is indisputable, but at least they can be associated with a quite phenomenal achievement in industrialising the country and even in laying the basis for much better living standards in the future. Historians have found it much more difficult to say anything at all on behalf of the 'revolutionary' policies of National Socialist Germany. There are, of course, those who still argue that the National Socialist régime was simply the agent of German capitalism determined to suppress the challenge of both Communism and Social Democracy, and hoping through conquest to gain new markets and new sources of raw material. Others again would see Hitler and his immediate entourage as simply a gang of evil madmen whose own personal proclivities determined the whole policies and orientation of German society.

Let us try to look more closely into the nature of German society as it had developed by the 1930s. The trauma of defeat, the incomplete nature of the 1919 'revolution', the apparent successes of ruthless business management in the 1920s followed by catastrophic economic collapse and unemployment reaching six million, in combination with developing tensions between, on the one side, rural workers who had suffered particularly seriously in the economic disaster together with the white collar lower middle class, which found its position further undermined in every unheaval, and, on the other, the whole of industrial society, meant that Germany, though potentially enormously powerful,

was a peculiarly unstable society. A National Socialist régime was in no
sense an 'inevitable' outcome. Hitler's popular vote was actually on the
wane in the election which preceded his being summoned to power.
But neither was the advent and consolidation of a National Socialist
régime merely the triumph of a few perverted personalities, nor a matter
of miscalculation on the part of German capitalists. Indeed it is clear
that a good deal of success attended the Nazis' deliberate wooing of the
working-class vote – the industrial workers after all were the principal
victims of the economic crisis. The goals of National Socialism were
not always consistent, coherent, or even comprehensible, but together
they embraced views widely held in German society and, indeed, elsewhere. Though business interests were willing enough to finance Nazism,
and the Nazis were willing enough to accept the support of these interests, the basic support for National Socialism lay in other quarters: it lay
indeed with these very rural and lower-middle-class interests which
were hostile to the developments of modern capitalism. In power
National Socialism exacted from industry concessions as no other party
had done, and, in fact, business tended to prosper to the extent to which
it was prepared to co-operate with the régime.

National Socialism postulated ideals of racial purity and racial
superiority which, alas, can now be seen to have too firm a hold on
the human psyche everywhere, not just in Germany with its long tradition of Slavophobia and anti-semitism. National Socialism argued that
democracy was an effete sham: given the state of Germany at the
beginning of the 1930s and of the west throughout the decade, this was
a far from absurd proposition, and as an argument it had a special
appeal for all classes in Germany where the democratic instinct was
never strong, and where nationalists had worked successfully to associate democracy with national defeat and economic disaster. National
Socialism glorified violence and the supremacy of emotion over rational
calculation – an approach with a wide appeal in the Europe which
emerged from the First World War. The revolutionary social and economic changes implicit in National Socialism only became clear as
National Socialism established itself inside Germany, and *vis-à-vis* the
other powers: they were rooted in doctrines of extreme German
nationalism and racial supremacy, of the need for complete economic
self-sufficiency ('autarky'), of German expansion into the territories
of inferior races, but also in notions of the unity of the German people,
of opportunity for the little man, and of the re-establishment of the
values of rural society and of the traditional German home as against
those of international capitalism. But first, last, and all the time, National

Socialism embodied the leadership principle, that the actions and intuitions of Adolf Hitler in some semi-mystical way embodied the popular will of the German people: the appeal to leadership, a potent one at any time, was particularly strong for a baffled, battered people tiring of the responsibilities of self-government.

Hitler became Chancellor of Germany in 1933 through the due constitutional procedure of an invitation from the President of the Republic, Hindenburg. His first government consisted mainly of Nationalists, together with a few of his own National Socialists. Once in office he insisted on a general election in which, aided by emergency decrees, control of broadcasting, and naked violence, he increased the National Socialist strength in the Reichstag from 196 to 288 (a popular vote of 17 million, 43·9 per cent of the electorate – not a striking victory by any means, given the resources at Hitler's disposal). By the end of the summer of 1933 the right to strike had been abolished, the trade unions dissolved, and a one-party National Socialist state established.

In the earlier days the main organ of Nazi violence had been the S.A. (*Sturm Abteilung*, storm detachment). Within the S.A. there developed the select, more tightly organised S.S. (*Schutz Staffeln*, defence squads). In 1934 the S.S. was the main agent in carrying through, partly on behalf of the army which detested the S.A., a bloody purge in which the leadership of the S.A. (all Nazis of genuine left-wing leanings) were liquidated along with many others. When Hindenburg died in August 1934 the offices of President and Chancellor were merged. The army now took a personal oath of allegiance to Hitler, who at the same time had himself declared 'Führer and Chancellor'. In theory the officer corps continued to act on the principle that their higher duty was to Germany, rather than to any particular ruler, but in practice Hitler secured closer co-operation with, and loyalty from the army than had any previous régime. Officially the policy towards all institutions and groups within Germany was one of *Gleichschaltung* (co-ordination). From March 1933 the independent power of the individual states began to be severely restricted so that for the first time Germany became a strongly centralised state. Eradication of all overt opposition was secured through the systematic violence of the S.S. and the secret police (Gestapo). Inculcation of the goals of the régime was secured through the Ministry of Public Enlightenment and Propaganda, headed by Goebbels, and through his Reich Chamber of Culture.

National Socialism's greatest success lay in the sphere of unemployment, which was brought below a million in 1937, and practically abolished by 1939. This achievement was the result of the deliberate

drive towards economic self-sufficiency, the build-up for military purposes of the heavy and chemical industries and the launching of such
massive public works' programmes as the building of the *Autobahnen*;
military service (for young men) and Labour Service for both sexes
also helped by removing young people from the labour market. Since
government policies were essentially those of guns *and* butter, real
living standards started moving upwards from the middle of the decade,
though the nature of totalitarian control over labour is seen in the fact
that Germany was unique among all the major countries studied in this
book in that real wages actually fell slightly between 1932 and 1939.[6]
Socially, the National Socialist régime has often been seen as merely
perpetuating and intensifying the dominance in the class structure of the
Junkers, generals and industrialists. In practice this was very much the
case; but at the same time there was considerable upward mobility in
the manner in which important functionary roles were occupied by party
officials, often from the humblest origins. Certainly the National Socialist
revolution did destroy many of the major institutions of the older
society, particularly the political parties; and the universities and the
churches were brought within the ambit of co-ordination. With the
replacement of the trade unions by the Labour Front, labour lost not
only the right to organise and to collective bargaining, but also freedom
of movement and freedom in choice of job. Dr Schoenbaum has suggested that these losses might not have seemed so severe to younger
workers, whose first adult experience had been of unemployment, as to
older workers. It can be pointed out, too, that many of the restrictions
were shared by employers.[7] Professor Guillebaud attempted to pinpoint
the nature of the change in class relations in Germany by citing the
case of an ex-Communist house painter who described National Socialism as a movement which would enable him to meet his employer outside
working hours on an equal basis while allowing himself, if he had the
ability, to work himself out of the ruck and thus benefit his family.[8] As
late as December 1944 a mining family whose son had recently been
killed in action expressed thanks to the commander of an Adolf Hitler
school 'for the splendid hours that our Helmut was allowed to spend at
the highest school of the Reich: . . . something we could not have
afforded to offer him ourselves'.[9] Of course these are, in themselves,
trivial examples, but the point that does have to be made is that thousands of Germans believed that National Socialism offered opportunity
even for those down at the bottom of the social scale; and there were
enough party members of humble origins seemingly performing elevated
functions to give apparent substance to the belief.

There were not many significant developments in social welfare policies, though, as in Soviet Russia, there was a great extension of the idea of holidays with pay. Large families, too, were encouraged and helped by marriage loans and baby bonuses; and there were important extensions to the labour laws protecting women and girls. The conservative aspects of National Socialist theory aimed at a return of workers to the land, and of women to the home. Such were the pressures of modern industrialism that in fact little was achieved in either direction.[10] Agricultural wages remained lower, and hours remained longer than those in the towns.

The National Socialist state was quite clearly orientated towards expansion in central and eastern Europe. It had a viciously repressive régime which carried through its own massive purges in 1934, and which, from the time of the Nuremberg Laws in 1935, initiated a campaign of brutality against the Jews which after 1938 escalated towards total inhumanity. At the same time it sought to achieve the contentment of most Germans through the establishment of full employment and provision of consumer goods. Rearmament was only carried out to the extent necessary for the waging of short blitzkrieg wars; to have rearmed for total war would have been to impose demands upon the German worker which Hitler did not desire. Germany, then, was not, as was sometimes said at the time, and since, prepared for a full-scale total war. But she was already on a sort of permanent semi-warlike footing, fully ready to fight brief aggressive wars, which could be conducted without serious inconvenience to her civilian population. This particular state of organisation and preparedness will be a most important consideration when we try to assess the impact of the Second World War on German society.

Behind the imposed national unity were numerous conflicts and tensions. Many of those which had made the advent of National Socialism possible were certainly not solved by the régime; other tensions were fostered by the openly revolutionary policies pursued. Hitler could not build up a new society and a new economy, as it were, from scratch as Stalin could. (In an earlier chapter we noted how Lenin modelled some of his economic policies on those of imperial Germany at war; now, in an odd reversal of fortunes, Hitler, privately, was a sincere admirer of Stalin and his policies.) While success lasted and terror mounted, potential centres of opposition were not very obvious. But they existed, so that there were limits upon the sacrifices Hitler felt able to call for from the German people as a whole. High policy was very much a matter of the Führer's intuition and the Führer's will. Much detailed and local policy-making lay within the province of individual National Socialist bosses both at national level and at the level of the district leaders, the *Gauleiter*. There was much conflict, confusion, and, therefore, of course, inefficiency. Economic policy, for example, was a matter of continuous conflict between Goering, whose grandiose title was General Plenipotentiary for the Four Year Plan (launched in 1936 with the aim of making Germany economically self-sufficient), the Economics Ministry, the Reichsbank, and the Labour Front. In a comment pregnant with significance for a study such as this, a perceptive German critic at the time noted of the National Socialists, 'These people have no idea what a state is like. Such an apparatus is incapable of surviving the test of war.'[11]


## II   The War and German Society

Most studies relating to Germany and the Second World War, apart from purely military ones, tend, very reasonably, to cover the whole span of occupied Europe, or to consider aspects of Hitler's 'New Order'. The purpose of this section, however, is purely to consider the effects of the war on German society; the impact of invasion and occupation on other countries will be discussed in Chapter 6. Events in Germany were so cataclysmic as perhaps to cast great doubt on the adequacy of my four-tier model to cope with them: from a period of easy victories in which living standards were maintained and even enhanced, Germany moved to a time of almost incessant aerial bombing of unprecedented intensity, to a culminating period of invasion accompanied by an almost complete collapse of society, and on to an immediate post-war period of grim privation in a divided Germany, which was accompanied by an exposure of the atrocity of German wartime policy towards the Jews and other nationalities, and from there, eventually, to another 'economic miracle' from which West Germany emerged as the world's most prosperous country.


### The First Phase: September 1939 to Spring 1942

As was stressed in the previous section, the first consideration to be taken into account in beginning a discussion of the impact of the war on German society is the extent to which that society was already organised to fight a certain type of war. In other countries the war forced immediate changes; in Germany, as long as the successful blitzkrieg wars which Hitler had envisaged continued, life went on much as before. Let us look quickly at this phase, which covers the invasion and conquest of Poland (October 1939), the occupation of Denmark and Norway (April 1940), the defeat of France (June 1940), the crushing of Yugoslavia and Greece (March and April 1941), and the series of astonishing victories in Russia which seemed to herald the fall of Moscow (June to September 1941).

National Socialist Germany was organised in such a manner as to minimise the *disruptions* of the only sort of war Hitler contemplated fighting; indeed it was organised to profit directly from war. The building of autobahns and the planning of grandiose public buildings continued unabated; and party functionaries maintained their lavish private expenditure. Rationing, it is true, was extended to almost all commodities from the start of the war, and there was a slight fall in standards of food available over the period to May 1940. Thereafter there was a slight improvement as the ordinary German benefited both from the systematic requisitioning sponsored by his government and from private enterprise looting. While Hitler used some of the cultural spoils of war to endow public galleries, party officials, from Goering downwards, assiduously feathered their own nests. There was no total domestic mobilisation; the blitzkrieg strategy simply depended on building up the particular industrial sectors needed for each particular war. From the outbreak of war to May 1942, 7,805,000 men were drafted from civilian occupations into the armed forces.

To the restrictions on mobility of labour already existing was added, on 1 September 1939, a new decree restricting changes of employment. But still the German labour market remained relatively insulated since by this time well over four million foreign nationals had been recruited forcibly or otherwise to the German labour force. Among Germans there was little redeployment of labour and no large scale mobilisation of women. In fact the number of women in the civilian labour force actually decreased by 249,000. Top Nazis continued to believe, at least in public, that work by women outside the home would damage their 'psychic and emotional life' and impair their ability to bear children, though this may just have been a gloss on the embarrassing fact that many women were unwilling to take employment anyway.[12] In this first period the total number of domestic servants was cut by only 165,000. By May 1942, then, when other belligerents were straining every sinew to maximise their manpower, the total German labour force was down by almost four million on the pre-war figure.

During 1940 the British R.A.F. Bomber Command mounted occasional daylight raids on strategic centres in Germany, with one raid on Berlin in August, intended as retaliation for the London blitz. In the autumn, because of the vulnerability of bombers in daytime, the British switched to night attacks on strategic centres. It was soon suspected that 'precision bombing' at night was wildly inaccurate, and this was confirmed by a study of photographic evidence undertaken in August 1941. Thereafter, partly because of these findings, partly because of a desire on the part of the British to hit back at the Germans somehow, precision bombing was abandoned for 'area bombing': that is to say, instead of aiming at strategic industrial complexes and military installations, bombs were now being directed indiscriminately at civilian housing. Even so, these raids were not particularly damaging, so that by the end of the first period bombing had not really had any seriously disruptive effect on German society.

In National Socialist ideology war was quite unashamedly regarded as a 'test' in the obvious, value-loaded sense which I have explicitly disavowed in my usage of the word. The National Socialist state was organised towards the expansion of German territory through a series of blitzkrieg wars which would leave unimpaired the standard of life and norms of behaviour established in the 1930s. Up till the spring of 1942 Germany, in most respects, did outstandingly well in this test, and in fact German territorial expansion continued till the autumn of 1942, when it reached its furthest extent (see Map 2).

However, the invasion of Russia, and the hazards encountered there after September 1941, undoubtedly imposed new stresses on German society. Food conditions became suddenly worse in the autumn and winter of 1941–2. Yet, for the time being, the effect of this domestic crisis was simply to demonstrate the strength of National Socialist institutions. Even Max Seydewitz (a leading German Social Democrat in exile in Sweden who compiled, mainly from the German newspapers, a contemporary account of the German home front), was forced to make a favourable comparison between the reactions of the National Socialist régime and those of the Kaiser's government in the previous war.[13] Hasty but energetic measures were taken, which eventually merged into the more thorough reorganisation of the second phase of the war. While the imperial government had never fully admitted its difficulties, the National Socialists now publicly admitted that times were hard and called for the utmost effort from everyone in the community.

Here was the *participation* effect at work in a minor way: but any full analysis of the participation effect of war in Germany (or for that matter in Russia) must take into account the extent of totalitarian control of labour. While things went well for Germany there was little scope for unguided forces to come into play, and the main significant factors continued to be Hitler's memory of how material deprivation in 1917 and 1918 had brought a collapse in morale and his determination to avoid a recurrence of that situation. For rationing purposes German civilians were divided into four categories: normal consumers, workers doing overtime and night work, workers doing heavy work, workers doing very heavy work. Up till the spring of 1942 main rations in grams per week were as shown in Table I.

|                                         | Bread | Meat | Fats |
| --------------------------------------- | ----- | ---- | ---- |
| Normal consumer                         | 2250  | 400  | 269  |
| Worker doing overtime and night work    | 2850  | 600  | 289  |
| Worker doing heavy work                 | 3650  | 800  | 394  |
| Worker doing very heavy work            | 4650  | 1000 | 738  |

TABLE I

The crude manner in which participation in the war effort brought basic rewards is driven home by the fact that material standards in the armed forces were considerably higher.[14]

The most interesting aspect of the immediate *psychological* impact of the war is its remarkable similarity to that which obtained elsewhere in Europe. Whereas jingoistic enthusiasm had been the keynote in August 1914, resigned and often apprehensive acceptance of the inevitable was the predominant emotion in September 1939. Albert Speer comments in his memoirs:

> Because of the general nervousness a false air-raid alarm was sounded in Berlin early in September. Along with many other Berliners I sat in a public shelter. The atmosphere was noticeably depressed; the people were full of fear about the future.
>
> None of the regiments marched off to war decorated with flowers as they had done at the beginning of the First World War. There was no crowd on Wilhelmsplatz shouting for Hitler.[15]

Even after the fall of France, Speer was wondering 'at the apathy I thought I observed in the public despite all the grand triumphs', though it should be noted that the film evidence certainly shows the Germans enthusiastically rejoicing over these 'grand triumphs'. For the time being the war seems to have served the useful purpose for the ordinary German of distracting his attention from those aspects of the régime over which he might well have had doubts and of canalising his energies behind the government.

But there is a much more horrific dimension to the psychological aspect of the opening phase of the war. Addressing the Reichstag in January 1939, Hitler had declared that 'if the international Jewish financiers . . . succeeded in plunging the nations once more into a world war the result will be . . . the obliteration of the Jewish race in Europe'.[16] Of course National Socialist policies towards the Jews were brutal enough in pre-war days, yet there does seem to be a clear link between the mounting intoxication of war and the steady movement from extreme brutality to out-and-out genocide. Success in war, which meant success for National Socialist ideas, both intensified the drive towards a truly 'revolutionary solution' to the 'Jewish problem', and provided the opportunity for such a solution, since every victory brought more and more of Europe's Jewish population under German control. First, in 1939–40, official ghettoes were established in Poland; then, in 1940–1, there were plans for transporting all Jews to the French colony of Madagascar; finally, in the midst of the astonishing military successes in Russia, plans were formed for a 'final solution'. In 1941–2 four extermination camps were built in Poland and the Auschwitz concentration camp was converted into an extermination camp. Reports of the camps reached the west during 1942, but, in a final twist to the psychological consequences of the previous war, they were generally discounted as mere war propaganda.

## The Second Phase: Spring 1942 to Spring and Summer 1944

However remarkable the German success in Russia, it was becoming painfully apparent by the spring of 1942 that the blitzkrieg strategy could not be successful in the vast spaces of Russia, in face of freezing temperatures and the surprising counter-attacks of the Russians. No longer could Germany continue on the semi-warlike footing of peacetime. Now, as the pressures of war really took hold, some of the mechanisms of change began to come fully into play. No longer were events entirely within the guided control of the National Socialist leadership, though, of course, their totalitarian power through S.S. and Gestapo continued to be exercised right to the end of the war. By December 1941 German casualties in Russia were already running at twenty-five per cent. The German armies enjoyed spectacular successes again in the spring and summer of 1942; in the autumn it seemed as though they might well take the vital strategic and industrial centre of Stalingrad.

But in the end the German armies had to face superior forces, better equipped; the German surrender at Stalingrad on 2 Februaury 1943 was one of the great military turning points of the war.

The *disruptive* effects of this new phase showed themselves clearly in the changed labour situation. The newly-appointed Plenipotentiary for Labour Allocation, Sauckel, began a really massive transfer of foreign labour to Germany: by the end of May 1943 there were 6·25 million foreign workers in Germany. Economic necessity could not suppress the prurient racism of National Socialism: on 15 February 1942 Goebbels was noting in his diary the danger 'that intercourse between these workers and German women will cause a gradual deterioration of our race'. However, a few days later, Goebbels was commenting on a slightly different, though related, issue:

> By a decree of the Führer all intercourse with Polish girls by soldiers stationed in Poland is forbidden and punishable. I doubt very much whether this decree is practical. . . . As long as German women are forbidden to follow the armies in these areas one can't be too severe, for in one way or another nature will claim its rights in the end.[17]

All foreign labour was rigidly segregated, being housed in squalid, inadequate camps. Theoretically foreign labour from the western countries was supposed to get the same rations as German civilian labour, but in practice this was never so. Eastern workers were simply treated as subhumans. This notorious remark made by Himmler to a group of S.S. Generals at Posen on 4 October 1943, makes the point:

> What happens to a Russian, or to a Czech, does not interest me in the slightest. What the nations can offer in the way of good blood of our type, we will take, if necessary by kidnapping their children and raising them here with us. Whether nations live in prosperity or starve to death interests me only in so far as we need them as slaves for our Kultur: otherwise, it is of no interest to me. Whether 10,000 Russian females fall down from exhaustion while digging an anti-tank ditch interests me only in so far as the anti-tank ditch for Germany is finished. . . .[18]

At the end of May 1943 the total German civilian labour force was up a million on the previous year, despite increased mobilisation to meet the heavy losses of the Russian campaigns. A decree of 13 June 1942 prohibited all changes of employment except on the order of the Labour Offices. In January 1943 it was decreed that all men between 16 and 65, and all women between 17 and 45, excepting certain categories of married women, were to register for work of national importance. But already Germany's labour resources were under severe strain: the new registration brought forward 3·5 million additional persons, almost 2·75 million of them women who for family reasons were not able to work a full week. In March 1943 it was decreed that all firms not directly concerned with the war effort should be closed down or drastically concentrated. By the autumn of the same year younger skilled workers were being called up. Basic food rations were cut on 6 April 1942: the 'normal' bread ration to 2000 grams, the meat ration to 300 grams, and the fats ration to 206 grams. There was a temporary restoration of the bread and fats ration in October, together with a partial restoration of the meat ration.

The *destructiveness* of this phase of the war, however, came in the most direct fashion: aerial bombardment. In face of criticism of the ineffectualness of the previous period of area bombing, Lord Cherwell, Churchill's adviser on scientific matters, argued for an intensified programme to turn the Germans 'out of house and home'. In 1942 the new head of Bomber Command, Sir Arthur Harris, deliberately mounted a series of spectacular raids, aided by new navigational devices and by the development of the Lancaster bomber. In May 1943 the American Strategic Air Force joined in, but concentrated on daytime precision bombing. The new British offensive opened with the raid on Lübeck of late March 1942. Very severe damage was caused to the historic centre of the town, and the shock to German confidence was considerable. All in all 1425 houses were completely destroyed, 1976 heavily damaged, and 8000 slightly damaged; 312 people were killed and 136 severely wounded out of a population of 160,000. The port of Lübeck suffered such heavy damage that the whole port area had to be closed for ten days, and there was severe damage to food and consumer goods in shops and warehouses. Yet recovery was speedy. Factories resumed work in other premises and within a week production had reached eighty to ninety per cent of normal. On the whole the civil defence system of 'self protection' set up before the war, whereby ordinary citizens, encouraged by the local National Socialist party organisations, worked together under a warden, operated efficiently.[19]

The next big raid, in April, was on Rostock. Seventy per cent of the old city was destroyed, and Goebbels, in his diary (p. 151), spoke of 'a gruesome picture of destruction; 100,000 citizens were evacuated to surrounding villages. Yet again the main story is the same as for Lübeck: by the end of the month all the principal factories were back to full production. There now followed Sir Arthur Harris's spectacular 'thousand-

# PLATES

PLATE I  BERLIN BEFORE AUGUST 1914

The still well captures the flavour of the film: the old world that was destroyed by the First World War.

Film-still from *Bilder aus Alt-Berlin*; undated, pre-1914; production company unknown, Bundesarchiv Koblenz: Magazin no. 15064/1.

PLATE II  WAR AS SPORT CONTINUED BY OTHER MEANS

This war-loan appeal cartoon shows how the 'sporting' image of war continued to be presented to domestic audiences.

Film-still from *Stand by the Men who have Stood by You*, 1918; Kincartoons. Imperial War Museum, London, Film Department Can 542.

PLATE III     WE ARE MAKING A NEW WORLD

Paul Nash (1889–1946).

Imperial War Museum, London.

PLATE IV   LONDON IN THE BLITZ

Original record film, used in many different compilations.

Film-still from *London Fire Raids*, 29–30 September 1940; London Fire Force Film Unit. National Film Archive, London, and G.L.C. Fire Brigade Department.

PLATE V    THE AIR-RAID WARNING

A scene from a remarkable acted documentary which brings home the horrors of a bombing war.

Film-still from *The Warning*, March 1939; produced by British National Films under the aegis of the National Defence Services. National Film Archive, London.

PLATE VI   DRESDEN, FEBRUARY 1945

This photograph, by Herbert Hoffman, shows the collecting of dead
bodies on 13 February 1945 after the great 'fire storm' bombing
of the city.

bomber' raids, first on Cologne, then on Essen (in fact the attack was dispersed over the Ruhr) and Bremen, and finally (in 1942) on Düsseldorf. In the Cologne raid 3330 houses were destroyed and 474 people killed. In Düsseldorf 428 houses were destroyed and 1921 seriously damaged; 33 factories and 26 public buildings were destroyed; 379 people were killed, and 1464 seriously injured. There was some evidence of panic, particularly in Cologne. Yet, again, both cities were functioning almost normally within a very short space of time.

In 1943 five times as many bombs fell on Germany as in 1942, resulting in the killing of 200,000 people and the destruction, or damage beyond repair, of 212,000 buildings. The main attacks were, in the spring, on the Ruhr, in the summer, on Hamburg, and in the autumn and winter, on Berlin. The Hamburg raid was the most destructive yet seen in history, and the first to reveal in full the awful power of fire raids, producing a series of irresistible fire storms which simply sucked everything, non-human and human, into their centre. In Britain, throughout the whole of the Second World War, 51,509 people died from enemy air raids; in Hamburg, in the summer of 1943, 243,000 people out of a population of 1·5 million were killed in one week, while almost a million people fled to the surrounding villages. Hamburg fire-storm conditions were reproduced in Kassel, where 5248 people were killed out of a population of 228,000 (just under 3 per cent of the population, compared with just over 3 per cent in Hamburg) and 91,000 people were rendered homeless. The extent of the evacuation caused by the raids on Berlin can be seen in the population figures: 4,090,953 in March 1943, 3,300,204 in September 1943, and 2,920,095 in March 1944.

In his report on the Hamburg fire raid, the Police President remarked that his account, 'even though illustrated by figures, maps and photographs' could not give 'any idea of the destruction and terror'. Actually there does exist in the Imperial War Museum in London some captured film, presumably shot by the Hamburg fire department, which adds something to our understanding of this horrific event (brief excerpts can be seen in two Open University 'War and Society' Films, *Archive Film in the Study of War and Society* and *The Strategic Bombing of Germany*). But the written report is powerful enough to merit further quotation:

The streets were covered with hundreds of corpses. Mothers with their children, youths, old men, burnt, charred, untouched and clothed, naked with a waxen pallor like dummies in a shop window, they lay in every posture, quiet and peaceful or cramped, the death-struggle shown in the expression on their faces. The shelters showed the same picture, even more horrible in its effect, as it showed in many cases the final distracted struggle against a merciless fate. Although in some places shelterers sat quietly, peacefully and untouched as if sleeping in their chairs, killed without realization or pain by carbon monoxide poisoning, in other shelters the position of remains of bones and skulls showed how the occupants had fought to escape from their buried prison.

No flight of imagination will ever succeed in measuring and describing the gruesome scenes of horror in the many buried air-raid shelters. Posterity can only bow its head in honour of the fate of these innocents, sacrificed by the murderous lust of a sadistic enemy.

The conduct of the population, who at no time and nowhere showed panic or even signs of panic, as well as their work, was worthy of the magnitude of this disaster. It was in conformity with the Hanseatic spirit and character, that during the raids, friendly assistance and obligation found expression and after the raids an irresistible will to rebuild.[20]

The last phrase, if true, certainly accords well with one of my main arguments with regard to the 'reconstructive syndrome' touched off by the destruction of war. Obviously one must take into account the police chief's desire to pass on the sort of information that he knew his superiors would wish to hear. Yet the hard evidence surely speaks for itself. In all the cities subjected to devastating raids, return to normal levels of production was achieved within weeks. In fact arms production was not only maintained, but was considerably increased during the first half of 1943; thereafter it remained steady, with a slight fall at the end of the year; then, in the first half of 1944 it rose steeply again, to reach its highest point in the summer. Serious economic damage was caused by the American 'precision' attacks, which culminated in the October raid on the ballbearings plant at Schweinfurt. A few more attacks of that sort, and the German economy might well have been completely disrupted. But in fact the cost to the American Strategic Air Force was too high to be borne, heavily laden bombers being relatively easy prey for rapid fighter planes.

Albert Speer wrote this account of one of the British winter raids on Berlin:

We drove over streets strewn with rubble, lined by burning houses. Bombed-out families sat or stood in front of the ruins. A few pieces of rescued furniture and other possessions lay about on the sidewalks. There was a sinister atmosphere full of biting smoke, soot, and flames. Sometimes the people displayed that curious hysterical merriment that is often observed in the midst of disasters. Above the city hung a cloud of smoke that probably reached twenty thousand feet in height. Even by day it made the macabre scene as dark as night.

Speer had also remarked that neither the raids themselves, nor the hardships which resulted from them, had weakened morale. On the contrary, Speer derived from his visits to arms factories and from his 'contacts with the man in the street' an impression of 'growing toughness'.[21] In his study of bomb disaster, F. C. Iklé points to the distinction between 'passive morale', which shows itself in personal bearing and in private relations and which, as a result of bombing, was generally low, and 'active morale', that concerned with public and job activities, which was not adversely affected.[22] The distinction perhaps has special validity for Germany, where public activity (and much private) was subject to such rigorous control. The evidence drawn from social psychology and sociology, as well as from historical studies, does not permit the generalisation, sometimes loosely bandied about, that bombing always intensifies civilian morale, though it may, for a short time at least, do so. In Germany any natural human resilience which we may presuppose was greatly assisted, on the one side by the encouragement of an efficient civil defence system, and on the other by the coercive powers wielded by the National Socialist state. Apart from special fire-fighting services, often composed of First World War *Luftwaffe* veterans, convoys of lorries or special trains were mobilised to serve as relief columns. Equipped with kitchens and refrigerators, together with supplies of food and other necessities, these were capable of supplying up to 30,000 meals a day. 'Community kitchens' were established and, where necessary, compulsory billeting for the homeless was strictly enforced. It was a German boast that their services were directed towards saving lives, not, as in Britain, property, and the two leading British authorities on the strategic bombing of Germany have concluded that rescue services provided through National Socialist party agencies were performed with 'humanity and commonsense'.[23] There was a much greater provision of strongly-built deep shelters than in Britain. Cellars, sometimes extended under several buildings, were turned into highly reinforced shelters. Small concrete bunkers were built in open spaces, but there was no provision for personal shelters. Many Germans took to living night after night in the deep shelters, though they did not always provide secure protection against fire storms, in which 70 per cent of deaths were caused by carbon monoxide poisoning, and 15 per cent by burns and inhalation of hot gases.

In the early stages of the war there had been great reluctance to make use of such evacuation facilities as existed. In 1942 the facilities were greatly increased, with use again being made of Party organisations: the 'National Socialist People's Welfare' and the 'Extended Child Evacuation Scheme' (this developed from a pre-war experiment in providing free holidays for city children). The main reception area was Bavaria, which became known as 'the air-raid shelter of the Reich', and evacuation remained unpopular. In 1943 other, less remote, areas were brought into use. Evacuation was still not compulsory, though teachers were compelled to go with their schools. Indiscriminate 'self-evacuation' from the danger areas, on the other hand, was controlled through a system of 'departure certificates'. More than this, long-term relief services, food tickets and so on, were supplied through places of work, so that people had to return to their jobs. Behind all that stood the S.S. and Gestapo, ready to deal with any sort of 'defeatism'. Goebbels's own private comment of 16 November 1943 is heavy with meaning: 'Morale among our people at present is excellent. This is partly owing to our good propaganda, but partly also to the severe measures which we have taken against defeatists.'[24]

This second phase of the war was undoubtedly a *testing* one for Germany, and no longer in the sense in which National Socialists gloried. The semi-war footing which worked admirably as long as Hitler could dictate the style of war, was no longer adequate when war itself remorselessly became the dictator. It was now that Albert Speer emerged as the reorganiser of the German economy. The first steps had been taken at the beginning of 1942 by Speer's predecessor at the Ministry of Armaments and Munitions, Fritz Todt, whose death in an air crash left the way open for the translation of Speer from being Hitler's favoured architect, to being the single most important influence in developing the German war economy. Speer himself identified the originator of what he called 'industrial self-responsibility' as Walter Rathenau, the great pioneer of industrial reorganisation during the First World War. Essentially the system Speer attempted to develop was that same kind of managed capitalism to which Britain and the United States also had resort at this time. But if Speer could rely on special support from National Socialist devices of coercion and totalitarian control, he also had to overcome far greater resistance than faced politicians in any of the democracies. In the spring of 1942 his Ministry took over the Wehrmacht's War Economy Branch; but it was only the dire implications of the Stalingrad defeat which enabled Speer gradually to extend the influence of his Ministry in other spheres. It took control of naval production in the summer of 1943, but did not control aircraft design and production till March 1944. Goering's Four Year Plan Office continued throughout to be at least a minor nuisance. The National Socialist gauleiters continued, usually successfully, to insist on preserving the interests of their own little fiefs, and to resist attempts to cut civilian consumption back further. The S.S. held on to, and indeed developed, its own private economic empire. Speer was unsuccessful in his bid to secure control of manpower, which instead remained within the jurisdiction of Sauckel, a dedicated old-style National Socialist. Sauckel and other dedicated party members detested Speer's policy of co-operation with big business, and obstructed his attempts to mobilise women. Eventually open disagreement arose between Speer and Sauckel over the use to be made of foreign labour: Sauckel held firmly to the National Socialist policy of transporting such labour into Germany itself; Speer saw that much higher productivity would be achieved by leaving workers to operate their own plant in their own countries.

Speer generally had the ear of Hitler, but in the jealous and barbarous maze of competing authorities which was National Socialist Germany, he could by no means count on Hitler's support. On 6 October 1943 Speer made a tough speech to the gauleiters:

> You will please take notes of this: the manner in which the various districts [*Gaue*] have hitherto obstructed the shutdown of consumer goods production can and will no longer be tolerated. Henceforth, if the districts do not respond to my requests within two weeks I shall myself order the shut-downs. And I can assure you that I am prepared to apply the authority of the Reich government at any cost! I have spoken with Reichsführer–S.S. Himmler, and from now on I shall deal firmly with the districts that do not carry out these measures.[25]

Many of the gauleiters found these threats so upsetting that they got thoroughly drunk that night and had to be helped to the special train taking them to Hitler's headquarters. But in fact the gauleiters won: little or nothing was done to curb their determination to maintain the supply of consumer goods. Responding to the test of war, Speer had brought to the surface the jobbery and corruption which was ultimately inimical to German success, though, in this case, he was not able to do much about it. Yet meantime, for all the resistances and difficulties, a remarkable transformation had taken place in the direction of a managed economy successfully producing weapons of war. From the spring of 1942 to the spring of 1944 overall German arms production rose threefold.

It is hard to discern any new gains made by any sections of the German people through their *participation* in this phase of the war, though, of course, the differential rationing system continued to provide higher rations for those whose contribution to the war effort was felt to be greatest. And it remained a fundamental element in National Socialist thinking that civilian standards should not be cut if at all possible. In practice there was still no serious privation before 1944, and standards remained well above those suffered in the comparable period of the previous war. But in the end living standards depended less and less on guided National Socialist policy or on broad unguided forces of change, but, as is classically the case in a community disrupted by war, on whether civilians had 'relatives on farms, whether they were friends with the butcher, whether they had access to the black market, whether they obtained gifts from soldiers'.[26]

## The Final Phase

In the hope of providing an assessment of the various *psychological* implications of the war, I want to turn now to the final phase of the war, in which, overwhelmingly, the single most important element is *destruction*. After February 1944 the advent of the P-51 Mustang long-range fighter plane made it possible for the American Strategic Air Force to begin the highly effective precision bombing of Germany's oil installations, and also enabled the Allies to win command of the air. At the same time Britain's Bomber Command intensified the area bombing of German cities: this policy culminated in the greatest holocaust Europe has ever seen, the fire-bombing of Dresden in February 1945 by the combined forces of Britain and the United States. One of Europe's most beautiful cities was turned to a charred moonscape; since Dresden was full of refugees from the Russian advance no one really knows how many German civilians were killed – anything from 35,000 to 140,000. The Normandy landings in June 1944 and the slow advance towards and into Germany imposed further direct disruptions of German life. The food supply situation became really serious, and, such was the havoc brought by bomb attacks, for over 26 million Germans the only places where food could be obtained were the communal food centres.

Up till this stage the most obvious psychological reaction was an underpinning of faith in the régime. Many Germans clearly retained faith in Hitler and his ideology to the end. The unsuccessful military bomb plot to assassinate Hitler of 20 July 1944, simply enabled the Führer to boast more loudly of his invulnerability, and set off a final wave of terror against all the conservative elements suspected of being implicated in the plot and many others as well. As late as February 1945 there were apparently attentive audiences for talks on such topics as 'Who shall win? Horst Wessel or Judah?' [27] Yet a rather different view emerges in this comment by a German observer: 'Pressure by the Gestapo succeeded for a long time in maintaining an artificial morale in spite of intense bombardment, but that a limit to this could be reached is clearly exemplified in the case of Dresden. When this catastrophe became known to the whole of Germany, morale disintegrated everywhere in spite of the best or worst efforts of the Gestapo.' [28]

During the first part of the last phase of the war underground factories were built: German workers, very reasonably, insisted on going to work there. In the very final stages of the war citizens actively discouraged the German forces from attempting to defend their towns since such 'defence' would make destruction by the Allies all the more certain.

Reactions higher up were a little different. In the final desperate phase there was a sharp swing away from Speer's business economy towards elemental National Socialist policies. For example, Speer's final attempt to grapple with the manpower problem was ruined by Hitler's insistence on recruiting a 'People's Army' of youngsters and old men for a death or glory defence of the homeland: thus virtually all remaining manpower was diverted away from arms production. Hitler called for a scorched earth policy in the face of the invading armies; Speer, concerned now for the state of Germany's economy after the war, put himself firmly in Hitler's black books by doing his best to circumvent this policy.

From the east the Russians reached Berlin in April 1945. On 30 April Hitler committed suicide in his bunker in the middle of the devastated capital. On 7 May the representative of Admiral Doenitz, named President by Hitler, accepted the Allied terms of unconditional surrender on all fronts. The National Socialist state, well prepared for one type of war, had collapsed in face of the test of a different sort of war. Soon after the war the German historian Friedrich Meinecke produced his agonised study of *The German Catastrophe*. But, of course, defeat and destruction were only one part of that catastrophe. The other part was only fully revealed in the west as the advancing armies reached the concentration camps: a little bit of their sense of shock can still be recaptured today from the record film shot at the time by army cameramen.[29] The post-war trials before the International Tribunal at Nuremberg publicised fully the horrific aspect of the German catastrophe. There is little virtue in dwelling on horror for its own sake but it would be an unbalanced account of Germany and the Second World War which did not conclude with some further reference to the camps which in the later stages of the war served the combined function of labour camps and extermination camps; nor, without this, would it be possible in the final section of this chapter to assess the full longer term effects of the war experience on German society.

Here, then, is the long extract quoted at the Nuremberg Tribunal from an Official Report on German Concentration Camps prepared by a special United States' Congressional Committee:

The treatment accorded to these prisoners in the concentration camps was generally as follows. They were herded together in some wooden barracks not large enough for one-tenth of their number. They were forced to sleep on wooden frames covered with wooden boards in tiers of two, three and even four, sometimes with no covering, sometimes with a bundle of dirty rags serving both as pallet and coverlet.

Their food consisted generally of about one-half of a pound of black bread per day and a bowl of watery soup at noon and night, and not always that. Owing to the great numbers crowded into a small space and to the lack of adequate sustenance, lice and vermin multiplied, disease became rampant, and those who did not soon die of disease or torture began the long, slow process of starvation. Notwithstanding the deliberate starvation programme inflicted upon these prisoners by lack of adequate food, we found no evidence that the people of Germany, as a whole, were suffering from any lack of sufficient food or clothing. The contrast was so striking that the only conclusion which we could reach was that the starvation of the inmates of these camps was deliberate.

Upon entrance into these camps, newcomers were forced to work either at an adjoining war factory or were placed 'in commando' on various jobs in the vicinity, being returned each night to their stall in the barracks. Generally a German criminal was placed in charge of each 'block' or shed in which the prisoners slept. Periodically he would choose the one prisoner of his block who seemed the most alert or intelligent or showed most leadership qualities. These would report to the guards' room and would never be heard of again. The generally accepted belief of the prisoners was that these were shot or gassed or hanged and then cremated. A refusal to work or an infraction of the rules usually meant flogging and other types of torture, such as having the finger nails pulled out, and in each case usually ended in death after extensive suffering. The policies described con-

stituted a calculated programme of planned torture and extermination
on the part of those who were in control of the German Government....[30]

## III    Russia and 'The Great Patriotic War'

On a superficial level there is one similarity between the German and
Russian experiences of the Second World War. Russia also had an easy
time in the first phase of the war when, under the terms of the German-
Soviet pact concluded on the eve of the war, she annexed the Baltic
states, part of Poland, and (with more difficulty) part of Finland. But,
however deplorable in the eyes of westerners, these annexations were
essentially defensive in a sense in which the German aggressions manifestly were not. The Russian leaders knew that at some stage they
would have to fight the Germans, even if Stalin remained hopelessly
deluded till the last over the immediacy of German plans for the invasion
of the Soviet Union in July 1941. From then onwards Russia was fighting 'the Great Patriotic War', whose overriding salient characteristic in
terms of our model is *destruction*, which in scale, and accompanying
atrocity, exceeded anything suffered elsewhere in tortured Europe.
Hitler, in the final period of the war, declared: 'If the German nation is
now defeated in the struggle, it has been too weak. That will mean it has
not withstood the test of history and was destined for nothing but
doom.'[31] Stalinism, it must be stressed again, though essentially defensive in attitude to international policy, shared with Hitlerism a belief in
war's function as a 'test', in the evolutionary, value-loaded sense which
I have explicitly disavowed. Undoubtedly Soviet institutions and Soviet
organisation did stand up very well to the enormous demands made on
them; significant changes, particularly in the distribution of industry,
took place in response to the dire needs of war. Although the Germans
were able at times to appeal to anti-Soviet and national minority sentiment, *participation* in the war was probably more total than anywhere
else in the world. But, as with Germany, any discussion of the participation effect on social change and social levelling must be set within the
context of the totalitarian nature of Russian society, and must, above all,
be set against the enormous direct destructive effect. The *psychological*
implications of the Great Patriotic War were enormous; for this was a
war in which the Russians as a national grouping were second only to
the Jews as a target for systematic brutality on the part of the Germans
and which contained great legendary set-pieces such as the siege of

Leningrad and the victory at Stalingrad, and countless incidents, sung (literally) and unsung, of individual and group heroism.

## Destruction and Disruption

The first big city to fall under threat as the Germans marched into Russia on 22 June 1941 was Leningrad. Patriotic sentiment there was high: soldiers sang in the streets of 'the People's War, the Holy War'; on the first day of war there were 100,000 volunteers, with 212,000 by the end of the week. The uppermost fear was of a London-style blitz. At the end of June thousands of children were evacuated from the city; tragically many were evacuated to the south and west where they fell victims to the unexpected German advance.[32]

From the time of his return to Russia twelve days after the beginning of the German invasion, the distinguished *Sunday Times* and B.B.C. journalist, Alexander Werth, kept an almost day-to-day record of life in Russia throughout the war years. On the face of it, he noted, Moscow in July 1941 looked perfectly normal.

> The streets were crowded and the shops were still full of goods. There seemed to be no food shortage of any kind; in Maroseika Street, I walked that first day into a big food shop and was surprised by the enormous display of sweets and pastila and marmelad; people were still buying food freely, without any coupons. In their summer clothes the young people of Moscow looked anything but shabby. Most of the girls wore white blouses, and the men white, yellow or blue shirts, or buttoned-up shirts with embroidered collars.[33]

The Soviet gift for inspired poster propaganda was much in evidence. Among the posters – which, Werth said, were being eagerly read – was one of a Russian tank crushing a giant crab with a Hitler moustache, and another of a Red soldier ramming his bayonet down the throat of a giant Hitler-faced rat. Other posters made direct appeals to women: 'Go and Work on the Collective Farms, Replace the Men now in the Army.' Recruitment into the worker brigades (*opolchenya*) armed with rifles, as long as these were available, was brisk. But Moscow was also in the grip of a spy mania: 'speaking anything but Russian aroused immediate suspicion.' The French journalist Jean Champenois (author of *Le Peuple Russe pendant la Guerre*, published in France in 1948), smoking a cigarette in Gorki Street as dusk fell, was ordered by an auxiliary militia-woman to put it out, lest it was intended as a signal for German aircraft. However, air-raid precautions were being taken seriously, and from the second week of July the large-scale evacuation of children, and of some women, took place. Air attacks began on 21 July and continued throughout July and August.

In a book which he published at the time, Werth attempted a comparison between the Moscow and London blitzes:

> I wonder if Moscow is taking the blitz as well as London? People look grim; and there are mighty few bomb jokes. Perhaps people here feel *individually* more helpless than they do in London. Ambulances are comparatively scarce, and perhaps too precious to risk in a big blitz, and they therefore do not collect the wounded during a raid, but only after the all-clear has gone. Until then the wounded have only the local first-aid to rely upon. The fire-watching rules are very drastic, and a dangerous amount of sleep is lost ... nor are most of the shelters adapted yet for sleeping.[34]

There is perhaps a whiff of British myth-making about the London blitz here. However, there can be no doubt about the drastic nature of the Russian precautions: negligent fire-watchers were shot.

By the middle of July food shortages were very apparent. Food rationing was introduced for all the major cities: 800 grams of bread a day for workers, 600 for office staffs, and 400 for dependants and children; 2200 grams of meat a month for workers, 600 for dependants and children. But the big hotels and restaurants in Moscow were continuing to serve big meals at crowded tables; theatres and cinemas were also doing a roaring business.

Meantime the Germans were advancing rapidly on Leningrad; by 20 August they were in the outer suburbs of the city, and on 21 August Hitler decreed the encirclement of Leningrad as his principal immediate objective. Rocket attacks began on 4 September; air attacks began two days later. The long agony had begun, for Leningrad was now almost totally cut off from the remainder of Russia: supplies could be brought in only by air, or across Lake Ladoga (the large stretch of water to the north east in Leningrad's hinterland), at first by ship, then by surface transport across the frozen ice; for one month, between the German capture of the supply and communications centre of Tikhvin and its recapture by the Russians on 9 December 1941, even this route was cut.

Two questions in the realm of political and military history stand out: why did the Germans not completely crush and destroy Leningrad? and why did the Soviet leadership not make more strenuous attempts to raise the siege? Part of the answer to the first question is that the Germans were more than happy to leave Leningrad to starve slowly to death while they directed their energies towards Moscow; part of the answer to the second may lie amid the devious conspiracies and rivalries which riddled the Stalinist régime, though the main fact is that for long enough Russia simply did not have the military strength to raise the siege. However, our immediate concern here is not with such matters, but with the almost unimaginably catastrophic character of the siege. The winter of 1941–2 was appalling beyond description with deaths from starvation running as high as 50,000 a month. Loss of one's ration card meant certain death. Any offence against the food regulations was punished by summary execution. Desperate, hunger-crazed citizens resorted to murder to gain food and ration cards, and to cannibalism. Frozen corpses were to be seen everywhere. Conditions lightened only slightly in the spring, when it was possible to evacuate about a million of the survivors. The remaining population, about 1,100,000 out of a pre-war total of 3 million, settled down to face the second winter of blockade. Now, though conditions were still desperately hard, better order was maintained. The streets had been cleaned up, and some of the trams were running again. Yet in July and August 1943, with the population down to a select, proud, and still near-starving 600,000, there came the worst shelling of the whole war: new street signs went up: 'Citizens: in case of shelling this side of the street is the most dangerous.' The military success which finally broke the siege did not come till January 1944. At least a million Leningrad citizens had died of starvation; another 20,000 or so from bombing and shelling.

Leaving Leningrad to starve, the Germans in October 1941 were rapidly advancing on Moscow. On 16 October many top Moscow citizens took to flight. However, Stalin remained; and Moscow, in fact, did not fall. Moscow's winter was not as desperate as that of Leningrad, but 'many individual stories were grim – stories of under-nourishment, of unheated houses, with temperatures just above or even below freezing point, with water-pipes burst, and lavatories out of action; and in these houses one slept smothered – if one had them – under two overcoats and three or more blankets.' In June bread was selling on the open market at 150 roubles a kilo (£1·50 a pound). Milk, sugar, fats and tobacco were all very hard to come by. Cabbage and other vegetables had disappeared, having been commandeered either by the German or the Russian armies. Werth noted 'a peculiar form of profiteering which had developed in Moscow during the spring, when the owner of a cigarette would charge any willing passers-by two roubles (nominally equivalent to the then British shilling) for a puff – and there were plenty of buyers'.

People in the Moscow streets looked haggard and pale, and scurvy was fairly common. Consumer goods were almost unobtainable, except at fantastic prices, or for coupons, if and when these were honoured. In the big Mostorg department store strange odds and ends were being sold, such as barometers and curling tongs, but nothing useful. In the shopping streets like the Kuznetsky Most, or Gorki Street, the shop windows were mostly sand-bagged and where they were not, they often displayed cruel cardboard hams, cheeses and sausages, all covered with dust.

There were other deplorable shortages. In dental clinics – with the exception of a few privileged ones – teeth were pulled without an anaesthetic. The chemists' shops were about as empty as the rest. . . .

Moscow itself was very empty, with nearly half its population still away. Only half a dozen theatres were open in June, among them the *Filiale* of the Bolshoi, and tickets were easy to obtain. In the buffet, all they sold, for a few coppers, was – glasses of plain water. The Bolshoi itself had been hit by a ton bomb, and was out of action. There was a good deal of other bomb damage here and there, and the sky was dotted with barrage balloons.[35]

Retreating in face of the German invasion, the Russians by the end of November 1941 had lost territories containing 63 per cent of all coal production, 68 per cent of pig iron, 58 per cent of steel, 60 per cent of aluminium, 41 per cent of railway lines, 84 per cent of sugar, 38 per cent of grain, 60 per cent of pigs. A broad view of the extent of the losses can be seen from a comparison of output in 1942 with that of 1940: pig iron, 4·8 million tons (14·9 million tons in 1940); steel, 8·1 million tons (18·3 million tons in 1940); coal 75·5 million tons (165·9 million tons in 1940); oil, 22 million tons (31·1 million tons in 1940); electricity, 29·1 milliard kWh (48·3 milliard kWh in 1940). From the very start of the war the Soviet Union embarked on a massive policy of transferring supplies and whole industrial enterprises eastwards. Werth had the opportunity, at the time, to talk to many of the workers, both men and women, who were evacuated to the Urals or Siberia during the grim months towards the end of 1941.

In most places, living conditions were fearful, in many places food was very short, too. People worked because they knew that it was absolutely necessary – they worked twelve, thirteen, sometimes fourteen or fifteen hours a day; they 'lived on their nerves'; they knew that never was their work more urgently needed than now. Many died in the process. All these people knew what losses were being suffered by the soldiers, and they – in the 'distant rear' – did not grumble much; while the soldiers were suffering and risking so much, it was not for the civilians to shirk even the most crippling, most heart-breaking work. At the height of the Siberian winter, some people had to walk to work – sometimes three, four, six miles; and then work for twelve hours or more, and then walk back again, day after day, month after month.

Werth goes on to quote an account from *Pravda* (18 September 1942) of how two buildings were erected in a fortnight to accommodate machinery evacuated from the south (no doubt there is a touch of mythology about this too):

... the people of the Urals came to this spot with shovels, bars and pickaxes: students, typists, accountants, shop assistants, housewives, artists, teachers. The earth was like stone, frozen hard by our fierce Siberian frost. Axes and pickaxes could not break the stony soil. In the light of arc-lamps people hacked at the earth all night. They blew up the stones and the frozen earth, and they laid the foundations. ... Their feet and hands were swollen with frost bite, but they did not leave work. Over the charts and blue prints, laid out on packing cases, the blizzard was raging. Hundreds of trucks kept rolling up with building materials. . . . On the twelfth day, into the new buildings with their glass roofs, the machinery, covered with hoar-frost, began to arrive. Braziers were kept alight to unfreeze the machines. . . . And two days later, the war factory began production.[36]

Agricultural production was very seriously disrupted. Almost the entire production of sunflower seed (for vegetable oil) was located in the occupied regions. Potato production dropped by two thirds. The overall effects on grain production can be seen from Table II.[37]

|  | 1940 | 1941 | 1942 | 1943 | 1944 | 1945 |
|---|---|---|---|---|---|---|
| Area sown (million hectares) | 110·5 | 81·8 | 67·4 | 70·7 | 81·8 | 85·1 |
| Yield per hectare | 8·6 | 6·9 | 4·4 | 4·2 | 6·0 | 5·6 |
| Total harvest | 95·5 | 56·3 | 30·0 | 30·0 | 48·7 | 46·8 |

TABLE II

Even when, in 1943, Russia was back on the offensive there was no direct recovery of lost productive resources, since the Germans carried out a policy of systematic destruction as they retreated. Within the territories they had occupied, 65,000 miles of railway track, half of all bridges, 15,800 locomotives and 428,000 goods wagons were totally destroyed or severely damaged. 20 million out of 23 million pigs were slaughtered or taken away, as were 7 million horses out of 11·6 million. Vast quantities of tractors and other farm equipment were destroyed, as were 3·5 million dwellings in rural areas. In towns nearly half of all housing was destroyed. The real human cost is incalculable, but it seems clear that something like 20 million Russians lost their lives as a direct result of the war.

The Second World War, then, caused enormous dislocation in Russian life, even greater in scale and atrocity than that of the First World War. There was a further ironic twist in the last stages of the war as Russian soldiers marched forward into Rumania, Poland, Hungary and Germany itself. German cities had already been flattened, but such cities as Bucharest proved a revelation to ordinary Russians of what bourgeois life and bourgeois shops could look like, providing them with a new standard of reference. Something like twelve million men served in the Russian armies; women too served as non-combatants and as combatants. But war, in a direct way, impinged on the lives of almost all Russians. The Germans as we have seen, carried out wholesale deportations in order to provide labour for German industry; apart from the massive evacuations to serve industry in the Urals and in Siberia, the Russians carried through their own deportations in the name of national security. A number of national minorities, including, in particular, the Volga Germans were forcibly moved many hundreds of miles.

*Test*

How far is it proper to make the contrast between Soviet Russia surviving the test of war and National Socialist Germany failing it? In the end Germany was faced with an overwhelming combination of Allied might; and, in the final analysis, the geographical differences discussed in Chapter 1 were of great significance: the Russians survived by withdrawing into their vast hinterland; in 1945 there was nowhere for the Germans to go. Yet it remains true that as early as 1942 the National Socialist system was showing grave flaws in face of the strains of total war; at the same time the German people, and some of the German social services, showed an amazing resilience in face of devastating bomb attacks. Russia, in the first year of direct conflict with Germany, suffered a shattering series of defeats, with the desperate human consequence we have already noted. This was due partly to the near fatal dependence of the entire nation upon Stalin's whims and miscalculations; partly, in the aftermath of the purges, to a shortage of decent military talent; and partly to the Russian inferiority in military equipment. The follies of German cupidity, arrogance, and racism have to be brought into the account too. Many of the Russian minority nationalities would have been ready to welcome the Germans as liberators, as would many peasants still unreconciled to the oppressions of collective farming. But the wholesale brutalities perpetrated in occupied territory, and the continuance of the collective farming system in order to maximise food deliveries for Germany and the German army, soon lost the invaders whatever support and sympathy they might have been able to call upon. Russia, furthermore, received vital supplies from the west. According to the official Soviet history Russia herself produced 489,000 guns, compared with 9600 from the United States and Britain, 136,800 planes, compared with 18,700 from the west, 102,500 tanks and self-propelled guns, compared with 10,800 (some of them obsolete) from the west. Even if the figures are not completely accurate in detail, it remains true, Professor Nove has concluded, 'that the U.S.S.R. produced the bulk of what was used': and 'that the vast majority of the best aircraft, tanks and guns were of Soviet manufacture'.[38] Anyway, if we are to continue the direct comparison between Russia and Germany, the vast territories and industrial potential sprawling across Europe, which the Germans could exploit until finally pushed on the defensive, must also be included in any reckoning. One area in which pre-war Soviet weakness was exposed by war was that of vehicle production; but for supplies under the American lend-lease agreements Russia might not have been able to cope with the special requirements of mobile land warfare. Supplies from the west of machine-tools, locomotives, non-ferrous metals and cable and wire also played an important part in smoothing out potential interruptions in the Russian war effort.

None the less, when set in the context of German occupation and conquest, the statistics of the Russian wartime achievement are truly impressive. Throughout the war the State Committee of Defence (Molotov, Malenkov, Beria and Voroshilov sitting under Stalin's chairmanship), effectively acted as supreme authority on all matters. Centralised control was stricter and more detailed than ever before, even in Russia's recent history. Inevitably there were many mistakes, many of them directly attributable to Stalin and the 'cult of personality'. But undoubtedly also, in this extreme time of trial, Russia was able to draw (in a manner in which National Socialist Germany could not) upon the experience of centralised planning of the previous decade. Indeed only one other country approached the Soviet Union in the extent of its organisation for war: Great Britain. The Russians had long-term plans, emergency plans, quarterly plans, and monthly plans. In the first months of war, from July to November, over fifteen hundred industrial enterprises were evacuated to the east. Along with the transfer of factories, equipment, fuel and other materials, went ten million Soviet citizens. By 1942 55 per cent of the national income was being devoted to war purposes, compared with 15 per cent in 1940. A blunt but clear measure of Russian difficulties and Russian achievements can be taken from Table III, quoted from Nove (p. 272 – in each case 1940 equals 100).

|  | 1941 | 1942 | 1943 | 1944 |
|---|---|---|---|---|
| National income | 92 | 66 | 74 | 88 |
| Gross industrial output, of which: | 98 | 77 | 90 | 104 |
| Arms industries | 140 | 186 | 224 | 251 |
| Fuel industries | 94 | 53 | 59 | 75 |
| Gross agricultural output | 64 | 38 | 37 | 54 |

TABLE III

It can, therefore, scarcely be denied that the Stalinist system withstood the test of war, as the Tsarist system had manifestly failed to withstand the test of the previous war. The final triumph was as much that of a whole people as of a political system, but undoubtedly the system succeeded in mobilising the sympathies and energies of the people. Perhaps under a more efficient and less inhumane system their sacrifices need not have been so great.

But let us move from that rather crude question to the particular changes, if any, brought about in Soviet society by the test of war. They are of two sorts. First, at the very time when so many of her productive resources were being destroyed, Russia had to maximise her productive capacity. In the event an enormous stimulus was given to development in hitherto backward areas. The Urals, where 3500 new industrial enterprises were built during the war, is a particularly significant case in point. Responsible for one fifth of Soviet metal production in 1940, by 1945 the Urals was producing well over half of the total output. Coal production rose from 12 to 257 million tons, and electricity generation doubled. At the same time the Soviet Union had now to resort to extensive use of mass production techniques. Secondly, whereas in most respects discipline had to be tightened still further, there were areas in which the rigidities of Soviet practice had to be modified in face of the realities of war. In particular, the incompetence of the 'political' generals meant that there was a rapid move away from political reliability to professional competence as the criterion for military promotions. In the desperate conditions of war, too, control over collective farms was in practice greatly relaxed. If officials, who were overworked in other directions in any case, were to have any chance of securing the necessary procurements, farmers had to be left to make their own decisions, even if these were in breach of the rules governing collective farms.

## Participation

Rumours were widely circulated that as a reward for participation in the victorious war effort the collective farm system would be greatly relaxed, or perhaps even abolished. Nothing of the sort actually happened; indeed in September 1946 the regulations governing collective farms were restored with all their old rigour. Once again it is a case of gains due to wartime participation being severely curtailed by totalitarian control. They were also curtailed by the very destructiveness of the war. In the light of the conditions I have already described with regard to, say, Leningrad and the Urals, it would need a singular obtuseness and insensitivity to maintain that participation (there was, of course, no choice) in the war effort brought anything but misery and privation, though, at times, too, there may well have been a special kind of exaltation. The key-note of the Russian effort was intensified discipline. In 1941 all workers in war industries, and all workers in transport, were rendered subject to military discipline. When holidays were cancelled in June 1941 compensation was provided, but this too was cancelled in April 1942. Anyone not directly helping the war effort was liable to be sent to the front; there was no freedom to move from job to job; overtime was compulsory. Earnings rose, but there was no appreciable upward movement of real wages, though some groups of workers did benefit from retraining and upgrading. Since the Russian revolutionary tradition welcomed the employment of women, as the German opposed it, Russian women served as non-combatants, and even as combatants, as well as in every type of civilian occupation. In 1945 51 per cent of all industrial workers in Russia were women.

Very difficult to quantify, yet very striking all the same, was the change in official rhetoric, and even in ideology, which accompanied the effort to mobilise all resources against the Germans. Anti-religious propaganda disappeared, and German persecution of the churches was even used for propaganda purposes. More important, Marxist jargon tended to give place to the old patriotic slogans. For all the ruthless discipline, a new unity in national patriotic feeling seemed to be opening between party and country. The boundaries of party membership were greatly extended, taking in, above all, soldiers who distinguished themselves in active service. A special type of participation was that of the Russian partisans operating in German-occupied Russia. Here the paradox is highlighted. Most partisans were patriots, or merely peasants seeking escape from German brutality, rather than dedicated Communists. Yet, as elsewhere throughout the national effort, the only effective organisations were those of the Communist party. Thus nationalism and party came together. Though some partisans later encountered the full weight of Stalin's mistrust, usually a successful partisan career led to political and social advancement in post-war Russia. Certainly partisan activities became a great source of inspirational legend.[39]

## Psychological Aspects

And here, in part, we move into the psychological realm of the arousing of 'in-group' feelings. In general the effect of the war clearly was to foster national solidarity. Stalin's appearance on newsreels in the cinema was instantly greeted with frantic cheering – Werth reckoned this enthusiasm to be genuine, since dissenters would be hidden in the dark, but he perhaps underestimated the potency of the group instinct.[40] (Churchill was similarly greeted, even when people were preparing to vote him out of office.) The ruthless cruelty of the Germans, unprecedented since the Tartar invasions, produced an emotional reaction of pity and pride which burst out in the music and literature of 1941 and 1942. Dmitri Shostakovich had volunteered for active defence of his native Leningrad in July 1941; instead he was allocated to air-raid duty. Refusing to leave the beleaguered city he composed the first three movements of his seventh symphony between July and October. Only then did he obey orders to move to Kinbysher, where the symphony – 'The Leningrad' – was completed the following year. With Neilsen's 'Inextinguishable' it ranks as one of the greatest musical works ever called forth by the torment of war. Representative of the same feelings are certain of Boris Pasternak's poems, written in 1941, though not published till 1945.

> Do you remember that dryness in your throat
> When rattling their naked power of evil
> They were barging ahead and bellowing
> And autumn was advancing in steps of calamity?

Naturally, the painting, literature and music which best caught the mood of the time were not necessarily of much significance as art. The most popular poem in Russia from its publication in the autumn of 1941, right through 1942, 'which millions of women recited to themselves like a prayer', was Simonov's banal 'Wait for me'.

The experience of the Leningrad siege fostered a special in-group feeling, a local Leningrad patriotism. Even as the city was being destroyed great plans were being drafted for the rebuilding of a still finer Leningrad which, looking away from Moscow, was to be a 'window on Europe'.[41] Widespread throughout Russia among thinking men of all sorts was a hope that the Great Patriotic War in which, despite its own iron discipline, there had been a broadening of party membership and a loosening of party rules, would lead to a better and freer Russia – the hope so often evoked by the holocaust of modern war.

9 May 1945 was the day of victory, an 'unforgettable day' bringing forth a 'spontaneous joy . . . of a quality and a depth' Werth had never seen in Moscow before. People hugged each other; they were so happy they did not even get drunk (which seems unlikely since they apparently also urinated in public). 'Nothing like *this* had ever happened in Moscow before. For once, Moscow had thrown all reserve and restraint to the winds.'[42]

## IV   The Aftermath of War

One of the most sharply compelling documents of any description that I have come across in my ventures into the study of war and society is a film made by the Friends' Relief Service in Germany in the months after the German surrender. The commentary is badly-spoken, but unobtrusive and to the point. Editing devices are minimal, with the screen frequently fading to a simple black between shots. There is no propaganda message till the end titles (and then it is simply to state the inter-denominational character of Christian Relief action in Germany) – indeed the most loaded thing in the whole production is the title, *While Germany Waits*.[43] The film is in fact a first-class piece of reportage showing the condition of Germany in the immediate aftermath of war in a way in which no other type of historical source could do. Starting off with Dortmund, the film shows a number of German towns. They have not been razed to the ground, since walls, factory chimneys, whole façades still stand; but they are empty shells, surrounded by heaps of rubble. All classes of housing, clearly, were devastated in the air attacks; the commentator suggests that the most drastic destruction was to the working-class housing near the station in Dortmund, but the visual evidence itself rather points up the universality of the damage. We see people living in cellars, or in crazy habitations perched up in the ruins. We see them about to eat the day's 'special', turnip thinnings.

It was to the countryside that the townsfolk constantly had resort in their search for food, for, as the film shows, most of the German countryside in the aftermath of war, remained largely undamaged. And here we have a first basic contrast with the condition of Russia, where virtually the whole of the west and south west of the country (a good half of European Russia), together with a total of 70,000 villages, had been laid to waste. Russia, certainly, was now a triumphant conqueror, the occupying power for the whole eastern half of defeated Germany. Russia, in the following years was steadily to consolidate the position bequeathed to her by the war as one of the world's two super-powers: by 1949 she had the atomic bomb; in 1957 she put the first satellite into space. Germany, too, was to make an astonishing recovery. Before we can sort out the relationship, if any, between these two indisputable developments and the war, we must stress that for both countries the immediate aftermath of war was destruction on a scale never previously experienced, and desolation and privation on a scale not experienced for many centuries.

And yet, in order not to weave fantasies and miracles where none exist, we must stress yet again one of the central paradoxes of modern war: in waging war, in attempting to surmount the effects of destruction, both nations had greatly developed their industrial capacity. In a revealing part of *While Germany Waits* we can see in the background the Hermann Goering works at Barbecke, obviously in full production. Even under the ruins, as had proved to be the case time and again during the war, plant remained relatively undamaged, so that it could again be rapidly put to productive purposes. Despite bomb damage (equivalent to 28 per cent of German productive capacity in 1936) and the dismantling of German industry carried out by the Allies immediately at the end of the war (5·7 per cent of 1936 capacity), fixed assets in Germany's industry in 1946 were still 14 per cent higher than in 1936 and about equal to what they had been in 1939[44] – with considerable extra potential once repairs had been put in hand.

In organising this book I have twice put Russia and Germany together in the same chapter, though they fought on opposite sides in both wars. The Second World War brought a crude but apparently effective solution to the problem of Germany as both a central and east European power, and a west European power. Half of the Germany of 1937 became in 1949 the German Federal Republic. Its capital was established at Bonn 'amid vineyards not potatoes' as its first Chancellor, Konrad Adenauer put it, in expressing his own firm conviction that Germany's centre of gravity lay on the Rhine, and that she should face firmly towards France and the west.[45] In this western half of Germany the Catholics were in a slight majority. A quarter of old Germany fell, as the German Democratic Republic (D.D.R.), within the Russian sphere of influence. Berlin now stood on the eastern fringes of German territory, for a further quarter of the Germany of 1937 was divided between Poland and Russia. It was the West Germany of Konrad Adenauer which achieved the 'economic miracle' in which, by the later 1950s, the Gross National Product was 125 per cent up on that of the whole of Germany in 1938.

In discussing the economic consequences of the First World War I found it difficult to decide how far the immediate effects of the war could be sorted out from the effects of the slump, and how far the economic crisis of 1929–31 could be treated as an independent variable and how far it had, in turn, to be related back to the war. A similar, though, happily, opposite problem exists for the period since 1945. During that time the countries of western Europe went through a further discontinuity, the onset of the period of affluence, with life styles determined by high levels of consumer spending and by the new technologies and their products (including oral contraception). Is this phase to be taken as itself a direct consequence of the war, or is it an independent variable? As with the 'discontinuity' of 1929–31 I believe it must be taken both as an independent phenomenon, separable from the immediate after-effects of the war, and as one in itself related to the longer-term working-out of some of the consequences of the war. Russia and East Germany, to begin with, did not share in this phenomenon, though, later, hints of it are to be found there too.

### The Four-Tier Model

Let me now try to summarise how I see the four tiers of my model coming into action with regard to Russia and Germany. I have already deliberately stressed the negative consequences of the *destructive* aspects of the war. Though I believe both countries demonstrated in full measure the way in which after the disasters of war creative energies can be released and opportunities to rebuild can be exploited, we have to handle with extreme caution the popular notion that since Germany was forced to build up her economy from scratch she could thus re-equip in the most up-to-date and efficient manner.

In a crude sense Russian institutions came through the *test* of war, and were therefore reinforced rather than changed. German institutions collapsed, and that is the real basis of the sweeping changes after 1945.

But at the same time the test of war brought improved industrial capacity to both countries, a key factor in subsequent economic developments. For West Germany the aftermath of war imposed a special test of its own: in reconstructing their country, now that the National Socialist leadership had disappeared, Germans were forced to develop real organs of discussion and consent (though, of course, direction and control at the top came from the Occupying Powers). More than this, the Germans had to meet the challenge of defeat: in the longer term that challenge produced an immensely constructive response.

Because of the constraints imposed by totalitarian rule, and because the negative effects of the war's destruction were so great, the *participation* effect played the least part in bringing about positive social change, though it can be seen at work everywhere in further developments in the status of women and of young people. Russia remained a repressively disciplined society in which even material standards took long to rise above pre-war levels. The major social changes in East Germany had little to do with participation. There were minor signs of the participation effect in West Germany, though where there was a guided policy of 'social rewards' this was rather for participation in post-war reconstruction than for participation in the war itself. Though showing a laudable humaneness in some respects, West Germany was to emerge as the most brashly American of all European societies, firmly set against community welfare and deliberate social levelling.

The *psychological* impact of the war, was immense, and even greater on Germany than on Russia. As remarked above (there is overlap here), it is in German reactions to defeat that one of the keys to Germany's subsequent economic expansion is to be found.

## Social Change – Geographical Aspects

The political decisions which settled national frontiers after the war were very much the inevitable outcome of the geopolitical situation brought about by the Allied policy of waging war right up to Germany's unconditional surrender, but we shall, none the less, have to try to keep in mind the distinction between changes brought by the war experience itself, and changes brought by post-war political decisions. Russia, naturally, consolidated and extended her frontiers, retaining the Baltic, Romanian, Slovak and Polish territories acquired in the opening phase of the war. Theoretically the Allies recognised the 1937 frontiers of Germany, and foreswore the dismemberment that they had previously favoured. In practice the whole body of Poland was given a shift westwards; German territory beyond the Oder–Neisse line was 'under Polish administration', while former East Prussia, as well as former Polish territory in the east, became Russian. *De facto*, Germany was divided between Soviet, American, British and French occupation zones; with the Allies unable at Potsdam to agree on any long-term settlement, partition into East Germany and West Germany became a fact. Berlin was itself partitioned into eastern and western sectors. The military situation as it existed at the end of the war set firm as the whole of eastern Europe, save for Greece, remained within the Soviet sphere of influence.

From the British or North American point of view the Second World War can, since there was no exact equivalent of the squalid slaughter in the western trenches, still often seem less catastrophic than the First, but for central and eastern Europe it was a gigantic demographic upheaval, whose dimensions can be roughly sketched, but whose precise implications are very hard to work out. The total Russian population loss (deaths plus loss of potential births) has been estimated at 30 million, or perhaps more. German losses seem tiny by comparison: 600,000 civilian victims of Allied bombing, 3·5 million servicemen killed; German service losses, in turn, were almost two-thirds of all European service losses outside of Russia, and almost fourteen times the British service losses. Inevitably policies of indiscriminate warfare and extermination meant that Russian (and other east European) deaths fell among women and children as well as men; indeed it was a universal feature of this, compared with the first total war, that a far higher proportion of civilians were at risk. However, the fact remained that, in the end, the highest proportion of all deaths fell among men of military age. In Russia, especially in the villages, millions of widows and orphans had to rebuild their lives as best they could alone.

Population changes were much greater this time, yet there was much less attempt at a careful spelling out of the implications than in the clauses of the Versailles Treaty; the Potsdam Conference simply decreed that 'any [population] transfers that take place should be effected in an orderly and humane manner'.[46] From areas taken over by Russia and Poland, from ancient German settlements in Hungary and Romania, and from Czechoslovakia Germans were forced to leave for, or simply fled to, West Germany: there were 10 million such 'displaced persons'. While many of the survivors of the German labour camps were able to make their way back to their native lands, there remained 250,000 or so who for various personal or political reasons had nowhere to go, and so remained aliens in Germany, nursing an understandable hatred for the Germany around them. The influx into battered, hungry West Germany was in the long term to have remarkably beneficial results for the West German economy, but more immediately noticeable was the misery of expellees who might have spent anything from three to eight days travelling in trains which were often little more than cattle wagons.

In a grim way the war created not just the opportunity but the necessity for extensive urban redevelopment. All over Europe the destruction of war had remarkably little effect in bringing about a relocation of urban centres; everywhere the tendency was to build cities upon the ruins of the old. Russia, we have seen, did enter the post-war years with substantial new industrial complexes in the hitherto neglected Asiatic heartland. The great cities were rebuilt, though with factories having precedence over housing; Leningrad, despite the hopes of wartime, was the last of the great cities to be rebuilt, and then on plans rather less ambitious than those of wartime. In Germany, redevelopment to escape bombing did not have significant long-term effects; where there were changes this was rather due to partition than to the direct consequences of war. Thus Berlin, though the western part was eventually as booming and prosperous as the rest of West Germany, suffered something of an eclipse as a political, business and professional centre. In West Germany Frankfurt made significant gains – many industrial houses, banks and insurance companies, formerly sited in Berlin, set up their headquarters there. Frankfurt also became the new centre for much of the publishing business and the fur trade of Leipzig. Hanover benefited in a similar way.[47] In East Germany reconstruction was much slower, and, in the smaller towns, much of the physical appearance of older Germany remained intact. The quiet Rhenish university town of Bonn blossomed into the capital of West Germany, though it never became anything approaching a true metropolis. West Germany, with most rebuilding to do, and most American money to spend, led Europe in developing architectural monstrosities of the North American type.

*Economic Aspects*

The German economy before the war had been a strange mixture of capitalist reality and National Socialist fantasy; West Germany after the war eventually became a model of modern high-growth capitalism. As with other European countries, but to a greater degree, the initial recovery depended very heavily upon American finance. The world situation was propitious: there was a shortage of, and high demand for, goods of all types; and the experience of peace and of war was at last being used to prevent international trade seizing up as it had done in the inter-war years. Much of the new industrial capacity of wartime was ready, or almost ready for use; the Germans were specially well practised in setting bomb-damaged factories to work again in the minimum time. With so much else in ruins, the Germans turned to hard work and entrepreneurial enterprise. Where plant was destroyed, it was renewed with the most modern and productive machinery. But the devastation which Germany had suffered brought a much more important spin-off. The Germans simply had to throw all their energies into rebuilding; after political and military catastrophe, self-respect could only be regained in economic success. All older systems of industrial relations were in ruins; now that the opportunity existed to rebuild the trade union movement, it was rebuilt to a rational plan which would enable the unions to operate in raising productivity, not cut across it, as was to happen so often with Britain's older system of industrial relations. At first it seemed that the great influx of expellees could only add a further crushing burden to a shattered country. In practice extra supplies of labour, particularly of people desperate to rebuild their lives as quickly and as fully as possible, were exactly what was wanted.

These are all unguided forces arising out of the war, many of them applying to East Germany as much as West. Denied the expected reparations from all of Germany, Russia at first laid heavy burdens on East Germany: but by the late 1950s, though growth was nothing like as spectacular as that in the west, the expansion of the East German economy was further evidence of the amazing energies of the German people in the aftermath of war. It would be a mistake to think of postwar West Germany as a land of strange good fortune, or a land guided only by the divine principles of private enterprise. Free prices and free competition were given maximum rein by Professor Ludwig Erhard, Economic Director for the Western Occupying Powers, then first Finance Minister in the Federal Republic, but it was a guided economy all the same, not utterly different from the system Speer had tried to operate in the middle years of the war. Germany, too, like Russia, benefited from the general orientation towards the greater exploitation of science-based technology which came about in what had been the most scientific of all wars.

In Russia there were changes in detail in economic practice, none in economic theory. The war reinforced the belief that Russia must be an invulnerable, self-sufficient top industrial power; it demonstrated the need for, and pointed the way towards, changing the balance of industrial power away from the exposed west; a great stimulus had been given to the development of mass production techniques. A fourth Five Year

Plan was approved in March 1946, calling for heavy investment in the industrial areas developed during the war; industry in the west was merely to be restored to pre-war levels. While there is some evidence of post-war exhaustion, of a desire to enjoy the fruits of victory, which, in turn, perhaps provided some excuse for further pressure from above for higher production, it also seems that some of the exaltation of victorious war could be canalised behind a drive which, in practice, involved more severe discipline and greater repression than the period of rapid industrialisation before the war.

## Social Structure

By the same token there was no really significant change in the social structure of Soviet Russia. Those groups which had made gains during the war were pretty quickly forced back into their old roles; thus the heavy expansion programme of the post-war years again bore heavily on the peasants. On the other hand the régime had the renewed vigour and confidence to press ahead with its social policies. Given the size of the country and its history, illiteracy continued to be a problem, yet by the time Stalin died it was almost totally eradicated. Soviet claims to have achieved the most democratic educational system in the world were not totally unfounded.

> The bright, devoted and politically sound student was privileged and carefully tended in the Soviet Union. This is important because it meant that the straightforward class correlation which we find among students at universities in England, France and Germany was modified. Many of the students at Russian universities in the 1950s had parents who, though of high status themselves, were clearly of working-class origin. The Soviet educational system might be creating a new form of inequality in the long run, based on the possession of intellectual capital, but it did not reinforce existing lines of class differentiation established in the past.[48]

In Germany two societies, different from Weimar, different from the Third Reich, and different from each other, emerged. Only the cataclysm of war, or of revolution, could have created such a situation. West Germany became a middle-class society (with a prosperous working class aspiring to middle-class standards) in a way in which Weimar, with its preservation of the old élites, had never been. In East Germany there were major land reforms in which the pre-eminence of the Junker landowners, many of whom fled to the west, was finally ended. Professor

Dahrendorf has penned a neat, if slightly abstract, comparison between the D.D.R. and the Weimar Republic:

> In the Weimar Republic the role of the citizen was formally guaranteed to all, but this offer was undermined by the absence of the social preconditions of its realization. In the D.D.R. the preconditions are present, but the realization is made impossible by numerous formal restrictions on the citizenship rights that are part and parcel of the constitution of liberty. De facto, there is no universal, equal, free and secret suffrage, no liberty of the person and of political activity, no equality before the law; but there is a society that would enable its members to make effective use of these liberties, if only they had them.

Dahrendorf, too, stresses the error of seeing East Germany as ruled by a leadership clique imposed by Russia: 'in fact, a society with its own peculiar structure has emerged.' [49]

## Social Cohesion

The history of all Europe, 1938–48, could almost be written in terms of the psychopathic attempts, first of Germany, then of Russia, then of all the Slav nations, to establish racially homogeneous empires or nation states. The rise of German military power was accompanied by massive population movements; so was the fall of German military power, and the advance of Russia. Writing shortly after the war, the great authority on European population movements, Eugene Kulischer, believed that all pockets of German colonisation, some going back to the early middle ages, had been wiped out in eastern Europe. He failed to take account of the tenacity of the 'ethnic Germans', but the broad conclusion is valid that the war and the population transfers that accompanied and followed it ironed out much of the racial diversity of central and eastern Europe. Hitler's hateful policies had the same effect in regard to the Jewish communities. Did this then mean that Germany and Russia were racially more cohesive countries than they had been before the war? Up to a point, yes; though the very economic successes of West Germany were eventually to lead to an enormous influx of foreigners – Italian, Slav and Arab. In Russia, though the Leninist tradition of respect for Russian minority nationalities was theoretically preserved, it tended to deteriorate into mere sentimentality in face of the realities of the enormous forces of Great Russian patriotism and standardisation unleashed by the war. Russia had a long tradition of anti-semitism which had apparently been exorcised in the upheavals of the previous war. A sad irony in the aftermath of Hitler's defeat was the rapid growth in Russia of hostility on the part of the ruling establishment towards the Jewish community.

In West Germany the holocaust of war and the wholesale reconstruction of society seemed to have got rid of those fundamental social conflicts which underlay the rise of National Socialism, but which National Socialism had been unable to resolve. In the end affluent West German society was to throw up further sharp stresses of its own. Nothing yet has appeared, however, that is quite as threatening to social stability as the para-military movements of the post-1919 period. After the revolt of 1953, East Germany has presented the appearance of a fairly stable society, save for the thousands who demonstrated their alienation from it by seeking escape to the west.

## Social Policies, Conditions, and Behaviour

Russia in the triumphant, though stringently austere, aftermath of war carried further the 1917 ideas of a complete social welfare system. East Germany followed in the same direction with a classless education system and comprehensive social security provision. West Germany, on the other hand, pioneered the model of contemporary welfare capitalism, explicitly disavowing the concept of universality, but aimed at demonstrable need, incorporating from the start the idea of wage-related benefits, and deliberately encouraging privately sponsored welfare schemes.

Material conditions, after the immediate post-war misery, rapidly improved in West Germany – though the average working week remained at 48 hours till 1956 – while showing far less improvement in East Germany and in Russia. Attempts to exact higher work quotas from East German workers produced the risings of 1953. In Russia real wages began to move steadily upwards from 1947, but housing conditions continued to be pretty dreadful.

Most of the characteristic features of the customs and behaviour of our own age, in which sex has completed its progression to the centre of public debate, are mainly related to the advent of affluence, and therefore only indirectly, if at all, to the war. Without doubt the upheaval of the war, massively involving civilians in a way in which the First World War had not done, brought its own moral codes. Starvation conditions as in Leningrad's first winter, brought an almost complete cessation of sexual desire; later the citizens spoke of 'trench love'. Werth quotes a cynical Russian major's comment on the activities of the advancing Red Army at the end of the war: 'Many German women somehow assumed that "it was now the Russian's turn", and it was no good resisting. "The approach", he said, "was usually very simple. Any of our chaps simply had to say: *Frau, komm*, and she knew what was expected of her."'[50] In Russia the attempt to restore the older moral canons was well under way in the inter-war years, and this policy was intensified after 1945; however it seems clear from Soviet novels that, despite the Iron Curtain, Russia after the war shared in the world-wide loosening of the older conventions.

In an era of gas chambers, labour camps, and mass bombing there are, anyway, perhaps more crucial moral issues to discuss. Was the level of violence, barbarism and inhumanity suddenly and permanently stepped up as a result of the war? Stalin's ruthlessness towards his fellow countrymen marked a continuity based on his style of rule, rather than a change due to war. It is not surprising that individual Russians seized the opportunity for reprisals upon German soldiers and civilians, but Russian official policy towards the German people was characterised by, in the circumstances, a forbearance which suggests that Nazi morality was not necessarily infectious. As far as public law can express moral codes West Germany seemed to do its best to disavow any continuance of the excesses of Nazism: from the start, for example, it had no death penalty. One article of the Versailles Treaty had attempted, without effect, to deal with the question of war crimes. At Nuremberg in 1946 the Allies publicly prosecuted the major surviving National Socialist figures; it was left to the Germans themselves to deal with the minor ones. Sometimes, it was true, men of dubious past reputation were given positions of responsibility in Adenauer's Germany; but this was rather because of the premium which was placed on ability than any weakening in the disavowal of the past. Proper restitution could, of course, never be made to the Jews, but West Germany did at least accept the responsibility for making reparations both to individual Jews and to the state of Israel.

Despite the final shock of defeat, attitudes did not necessarily change overnight among the broad mass of the German people. Public opinion surveys conducted in the immediate post-war years by the United States Military Government produced some interesting results. A poll conducted on 19 August 1946 suggested that 'large numbers of post-war Germans in the areas under American control continued to express perceptions characteristic of National Socialist ideology'. Between November 1945 and August 1947 'the percentage of Germans describing National Socialism as a good idea badly carried out remained at a

fairly high number – starting at 53 per cent in November 1945, dipping
to a low number of 42 per cent in July 1946, and rising again to 55 per
cent by August 1947'.[51] However, despite the fact that western policy
finally decreed that West Germany should rearm and have an army,
the new economic situation gradually reacted with the memory of war
to produce a steady change in the climate of opinion. Golo Mann is a
shrewd and not overly pro-German observer:

The Germans of the late fifties were no longer 'subjects'. They had
lost their old respect for authority, both public and private. The officers of the new *Bundeswehr* could tell a tale about this. It was true
that university students still came predominantly from the middle
classes and that talent among the lower classes was insufficiently
mobilized. But whereas the universities of the Weimar period had
been centres of reactionary and romantic protest, in the fifties they
were, as in America, Britain, Japan and Spain centres of vigilant,
sober criticism, centres of progressive restiveness – a difference worth
mentioning. . . .

Criticism certainly exists in present-day German literature; criticism of the welfare society, of conformism, of corruption and also of
'alienation', more or less as in other Western countries. The fantasies
which had arisen in the first thirty-three years of the century from
the morass of social conflict – on the subject of left-wing revolution
and 'conservative revolution', glorification of war, of power, of an
heroic going under – did not reappear. It was as though Germany
was as tired of intellectual as of political orgies. . . .

Finally, German society has changed. A glance at leading German
newspapers, a glance at television programmes demonstrates this
daily. The stuffy, ignorant Germano-centric, spiteful tone of the
twenties has gone. The general attitude of the press is incomparably
more open to the world, more urbane, sober and critical. This applies
particularly to the generations which, if all goes well, will occupy the
key position in ten or twenty years' time. Among the older people
there are incorrigible cases. The young generation is new. If in
present-day Germany there is a struggle between a reactionary trend
– back to nationalism, to the vicious circle of frontier disputes, to the
authoritarian state, to an over-estimate of military matter, to intoler-
ance – and a really modern trend, the latter has an incomparably
better chance than in 1927. Anyone who knows the past and therefore
realizes that he cannot know the future, will say no more.[52]

Russia, like Hitler's Germany, but unlike post-war West Germany, still stages regular military parades. But there can be little doubt, too, about the deep revulsion against war among the Russian people. And, finally, however deplorable certain Russian actions in East Germany, Poland, Hungary and Czechoslovakia, it must be recorded that neither Russia nor Germany since 1945 has resorted to the kind of insensate brutality and needless destruction of life and property which characterised both Nazi policies and the Allied raids on Dresden.

## Intellectual Attitudes

In accepting the Nobel prize for literature in 1957, Albert Camus declared:

> Men born at the outset of World War I became twenty at the time both of Hitler's ascent to power and of the first revolutionary trial. Then, to complete their education, they were confronted in turn by the Spanish Civil War and World War II – the universal concentration camp, a Europe of torture and prisons. Today they must raise their sons and produce their works in a world threatened by nuclear destruction. Nobody, surely, can expect them to be optimists.[53]

It is, I think, less easy to make out a case for the Second World War as a watershed in the creative arts in the way in which the case (with all the reservations I expressed) can be made in regard to the First World War. Writers in the inter-war years had scarcely been optimists either. Still the pessimism was perhaps a deeper and more complex one than that engendered by the First World War. More truly than ever was it perceived that it was not enough just to see the evil in war, but that the basic evil lay in man. Naturally the war figured largely as subject matter for writers both during it, and in the aftermath. Cultural developments in Germany and Russia took particular directions. Sensitive Germans could not but be preoccupied with the causes, scale and consequences of the 'German Catastrophe'. Meinecke sought for his country 'a new existence – to be sure a bowed-down, but a spiritually purer, existence'. He wanted Germans to go back beyond the traditions of Bismarck to those of Goethe. 'The German state is crushed,' he wrote, 'and wide lands are lost to us. Rule by foreigners is our destiny for a long time. Shall we succeed in saving the German spirit? Never in its history has this spirit had to endure such a severe test.'[54]

In the event the moral climate of the economic miracle seemed to be that of the grossest materialism. Thus in one of the greatest and most genuinely historical of novels ever written, *The Tin Drum* (1959),

Günther Grass traced the destructive spirit of Germany from the rise of Hitler, through the war, past the currency reform and into the age of acquisitive materialism. In a sense the Marxist playwright Berthold Brecht had seen it all in advance; and in his East Berlin theatre he continued to set a theatrical style for both Germanies.

The Great Patriotic War had brought a release of creative energies, not all of the highest order. But immediately after the war a greater cultural freeze than ever before set in, with the inspiration of the war being cited in justification of the purge of writers and artists, as this statement by Zhdanov, Stalin's principal henchman in this matter, suggests:

> In Leningrad journals, there began to appear works . . . which relapsed to a position of idealess-ness and defeatism, I have in mind such works as those of Sadofyev. . . . In some of his poems, Sadofyev . . . began to cultivate moods of sadness, longing and loneliness. . . . Needless to say, such moods . . . can exercise only a negative influence on our youth with the rotten spirit of idealess-ness, of apoliticism, of despondency. And what would have happened had we educated our youth in the spirit of despondency and disbelief in our goals? We would not have won the Great Patriotic War.[55]

After Stalin's death in 1953 there was something of a cultural thaw. Not unnaturally war is a theme which looms large in many of the works most respected in the west:

> 'A young Moscow history professor, Razvodovsky, only just arrested and who of course hadn't been at the front, was arguing passionately and brilliantly – and convincingly too – that war had its good side. He produced a whole battery of political, historical and philosophical arguments to back up his case. And some of the boys in the cell, who had fought on every front, were so furious they nearly lynched him. I listened and said nothing. Razvodovsky had some good arguments. Every now and then I thought he was right, and I did remember some good things about the war – but I didn't dare argue with those soldiers. The professor, you see, had been spared from having to fight. And as a reserve artillery officer, so had I – at least compared to those men, who had been in the infantry. You know how it was, Lev, you were at the front yourself – you had a pretty easy war in your little Psychological Warfare outfit. You were never in the sort of fighting where you and your men had to hold out at all costs. It was the same with me, or very nearly so –

I never once led an attack. Our memory plays tricks with us, we
forget the worst....'
'I wasn't saying....'
'. . . And we remember the things we liked. But that day when a
Junker dive-bombed us and nearly blew me up near Orel – there
was nothing I liked about that. The only good war is one that's over
and done with.'
'I wasn't saying it was good, only that I have some good memories.' [56]

If political structures are the last to yield to the transforming pressures
of war, equally they are the most sensitive to the actual military and
political outcome of a particular war. Stalinism could boast of its
greatest triumph ever, so Stalinism was reinforced. As Russia has
become a more sophisticated society, it seems unlikely that Stalinism,
which had almost brought the country to disaster in October 1941, will
reappear. In Germany only the total collapse of National Socialism
made possible the creation of two utterly different systems, a one-party
unitary state in the east, a democratic federal republic in the west. Here
everything that could be done by means of a written constitution to avoid
the tragedy of the past was done: thus West Germany emerged as essentially a two-party parliamentary state with the Christian Democrats
(inheritors of the Centre Party tradition, but no longer exclusively
Catholic) in office throughout the economic miracle and after, faced
by the Social Democrats, who increasingly adjusted to the world of
modern managed capitalism.

Such meticulous analysis of the consequences of war perhaps has
the danger of reducing appreciation of the awesomeness of war. Many
commentators, anyway, particularly at the height of the Cold War,
lamented that one of the war's most obvious geopolitical consequences
was to bring Russia into the heart of Europe, and to make more rigid
the Communist system of government. This chapter, therefore, can
appropriately be concluded with the words of that eminently level-
headed historian, J. M. Roberts:

So much time has been spent bemoaning this result of the war
that it is important to remember the rewards of victory, for they
were very great. The greatest was the destruction of German power.
That destruction was a means to another end which was sought
without qualification by all the allies: the overthrow of the Nazi
régime and its dependent despotisms. This was an unambiguously
great and noble end, and it was successfully achieved. Nazism was
the worst challenge ever presented to liberal civilization and its

conception of the humane society. The horrors of the Final Solution, the lunacies of racialism and the brutalities of German occupation threatened all that had been laboriously built up since the eighteenth century – perhaps since the coming of Christianity. This challenge was the great justification of the war, though few people saw this when the war began.[57]

## Notes and References

1. Stanley Hoffman, 'The Effects of World War II on French Society and Politics', *French Historical Studies*, vol II, no. 1 (1961) pp. 29–30.
2. On newsreel in Britain see the two excellent articles by Nicholas Pronay, 'British Newsreels in the 1930s' pt I, 'Audiences and Producers', pt II, 'Their Policies and Impact', *History* (Oct and Dec 1971).
3. Janet Chapman, *Real Wages in Soviet Russia* (1963) p. 153, and Alec Nove, *An Economic History of the U.S.S.R.* (1969) p. 250.
4. Cited by Nove, pp. 250–1.
5. Quoted by L. Kochan, *The Making of Modern Russia* (1963 edn) p. 295.
6. G. Bry, *Wages in Germany, 1870–1945* (1960) p. 262. In general, in my attempt to assess the nature of National Socialist Germany, I owe an immense debt to the seminal works of Professor A. S. Milward.
7. David Schoenbaum, *Hitler's Social Revolution: Class and Status in Nazi Germany 1933–1939* (1966, 1967 edn) pp. 116, 118.
8. C. W. Guillebaud, *The Social Policy of Nazi Germany* (1941) p. 60.
9. Quoted by Schoenbaum, p. 286.
10 See in particular Jill McIntyre (now Stephenson), 'Women and the Professions in Germany 1930–1940', in *German Democracy and the Triumph of Hitler*, ed. A. J. Nichols and Erich Mathias (1971) pp. 175–213.
11. Quoted by Schoenbaum, p. 243.
12. Albert Speer, *Inside the Third Reich* (1970) pp. 220–1. I am indebted to Jill Stephenson for the additional point.
13. Max Seydewitz, *Civil Life in Wartime Germany* (1945) p. 126.
14. The information is conveniently summarised in Jürgen Kuczjnski, *A Short History of Labour Conditions under Industrial Capitalism*, vol. III, pt 2, *Germany under Fascism* (1944) p. 214.
15. Speer, pp. 166–7. Also see Seydewitz, p. 45.
16. International Military Tribunal, *Trial of the German Major War Criminals*, pt XXXI (1946–51) p. 65.
17. L. P. Lockner (ed.), *The Goebbels Diaries* (1948) pp. 50 and 57.
18. *Trial of German Major War Criminals*, pt II, pp. 290–1.
19. See Sir C. Webster and N. Frankland, *The Strategic Air Offensive against Germany 1939–1945*, Official History: U.K. Military Series, vol. II (4 vols, 1961) p. 238.
20. Quoted in Webster and Frankland, vol. IV, p. 316.
21. Speer, pp. 288 and 278.

22. F. C. Iklé, *Social Impact of Bomb Destruction* (1958) p. 121. In general see also I. L. Janis, *Air War and Emotional Stress* (1951).
23. Webster and Frankland, vol. II, p. 241.
24. *Goebbels Diaries*, p. 419.
25. Quoted by Speer, p. 312.
26. Bry, p. 264.
27. W. Prüller, *Diary of a German Soldier* (1963) p. 180.
28. The comment was made during interrogation on 23 July 1945 by the head of the Luftwaffe Experimental Station at Rechlin; quoted by Webster and Frankland, vol. III, p. 224n.
29. See the collection in The Imperial War Museum, London. Very brief excerpts can be seen in the Open University compilation, *Archive Film in the Study of War and Society*.
30. *Trial of German Major War Criminals*, pt II, p. 339.
31. Speer, p. 393.
32. Harrison E. Salisbury, *The 900 Days: The Siege of Leningrad* (1969, paperback edn 1971) pp. 168–9.
33. Alexander Werth, *Russia at War* (1964) p. 176.
34. Alexander Werth, *Moscow 41* (1942) p. 111.
35. Werth, *Russia at War*, p. 370.
36. Ibid. pp. 218–19.
37. Cited in Nove, p. 276.
38. Ibid. p. 274.
39. John A. Armstrong, *Soviet Partisans in World War II*, (1964) pp. 65–7.
40. Werth, *Russia at War*, p. 184. For the rest of this paragraph see ibid. pp. 272–4.
41. Salisbury, p. 680.
42. Werth, *Russia at War*, p. 961.
43. The film is in the National Film Archive, London.
44. Figures cited by M. M. Postan, *Economic History of Western Europe Since 1945* (1967) pp. 23–4.
45. Golo Mann, *The History of Germany since 1789* (1968) p. 505.
46. Quoted by E. Kulischer, *Europe on the Move* (1948) p. 282.
47. Leo Grebler, 'Continuity in the Rebuilding of Bombed Cities in Western Europe', *American Journal of Sociology*, vol. LXI (March 1956).
48. J. P. Nettl, *The Soviet Achievement* (1967) p. 200.
49. Ralf Dahrendorf, *Society and Democracy in Germany* (1967) pp. 422–3, 431.
50. Werth, *Russia at War*, p. 964.
51. OMGUS Surveys, cited by A. J. and R. L. Merritt, *Public Opinion in Occupied Germany* (1970) pp. 31 and 171.
52. Mann, pp. 526, 529, 535.
53. Quoted by A. J. May, *Europe Since 1939* (1966) p. v.
54. F. Meinecke, *The German Catastrophe* (1946) pp. xiii, 121.
55. Quoted by Vera S. Dunham, 'Sex: From Free Love to Puritanism' in *Soviet Society*, ed. Alec Inkeles and Kent Geiger (1961) p. 544.
56. A. Solzhenitsyn, *The First Circle* (1968, paperback edn 1970) p. 45.
57. J. M. Roberts, *Europe 1880–1945* (1967) p. 540.

# 5. The Second World War: Britain and the United States

## I The Impact of the Second World War on British Society

Britain's war experience seems to be clearly set apart from that of the nations of continental Europe. Britain did not have vast parts of her territory fought over and laid waste as did Russia; Britain (apart from the Channel Islands) was not occupied as was France; Britain did not suffer the trauma of defeat as did Germany. On the other hand, unlike the United States, she did suffer two periods of serious aerial bombing (though in the end the devastation was nothing like that endured by Germany), and for a time underwent the apparently real threat of invasion. There were no bloody conflicts of loyalty between partisans and government (as in Italy), no Resistance, no starvation – though direction and control of life and labour were probably more total (and more efficient) than in any other combatant country, save for Russia. There was no change in the British political system, though at the end of the war, and in the years that followed, there was much talk of a 'social revolution'. In 1943 a conservative publicist, in a pamphlet expressively titled *Benefits of War*, argued a familiar case: that war is a spur to a higher level of social attainment, destroying what is moribund, and bringing out the best qualities in a people.[1] Liberal historians, we have seen, naturally react against such views. The two most recent comprehensive studies of Britain in the Second World War have both taken a rather negative view of the consequences of the war for British society. Dr Pelling condemns those who have attributed social change after 1945 to the war as having 'failed to avoid the commonest of historical pitfalls, the fallacy of *post hoc, ergo propter hoc*'.[2] Dr Calder has maintained 'that the effect of the war was not to

For Notes and References to this chapter, see p. 182 below.

sweep society on to a new course, but to hasten its progress along the old grooves'. [3] Clearly such caution is highly desirable, yet in the end it does not do full justice to the complex range of human reactions touched off by war.

## Social Outline of the War

The domestic history of Britain during the Second World War can be readily divided into four phases: the period of the 'phoney war' or 'invisible war' in which society fenced with the shadows of the war envisaged by the experts of the 1930s; the period of the Battle of Britain and the blitz, in which the nation hung on the precipice of defeat; the long slog from late 1941 when for a further year the submarine menace to her vital supplies was still desperate, but in which increasingly there was time to think of issues other than immediate survival; this merges into the fourth phase, that of the 'White Paper Chase' when thought about social reconstruction took the explicit form of the preparation of a number of important government White Papers, and when there was much public discussion of the prospects for substantial social change. The culminating point was the general election of 1945, which brought the Labour Party to power with a real majority for the first time.

The declaration of war on 3 September 1939 brought none of the enthusiasm which had marked the early days of August 1914. There was no cheering, no dancing in the streets, but, journalists and psychologists alike agree, there was a general sense of moral release. War, everyone believed, meant bombing – as in Spain and Abyssinia. And true enough, within minutes of the declaration of war, air-raid sirens sent the people of London and the south east scurrying for inadequate shelter. But that warning proved to be a false alarm, and for the time being there was no other. In spite of that government plans for the expected bombing war proceeded. Shelters were built and sand bags piled up in all available spaces. Poison gas was an expected threat, so 'gas detectors' were placed in the streets and gas masks issued to civilians. A complete blackout had been imposed from 1 September: road casualties doubled. Conscription, also introduced on the eve of the war, went ahead and a National Register was compiled: yet at the end of 1939 there were still about a million men unemployed. Cinemas and theatres closed; but after a fortnight of war the cinemas were opened again; then, over the following weeks the theatres cautiously began to reopen. Football and other spectator sports, banned at first because of the fear of the damage to morale of a bomb attack on a place of public assembly, were also soon resumed. But, whereas cinemas and theatres were crowded, football never regained its former popularity during the war mainly because of the reduced standards necessarily presented by depleted teams.

Early in 1940 the press began to refer openly to the 'creeping paralysis' affecting the British war effort under the direction of Neville Chamberlain. In April came the German invasion of Scandinavia, followed by the failed attempt to land British troops in Norway. Norway was the flash-point for gathering discontents, and on 10 May Neville Chamberlain's Conservative government gave place to a national coalition under Winston Churchill. News of Churchill's accession to power was chased from the headlines by Hitler's invasion of the Low Countries, followed quickly by the fall of France and the evacuation of British and French troops from Dunkirk. Dunkirk brought home in vivid terms that the war for survival had truly begun, that invasion might come at any time. To confuse the potential invader, signposts and place names were removed or painted out. There was an immediate response to the government call for suspension of all holidays; late-coming and absenteeism practically vanished; phenomenally long hours were worked; productivity soared. The effects were temporary. Longer hours, as the First World War had amply demonstrated, do not over a period yield higher productivity. But the Dunkirk spirit, though temporary, was real enough. Immediately after Dunkirk there followed the Battle of Britain, Hitler's unsuccessful attempt to destroy the R.A.F., then the blitz, the attempt to destroy civilian morale. The Battle of Britain, uniquely in a war which was to be won by an entire people, was fought by an élite – 'the Few' of Churchill's famous speech. While those who lived in the south could see the fighting going on above them, the rest of the country could listen to the B.B.C., whose commentators somewhat ghoulishly described the struggle in the phraseology of a sporting contest.

Around five o'clock on a hot Saturday evening (7 September) the intensive bombing of London began. London was bombed for seventy-six nights on end; then more sporadically for a further six months. On 14 November the entire centre of Coventry was destroyed, and in November and December other cities suffered severe bomb attacks. One of the most important sub-controversies of the war concerns the reaction of the British people to bombing. Did bombing strengthen morale, consolidate support behind the British government, and increase a determined hostility towards Germany? Or did morale come close to disintegration? Was there hostility to, and resentment against, government and authority everywhere? While optimistic accounts of British civilians exulting in the dangers of the raids and rallying enthusiastically to their nation's call must be treated with extreme scepticism, there is on the other hand solid evidence that the incidence of psychological disorders actually decreased during the war, and there was no abnormal absenteeism. In Coventry, for instance, shop girls carried on immediately in temporary premises. One American commentator did believe that had the blitz continued much longer, morale would have cracked. Of course, there were signs of fear and panic; but the clear fact, on the basis of what actually did happen, is that, if on occasion morale faltered, it never cracked.[4]

But it is equally clear that the immense suffering created by the blitz, very largely concentrated in the poorer parts of the east end of London, aroused enormous criticism of the British authorities. It could scarcely be otherwise. British society in the 1930s was an unfair and unequal society; it was also an inefficient one. Shelters and air-raid precautions were inadequate; there was confusion and muddle. The clear evidence of bitter hostility to authority is no more surprising than that shown in many service-men's letters during the First World War.

Some of the psychological evidence is fascinating, even if at first sight it appears to the cynical historian as no more than an obscure glimpse of the obvious. Much of the material is systematically presented in two invaluable studies already mentioned in connection with the bombing of Germany: I. L. Janis's *Air War and Emotional Stress*, and F. C. Iklé's *The Social Impact of Bomb Destruction*. One group of psychiatrists, in practice during the blitz, presented certain conclusions in the *International Journal of Psychoanalysis* (though they admitted that there were grave imperfections in the way in which they had been able to collect their evidence). One of them offered the following observations.

During the first September raids people of naturally good spirit tended to be excited and elated by the experience of being bombed. They were very communicative about their experiences and escapes and laughed and joked with some excitement about 'still being alive'. But in the later heavy raids, the same types talked much less about their bombing experiences: they were preoccupied instead with the various claims they had to make, how to fill in forms, where to send them, in fact with the business of their material loss. . . . By contrast, people who were nervous in the earlier blitz showed much more signs of nervousness in later attacks, although by that time the 'safety conditions' were much improved. Whereas at first they may have been able to control themselves with an effort even when guns were firing outside the window, they were later inclined to cry and shake when sirens were heard even in the day-time.[5]

In general, there was adaptation to the new dangers of a new way of life, often involving various personal shibboleths and taboos over what kind of behaviour would invite destruction, and what would avoid it. Londoners from the heavily blitzed areas took to sheltering night after night in the tube stations. There is little hard evidence of physical mixing of the social classes. On the whole, middle-class observers were horrified by the squalor they saw in the early days of resort to the tube stations. Many of the very rich continued to lead very segregated existences. The first shelter census of November 1940 showed that, of the 40 per cent who resorted to shelters, 27 per cent used their own domestic shelters and only 9 per cent used public shelters; 4 per cent resorted to the tubes.[6] There are many personal records of friendliness and social contact which seemed to transcend normal social barriers. But in part this can be explained by a need, in time of danger, to communicate freely, and to avoid conditions of social isolation. Looting on a small scale was fairly widespread after air raids, though there seems to have been a general disposition to excuse this on the lines that otherwise the goods taken would have been lost anyway, or that they were some kind of reward for dangerous rescue work undertaken. Curiosity about the effects of raids was another characteristic, with people often coming some distance to view the results of a previous night's raid; sometimes even to the extent of interfering with rescue and clearing-up work.

There is a good deal of film shot both by newsmen, and occasionally by camera crews attached to the fire-services, showing the physical reality of the blitz; most of this material was edited into the various patriotic documentaries made about the blitz,[7] but the *London Fire Service Film* still exists as one of the most authentic records available to the historian. What film shows, as no other source material can, is the way in which ordinary citizens have been projected into the front line of a modern war of incendiaries and high explosives. However the point should not be pushed too far: the condition of soldiers in a front line subject to military discipline should always be distinguished from that of civilians still surrounded by many of the resources of ordinary life, and still able to move with relative freedom. Altogether sixty thousand British civilians were killed, and two out of every seven houses were destroyed or damaged by bombs. A wider sense of life in the blitz is well rendered in this extract from a diary kept by a successful journalist:

So we have got accustomed now [18 October 1940] to knowing we may be blown to bits at any moment. The casual scraps of news we get about results of raids bring this home better than statistics. Two girls go into a telephone box to send word they may be late home, as there is a raid on. Bombs fall close by. Both killed. A woman of ninety-four with six daughters in a large expensive house are taking shelter in the basement when the house is hit. Two of the daughters die. What a picture! A family creeps out of its garden dug-out to get some supper. They sit down at table. Next minute they are all dead. We know this may happen to any of us. Yet we go about as usual. Life goes on.[8]

Were there any long-term consequences? The expressions of exaltation and of social solidarity are to be found almost exclusively in the diaries and comments of middle- and upper-class people; but they are real enough, and it was after all that class which would be in the best position to give reality to such feelings. The expressions of hostility to an established system which had failed to provide adequate protection and post-raid services, are to be found among the working class, and also among the more socially conscious of their betters. Together these two trends of thought were to create a determination that a social system whose inadequacy had been so disastrously exposed should in some measure be reformed.

Directly linked to bombing was the whole social experiment of evacuation of civilians from the most dangerous urban areas into the relatively safe countryside. Plans had been carefully laid in the pre-war years, and a first evacuation began on Friday 1 September 1939 two days before the actual declaration of war. However most evacuees had drifted back by the end of the year. Then, with the coming of the blitz, a second, hasty, evacuation had to be undertaken. There was a third wave of evacuation during the flying bomb and rocket attacks of the summer of 1944. Again, there is some controversy over the deeper social significance of the evacuation experiment. A recent volume of reminiscences, *The Evacuees* (1968), edited by B. S. Johnson, lays stress on the psychological damage caused by separation from home and parents, and it has been authoritatively argued that the disruption of the family bond was the single most traumatic factor for children living under air raid conditions.[9] This aspect of evacuation cannot be disputed. Evacuation, too, clearly revealed the deep social division within British society. Many wealthy households evaded their responsibilities for providing accommodation; others were disgusted by the habits of the slum children billeted on them. Certain contemporary newsreels reveal a quite horrifying upper-class contempt for the unfortunate evacuees. One Movietone 'news item' actually includes an acted sketch by middle-aged comedians, dressed up as schoolboy evacuees, putting on an exaggerated display of vicious table manners and excessive greed.[10] Yet, to my mind, the ultimate significant fact about the evacuation experience was that it brought to middle- and upper-class households a consciousness for the first time of the deplorable conditions endemic in the rookeries and warrens which still existed in Britain's great industrial cities, and so, among an articulate few, aroused a new sense of social concern.[11] In this sense evacuation was a unique experience and one of the most significant social phenomena of the war.

As the most frightening period of bombing passed away, conditions of privation and austerity worsened: the Battle of the Atlantic, the battle to keep supply lines open, was intensified. By mid-1941 the weekly ration of certain basic foods amounted to no more than what in a comfortable pre-war household would have been thought sufficient for a single helping: a shilling's worth of meat (about 8 oz.), 1 oz. of cheese, 4 oz. of bacon or ham, 8 oz. of sugar, 2 oz. of tea, 8 oz. of fats (including not more than 2 oz. of butter), 2 oz. of jam or marmalade. The Ministry of Food provided recipes for all sorts of strange substitute dishes: Woolton pie (principally vegetables and potatoes), lentil roast, carrot tart – glazed with lemon jelly to make a pudding. Apart from the basic rations other foods were put on 'points', which allowed for a certain limited choice (purchase of these goods depended not on the money one had available, but on the points one had not yet used up). For the privileged few lavish meals were still obtainable in such places as Claridge's, but, in general, eating habits were levelled out and institutionalised. For the majority the best meals were to be obtained at 'British Restaurants' – the name Churchill coined for the new wartime cafeterias. Clothing was rationed (despite Churchill's declaration that he would not be a party to 'stripping the people to the buff') in effect to one complete outfit a year. Despite the occasional brilliant improvisation, the community as a whole sank to a common level of dowdiness.

By late 1941 a preoccupation with the problems of social reform was apparent in all levels of society. In that year were founded both the Conservative 'Post-War Problems Committee', and the '1941 Committee' of upper-class liberals and socialist intellectuals: in 1943 this Committee became the Common Wealth Party and, standing on a platform of radical social reform, proceeded to win a number of by-elections from Conservative supporters of the Coalition Government. The Federation of British Industries declared in May 1942: 'We are on the threshold of a new world, and the theories and practices of the past cannot be taken for granted in the future.'[12] William Temple, Arch-bishop of Canterbury from 1941, became a leading non-party advocate of social reform, while the mass circulation *Daily Mirror* made a special task of popularising current discussions and of pressing for immediate reforms. Most significant, perhaps, was the role of the Army Bureau of Current Affairs which distributed a fortnightly journal *Current Affairs* as a basis for discussions among the troops: from September 1942 *Current Affairs* shows a growing concern with the problems of recon-struction and social reform. In May 1941, in response to trade-union pressure, the government appointed a specialist committee to study 'existing national schemes of social insurance and allied services'. Opinions vary about the exact origins of the Beveridge Committee: my own view is that the government found Sir William Beveridge, who had been brought back as one of the 'experts' of the previous war, so tire-some and opinionated, that they were glad to shunt him onto this new and not particularly promising committee. But Beveridge was able to appeal to gathering public sentiment and his *Beveridge Report* recom-mended not only a comprehensive social insurance system for the entire nation, but also suggested that there was need for a national health service, avoidance of mass unemployment, child allowances, and en-lightened national policies for housing and education. Beveridge's blue-print for a 'universalist' welfare state (one in which social services would be available to all, rich as well as poor) became, despite Churchill's hostility, a matter of public debate and widespread enthusiasm.

The trade unions and the Labour Party played an important role of their own in producing policy documents for a welfare state. But there was no real cessation of industrial strife. The number of days lost due to strikes steadily rose throughout 1942, 1943 and 1944, dropping slightly in 1945, when it was still double what it had been in 1939. In part this reflected a confidence on the part of the workers in their own importance in time of war. But it also reflected the general war-weariness which characterises most personal accounts of the later stages of the war.

Throughout this period the main changes in social patterns, apart from those imposed by austerity and rationing, arose from the dispersal to various parts of the country of the staffs of the major government departments and cultural institutions (for example the B.B.C.), and from the concentration in former rural areas of large numbers of munitions workers (many of them women). The stationing of Polish soldiers in certain small towns in Scotland certainly had marked, if unquantifiable, demographic consequences; and the influx of a million American soldiers had a more obvious consequence in spreading the standards of American consumer society. For the first time, too, domestic British society was faced with 'the colour problem'. The delicacy of the situation is well reflected in the careful phrases of *Current Affairs* (5 December 1942):

> The attitude of the British people towards the coloured troops is important from many points of view. Of course, all Americans are welcome here, whatever their creed, national heritage or colour. They are our guests and allies and as their hosts we have certain responsibilities. One of the responsibilities of a host is to avoid embarrassing his guests – and that is one good reason for avoiding thoughtless talk about the Colour Problem. . . .
>
> It may well be that occasional cases will occur which might arouse the resentment and even anger of British troops and civilians who witness them. On the other hand, it is obviously highly unsuitable for the British to try to interfere in those instances. The troubles in India and Jamaica, racial relations in South Africa and the neutrality of Eire, are examples of our own unsolved problems which exist even though many of us see little of them face to face in this country.
>
> It can be seen therefore that any attempts to break down the various forms of social regulation accepted by the average American family, white or coloured, is not likely to achieve any good purpose, but on the contrary might well lead to trouble and even violence, especially where women are concerned.

Women were affected by the Second World War much as they had been by the first. This time the government did extend conscription to women, a measure believed to be imminent in the previous war but never actually carried through. There was much grumbling at, and a certain amount of evasion of, government attempts to control and direct women's war work, but on the whole, as with most of the other totalitarian legislation of the Second World War, the Act was administered with great respect for the need to maintain civilian support and morale. As a matter of fact conscription played a relatively minor role in the changes in women's employment during the war. In practice only single women of the age group 19–24 were called up, and they were given the choice of serving in the women's auxiliary services, in civil defence, or in certain specified forms of civilian employment. At the end of the war there were rather fewer than half a million women enrolled in the W.R.N.S. (Women's Royal Naval Service), the A.T.S. (Auxiliary Territorial Service), and the W.A.A.F. (Women's Auxiliary Air Force), and the larger proportion of these were volunteers not conscripts. In civilian

trades women's employment expanded most noticeably in light engin-
eering and in agriculture. By late 1944 48 per cent of all civil service
employees were women; and women's employment in commerce had
almost doubled to 62 per cent of the total number employed.

Again there is controversy as to the true significance of these developments. Did women achieve a kind of equality, or only a different kind of
inequality? In her book, *The Feminine Mystique*, Betty Frieden has
argued that in the United States after the war there was a strong reas-
sertion of the traditional feminine image, in reaction against the role
undertaken by women in the war years. Whether or not strong evidence
of the same sort exists for post-war Britain (on the whole, I think not)
the point is a rather misplaced one. There was no complete change of
social attitudes in the war years. As newsreels and propaganda films
bring out, perhaps more strongly than any other single source, the entry
of women into many occupations *was* considered unusual (hence the
constant publicity given to it), frequently the new jobs undertaken were
very much along traditional lines (often, women were simply forsaking
the domestic kitchen for the army cookhouse), there was great and
continuing stress on the importance of fashion, and great weight was
placed on the value of pin-ups as a booster to morale in the forces.[13] It is
wrong, then, to see a swing of attitude and opinion in one direction, followed at the end of the war by a sharp reaction in the opposite direction.
It is equally wrong to ignore the basic economic and social facts of the
situation, and the demands and repercussions which built up irrespective of deep social attitudes. In the Second World War there was nothing
quite like the 'votes for women' cry of pre-1914 days, but one special
issue – that of the employment of married women – was greatly affected
by the war experience. Before the war it was common practice in many
professions to sack women as soon as they married. During the war
scarcity of labour inevitably meant that married women were given
employment, and the old myths about their unreliability as employees
were clearly exposed for what they were. More than this, in a few cases
employers, encouraged by the government, experimented with the setting up of nurseries which permitted the employment of women with
young children. This was an irreversible trend: a survey conducted
among private business at the end of the war, showed a remarkable
swing round in opinion with regard to the question of the employment of
married women.[14] Of course many married women, dependent on the
miserable allowance paid to soldiers, were badly off: but in general the
war meant a new economic and social freedom for women, the experience of which could never be entirely lost.

And this debate over the question of the effects of the war on women really brings one to the heart of the whole question of whether the war brought about significant social and economic changes. In disagreeing with the views of Calder and Pelling, I turn again to the four aspects of war's interaction with society.

## The Four-Tier Model

Bombing and all its implications form the most obvious example of the *disruptive* and *destructive* effect. Another example is the billeting throughout most of the war of almost half-a-million foreign troops on British soil, rising to one-and-a-half millions at the time of the Normandy landings. Fathers were again called from home for armed service, mothers for work in the factories. By a sad mischance, the day set for the long overdue raising of the school leaving age to fifteen was the day war broke out. Undoubtedly the destructive influence of war produced a massive negative total to be subtracted from the social gains resulting from the operation of the other three tiers of the model. Yet, as ever, the cumulative effect of all the destruction was to render imperative massive action to make good the ravages of war. Nowhere was this more apparent than in environmental planning. As age-old slums fell to the ground, there rose in unexpected places a firm determination to build something rather better in their place: 'Bombs', declared the monthly journal of the Federation of British Industries (October 1940), 'have made builders of us all.'

The *test* effect of war is well exemplified by the case of the hospital system, which before the war had been rent by petty rivalries between the 'voluntary' hospitals, and the local authority hospitals. To deal with the sudden influx of air raid casualties the government had to create a unified Emergency Hospital Service, providing free treatment. Gradually the scope of the service was extended so that by the end of the war it provided a solid basis upon which a National Health Service could be built. The health and amenity of the community benefited too from the manner in which science, still sadly neglected in pre-war days, was fully exploited during the war. Even in private industry there was a growing appreciation of the value of welfare and personnel services in meeting the disruptions of war. Scientific expertise was called in by the government to ensure that despite all the food shortages the entire community, through provision of cod liver oil, orange juice, extra vitamins in certain basic foods, for the first time in history could enjoy a completely healthy diet (though no government on earth could prevent certain citizens from pouring their free welfare food down the drain).

The management of the British economy and some aspects of British industry also had to yield to the transforming pressures of war. In 1940 J. M. Keynes, an economic voice in the wilderness of the depression, was brought back into the Treasury. Under Keynes's influence control of the economy was much less crude than in the First World War: it proved to be much more enduring. In 1944 the government published the famous White Paper, *Employment Policy*, which in Keynesian language promised that future governments would as a matter of deliberate policy maintain national expenditure at a sufficiently high level to avoid mass unemployment. Inevitably taxation increased greatly, providing a mighty engine for levelling some of the grosser inequalities of income. The war, finally, gave a tremendous stimulus to the technological industries of the twentieth century – aircraft, motor vehicles, machine tools, drugs, plastics, electronics – industries in which Britain had lagged behind in the inter-war years. Some British institutions – notably the Civil Service, the system of parliamentary government, and local government – though severely tested by the war, did not change very much, since Great Britain did not suffer the wholesale impact of invasion and defeat. Indeed, there was a feeling that these institutions had stood the test rather well, and that therefore there was no need for change. This was particularly true of the structure of industrial relations. On the whole it did seem that management and labour had co-operated well in the effort which finally saw Britain emerge on the winning side: there was, therefore, strong resistance to change in the traditional structures of both trade unions and management.

The under-privileged groups in the community which benefited from being drawn into *participation* in the war effort were exactly the same groups as underwent a similar history in the First World War: the working classes, women, children and young people. The working classes benefited because of their strong market position when labour power was an essential ingredient to success in war; they benefited because the government knew it was vital to secure their full support and co-operation; they benefited because the government felt it necessary to recompense them for their sacrifice of life and limb in battle and of trade-union privileges at home. While the government tried to control the cost of living through food subsidies, wage rates steadily rose. Altogether average weekly earnings, standing at 53s. 3d. in October 1938 rose 80 per cent to 96s. 1d., in July 1945 (when the cost of living had risen by only 31 per cent). Wartime changes were confirmed in 1946 when there were general reductions in the working week from 47 or 48 hours to 44 or 45.[15] The labour market favoured young people, too, and many were able to secure good wages. These material changes have been eclipsed by the second great wave of material change which flooded British society in the late 1950s, creating 'the affluent society'; but that does not mean that historians should dismiss them out of hand.

We have already noted the various changes of opinion in social matters in different social groups during the war period. At the legislative level these changes were consolidated by virtue of the election of a Labour government in 1945. To my mind, the evidence firmly suggests that had the normal peacetime election been held in 1940, Labour almost certainly would not have been returned to power;[16] and I think the evidence is conclusive that had Labour by chance been returned to power in 1940, it was at that time not equipped to carry out the kind of social programme that it did carry out after 1945.[17] The war experience, then, played a critical role in two ways: it influenced opinion to the extent of ensuring Labour's return to power; and it influenced Labour politicians themselves by giving them the experience and confidence to carry through the social reform policy which created the Welfare State. This Welfare State suffered from many limitations and imperfections, but its characteristic feature was the observance of the principle of 'universality': in the assertion of this principle, heavily attacked from the late 1950s onwards, Britain's Welfare State of the late 1940s stood out from those of all other industrialised countries.

There is no simple explanation for the phenomenon of full employment, the basic pre-condition of social well-being after the war. Professor R. C. O. Mathews has recently demonstrated that deliberate government policy was not the sole and crucial factor, and Dr Pelling has used this argument to support his own view that the war experience itself was not significant in creating a full employment society. Actually Mathews does very clearly indicate the significance of the war:

> The economy was given a once-for-all hoist upwards during the war. When the war ended income was therefore high. Moreover, the capital stock was low as a result of the low level of investment during the war itself and also during the inter-war period. Hence there was great scope for investment. The feed-back from this investment combined with the favourable effects of the foreign-trade situation combined [sic] to keep income up and keep up the demand for more investment.

Furthermore Professor Mathews finds another reason for the absence of mass unemployment in the 'change in entrepreneurial attitudes'[18] during the war. In other words, working-class participation, the spirit of unity, and the new mental environment of wartime, rendered unacceptable an older tradition of ruthlessness in the hiring and firing of labour.

The rather serious, and perhaps slightly dull, attitude towards social problems which characterised many upper-class intellectuals in the last years of the war and the first years of the peace, is well brought out in the many film documentaries produced at the time.[19] Other changes had less to do with the good intentions of intellectuals and politicians. Qualitatively the big shake-up in the old class structure had come during the previous war; short of a total revolution and the achievement of a 'classless society' there was less scope for major change this time. None the less, within a framework which, once things had settled down, was recognisably the same as that of the inter-war years, important developments had taken place. Heavy taxation, rationing, a positive nutrition policy and high wartime wages had produced a levelling of standards – up as well as down. Education in the forces and self-education in the air-raid shelters had assisted the developing consciousness among the inarticulate. At the end of the war the majority had a clearer idea than ever before of what it expected from a modern, civilised, industrial society: decent living standards, income and health security, a taste of the modest luxuries of life; once the idea was defined it became in itself an agent of further change.

One aspect of the emotional responses to war deserves special attention. In the midst of the drabness of wartime life there came an astonishing revival of the arts, which was to endure into the post-war world. At the end of 1940 the government-supported Council for the Encouragement of Music and the Arts (C.E.M.A., rechristened the Arts Council at the end of the war) was founded. Encouraged by C.E.M.A. grants the major British symphony orchestras gave performances outside the normal limits of the main centres of population. During the crisis months of 1940 tours of the Old Vic theatre in Lancashire and Wales were given C.E.M.A. guarantees. Less ambitious concerts, theatrical performances and exhibitions were mounted in small communities throughout the country. The wartime National Gallery concerts organised by Myra Hess were famous. Bomb damage in 1941 chased the Sadler's Wells Opera company out of their London home, to the immense profit of the provinces, where the company had to remain continuously on tour for four years. This whole side of the war experience is perhaps best symbolised by the founding of the Edinburgh International Festival of Music and Drama in 1947.

Still, these were undoubtedly matters of concern only to a minority. In blunt terms the consequences for British society of the Second World War were rather similar to those of the First World War for France. Technically there was victory; and without doubt there were positive social changes. But there were heavy physical losses which made more difficult the realisation of the social aspirations aroused by the war. Above all there was the basic problem of 'we won didn't we', a reluctance to face the fact that the institutions which survived the battering of war were not necessarily, thereby, perfect institutions with which to meet the post-war world. Those who judge everything by the highest standards of human brotherhood and efficiency will continue to feel that there was little 'real change' in Britain. Those who accept the imperfections of human systems, and who appreciate that change is not necessarily always in the one direction, will perhaps recognise that even without the drama and tragedy of an occupation and resistance, none the less the Second World War did have a considerable impact on the British people.

## II    The War and American Society

In comparison with all the other major countries, the United States was the least affected by the direct impact of the war; for all that her involvement far exceeded that of the previous war and was absolutely crucial to the Allied cause, and indeed to the whole subsequent course of world history. In assessing the effects of the war on American society, and in comparing the American experience with that of other countries, it is also important to remember the vast size and variousness of the American nation and the special nature of American institutions (both discussed at the end of Chapter 1): though smaller than the Soviet Union, the United States were not pulled tightly together by a centralised dictatorship; on the contrary, and in spite of the innovations of the New Deal, they were subject to strong pluralist tendencies. In the United States, more sharply even than in the other industrialised countries, the contrast stands out between post-war affluence and pre-war depression. Thus in discussing the United States it is perhaps specially important to heed Henry Pelling's warning against the *post hoc ergo propter hoc* argument. American historians, on the whole, seem agreed in stressing the significance of the war in bringing about social change. In a standard short textbook, which digests the work of many other authorities, William Miller comments: 'Wartime prosperity sparked a social revolution in the United States which continued with increasing momentum in the post-war years.'[20] Two books in the characteristic genre of American popular history, John Brookes's *The Great Leap: the Past Twenty-Five Years in American History* and Richard R. Lingeman's *Don't You Know There's a War On?* both give much attention to wartime social changes, and the former, in particular, is quite precise in pinning down certain longer term effects to the war. In the only full scholarly survey, Richard Polenberg asserts that:

> World War II radically altered the character of American society and challenged its most durable values. The war redefined the relationship of government to the individual and of individuals to each other, and it posed questions about the relationship between civilians and the military, between liberty and security, and between special interests and national purpose which continue to perplex Americans.[21]

In the carefully argued pages of his book, the second, more open-ended sentence is rather more fully substantiated than the short, sweeping first sentence. Again my methodology can be of assistance in defining what changed, and what did not; and, as was the case with the First World War, the model applies both to the period September 1939 to December 1941, when the United States was still technically neutral, and then, with greater force, to the period of hostilities begun by the Japanese attack on Pearl Harbor and ended by the American atomic bombing of Hiroshima and Nagasaki. The most important mechanism of change, in my view, was the *test* effect of war, not surprisingly, perhaps, amongst a people given to economic and technological innovation, and practised in surmounting the challenge of new circumstances. The *psychological* effects of the war – given that, at the end of the day, the United States really was cast in the role of the last champion of democracy – were also considerable. Because of the immense differences within American society and the strong pull of particular interests, the *participation* effect, though important, never came fully into play. The war undoubtedly *disrupted* American life, but direct *destruction* is a relatively minor feature. Certainly the Japanese bombardment of Pearl Harbor in December 1941 was for the time being a crippling blow to American naval power. The cost of the war was phenomenal, and America bore the brunt of it – to the tune of $330 billion (compared with $32 billion in the previous war). Altogether about 14·5 million men and women served in the armed forces (compared with under 5 million in the First World War): there were over a million casualties, including more than 393,000 dead. But no one on the American mainland was killed by direct enemy action.

*Destruction–Disruption*

How one assesses the negative effects of the war on peacetime processes of social and community change will in part depend upon one's estimate of the New Deal. It was in keeping with liberal tradition that many of the American liberals who had been closely associated with the New Deal believed that the war had brought reform to an end and replaced it by a menacing totalitarianism. Writing in 1943, a leading contributor to *New Republic* remarked: 'It is possible that a fascist state could be instituted here without many changes in government personnel, and some of these changes have been made already.' The following year Archibald Mac-Leish a leading New Deal administrator, told a gathering of reformers: 'Liberals meet in Washington these days, if they meet at all, to discuss the tragic outlook for all liberal proposals, the collapse of all liberal leadership and the inevitable defeat of all liberal aims.'[22]

There can be no doubt that the immediate effect of the outbreak of war in Europe was to divert the attention of administrators away from social questions towards those of military supply. Once the United States was in the war, New Deal agencies were run down and replaced by ones concerned with the war effort; many New Deal figures lost their government posts. Two major spheres in which the war had an obvious disruptive effect were anti-trust legislation and child labour. As soon as the United States began producing arms for the western Allies there was a drop in anti-trust activity, lest that should interfere with productivity; and once she entered the war anti-trust legislation, a central feature of New Deal policy, effectively went into abeyance. The situation on the child-labour front is very reminiscent of Britain in the First World War: children were tempted by the opportunities for earnings offered by the war, and influential local employers had little compunction about breaking the child-labour clauses of the 1938 Fair Labor Standards Act. By 1944 nineteen states had altered their laws so as to permit longer working hours for children; since 1940 over a million teenagers had prematurely left school, and inspectors found some horrifying evidence of the long night-time hours and heavy labour being done by young children.

The mid-term congressional elections of 1942 seemed to provide the hardest evidence that the war had damped the fires of liberal reform. The Democrats, and particularly liberal Democrats, suffered heavily; thus the relative position of the conservative Southern Democrats, and the right-wing alliance between them and the strengthened Republicans was consolidated. Only 28 million people voted in this election compared with nearly 50 million in 1940: too many young voters were in the forces (where it required some effort to cast an absentee ballot); too many workers were employed in factories far from home and were working such long hours as to make voting a serious inconvenience; on both counts the Democrats suffered far more severely than the Republicans. Thus the dislocations of war did affect adversely both the liberal position and certain types of reform. Yet unless one makes rather exaggerated claims on behalf of the New Deal – which, by 1939 was clearly failing to get to grips with basic social problems – these developments can scarcely be treated as a fatal interruption in a triumphant progress of social reform.

Just as serious were the disruptions which took place in areas not subject to guided social policy. Serious problems arose in those communities where the establishment of a new war industry brought a sudden large influx of outsiders, often accommodated in insanitary trailer camps or shanty towns. Not only were local community services totally unable to cope, newcomers were usually met with active resentment and hostility by the local inhabitants. Even outside the war-boom localities, the departure of husband and father to the war, and of wife and mother to the munitions factory or other employment put a severe strain on family life. Children were often released from schooling and tempted, or pressured into employment. Juvenile delinquency both increased, and attracted to itself greater attention. Official reactions to other disruptions of war were wiser and more cautious than those of a generation before: soldiers were provided with prophylactics, but revived cries for prohibition (of liquor, which American puritans linked closely with sex) were ignored. Rationing of certain commodities had to be introduced, though the strength of entrepreneurial spirit, as against civic loyalty, continued to show itself in the extent to which the black market flourished.[23] Out of the enormous cost of the war came the most important long-term innovation, a new tax structure which brought nearly all American households into this form of economic citizenship (in 1939 there were only four million tax payers): here the most obvious parallel is with Britain and the 1914–18 war.

## War as Test

It is in the United States' reactions to the test of war that we find the major clues to the more important social changes which took place over the war period. The nine-and-a-half million unemployed on the eve of the war represented not only a great social blot, but a terrible waste of potential resources. The more obvious side of the government's attempt to deal with the need to increase production and reallocate resources can be seen in the large number of boards and commissions which were set up to direct and regulate most aspects of American life: the War Production Board, the War Manpower Commission, the National War Labor Board, the Office of Price Administration, the Office of Economic Stabilization and the Office of War Mobilization were the main ones. Not all of the agencies worked very well: there were problems of duplication, demarcation, vested interests and rivalries, over-bureaucratisation, and inefficiency. In any case it is important to note first of all the manner in which the economy was stimulated by the European war, before U.S. entry, and before most of these agencies were created. In 1941 U.S. industry was booming as it had not boomed since the 1920s: for example, a million more cars were produced than in 1939. It was the task of the War Production Board not just to increase production but to redirect it in keeping with the needs of war, a task described by the board's head Donald Nelson as 'not so much industrial conversion as industrial revolution, with months and years condensed into days'.[24] Nelson was a businessman, and most of the new agencies were directed and staffed by businessmen. Once again we have that same basic model of managed state capitalism which operated pretty smoothly from the start in Britain, and which Albert Speer struggled so hard to establish in Germany. As in Britain control was less crude than in the First World War: this time, for instance, the U.S. government did not take over the railways, which instead submitted voluntarily to centralised direction. As in Britain, the war seemed to provide a triumphant vindication of Keynesian economic theories: eventually the Employment Act of 1946 recognised the need for the federal government to maintain total levels of expenditure sufficient to avoid mass unemployment.

In economic terms this mixed war economy was an almost unmixed success. By the end of 1942 America was producing more war material than all of the enemy powers combined. 48,000 planes in that year became 300,000 at the end of the war – and these were bigger, faster and more destructive than any dreamed of four years before. By the end of 1942 8 million tons of merchant shipping had been produced, by the end of the war more than 55 million tons. In short, America was not only triumphantly fulfilling her own military needs, but those of her hard-pressed allies as well. An immense upward boost was given to the economy: 'As much new industrial plant was built in three years of war as in the preceding fifteen years, and nearly twice as much was manufactured in 1942 as in 1939.'[25] Because the early Japanese victories cut off rubber supplies from south-east Asia a completely new synthetic-rubber industry had to be created. The method employed was typical: the government spent $700 million on building plants, which were then leased for a nominal fee to the private companies, who then operated on the 'cost-plus' basis which was pretty well universal throughout American wartime industry. The 'Rubber Director' was William Jeffers, President of the Union Pacific Railroad, and he followed the standard practice of drawing his staff from within the rubber industry itself. The economic and military results, once again, were phenomenal: supply, by the end of the war, was actually exceeding demand.

The case of synthetic rubber was typical of the general impetus towards a further technological orientation for American society. New industries, and new industrial capacity, provided a fairly secure base for high levels of employment in the future (though there would remain pools of under-employment in older industries). The buoyancy of 'cost-plus' brought economic gains to all classes. There was plenty of work, and plenty of hours to be worked: the weekly earnings of industrial workers rose by almost a hundred per cent. Obviously we will need to turn to the question of participation before we can fully work out labour's gains and losses in the war; but here it must be stressed that, probably more significantly than in any other country, a major factor in improved living standards for the American people was the manner in which the economy was transformed to meet the needs of war. Psychological factors also come into play in bringing the birth, during the war, of the modern American business corporation with a 'friendly' rather than a predatory image, ready to co-operate along the lines established in the war in the maintenance of an expansionist economy rather than resort to the over-competitive or highly defensive methods of the inter-war years. Naturally, many criticisms can be made of this type of mixed economy dominated by vast business corporations. One particular, and some would say central facet, will deserve further analysis later: it was in this war that scientists, businessmen, government, and the military arm were brought into a new relationship, vital if this most scientific of all wars were to be won, but which was to lead directly to the 'military–industrial complex' of post-war years.

War, indeed, brought a change in civil-military relations in the United States quite different from the minor, and often temporary, modifications in other countries. The United States had had her militarist adventures at the turn of the century, and a great patriotic spree in the First World War, but isolationist and anti-military sentiments were strong in the inter-war years. Acts of individual violence, involving death or extreme injury, were much more numerous than in the other major countries, but there was no central military establishment wielding the power and prestige such establishments had in European countries. Until Roosevelt established one in the first year of war, America had no intelligence (espionage) agency. The real loss of American innocence[26] came in the Second World War when she had to adopt and improve upon the institutions of degenerate Europe. In taking decisions which were crucial to the history of the whole world, her military establishment acquired a power and prestige which was never again to be taken away from it.

But the main body of U.S. political institutions and relationships remained unchanged. During the war the United States had no dictator, no national coalition; she continued to hold elections, and the Republicans continued to function as an opposition. There are many instances of policies which were well adapted to the needs of the war effort being watered down, or abandoned, either because of direct opposition in Congress, or because Roosevelt himself felt it politic to glance over his shoulder at the electorate. This was in the nature of the United States' balanced constitution (which, certainly, made no provision for the suspension of elections); more important, it was in the nature of the United States' sprawling, pluralist society. However this is not the whole truth. Republicans recognised, if grudgingly, that in some circumstances Roosevelt needed executive powers going beyond what was acceptable in time of peace. And it is widely agreed that in the whole troubled era which has followed upon the war, U.S. presidents have tended in practice to wield greater power than was ever the case before the Second World War.

## *Participation*

Other things being equal, we should expect the participation effect of the war to produce major gains for three main categories: labour, women, and racial minorities, including, in particular the substantial Afro-American minority. The complete story of U.S. labour in wartime is not a straightforward one. The administration was conscious enough of the vital significance of labour's participation in the war effort; but, even if willing, it was far less able than the British government to make an open bid for labour's full co-operation and support, since it had at the same time to appease other important interest groups. In Britain Ernest Bevin could be seen to be a genuine spokesman of the people, just as control of prices was obviously in the interests of organised labour. The U.S. government, particularly after the establishment in October 1942 of the

Office of Economic Stabilization under the influential congressman James F. Byrnes, was itself remarkably successful in controlling the inflationary pressures of war, and this, in part, was motivated by a desire to maintain the support of the country at large. But it was in the nature of American historical development for governments to tend to make a distinction between the interests of consumers and those of producers. Thus labour policy was conducted within limits determined by a strong fear of wage inflation; governed at all times by a recognition of the need to secure maximum productivity, it none the less oscillated between blandishment, restriction and downright coercion. The greatly strengthened market position which the war gave to labour was limited by the very vastness and heterogeneity of American society (rendering it, in this respect, much less than a perfect market economy), and by weaknesses in trade union organisation – in particular the split between the American Federation of Labor and the Congress of Industrial Organizations. Above all the participation effect was not fully reinforced by the social mechanisms springing from the disaster and psychological upheaval aspects of the war. Genuine and significant enough expressions of national unity in face of war exist in plenty, but overall the strengthening of 'in-group' feelings brought about by the war tended to mean the strengthening of the self-consciousness of groups within society as much as, or more than, it meant a forging of national unity and partnership between business, labour and government.

Certainly the unions together with the employers did, on 23 December 1941, enter into an informal 'no-strike' and 'no lock-out' agreement with the President; this was by no means an ineffectual gesture, and the yearly number of days lost due to strike action dropped (during the war) to almost half of the peacetime norm. In return there was some official attempt to recognise the needs and aspirations of labour through co-operation on the National War Labor Board and through the encouragement at local level of Labour–Management committees. Much more important, however, were the unguided changes in labour's market situation. These were apparent well before the entry of the United States into active hostilities. Labour's consciousness of its new strength (and the employers' powerful resistance) was reflected in the industrial strife of 1941, which, with the exception of 1937, was the worst year for strikes since 1919. The advantage lay with the workers; and, of the major unions, the United Mine Workers, the Steel Workers Organizing Committee, and the United Automobile Workers, were all able to gain favourable terms. Furthermore, a particularly bitter strike throughout the autumn in the 'captive' coal mines of the Appalachians (so called because they were run directly by the steel companies) in effect destroyed Roosevelt's first attempt at controlling labour through the National Defense Mediation Board. While all this was going on the unions recruited a million-and-a-half new members.

There was relative tranquillity in 1942, followed by further outbreaks of industrial discontent in 1943. Two government actions highlight the complexity of labour policy. In the summer of 1942 the War Labor Board attempted to resolve the conflict between union demands for a closed shop and employers' hostility to this by introducing the 'maintenance of membership' scheme. This scheme, where applied, created a closed shop situation, with the minor saving grace of a fifteen-day period at the commencement of his contract in which the individual worker could deliberately opt out of union membership. On balance the system worked very much to the advantage of the unions; on the other hand the government could refuse to apply the scheme in cases where it objected to the policies of particular unions. The Smith–Connally Act of June 1943, passed against the President's veto, was a swingeing piece of anti-labour legislation. It laid down that before calling a strike union officials must obtain the support of a majority of their members and must observe a thirty-day cooling-off period; the encouragement of strikes in war-production factories controlled by the government was declared a crime; and political contributions from union funds were banned. In face of the realities of the industrial situation the Act was of little consequence: strike ballots simply demonstrated the power and solidarity of the unions and in practice little attempt was made to enforce the Act rigorously.

The strong position of the unions can well be seen in the railroad strike of 1943 and in the coal strikes of the same year. Because it could not risk the disruption to the war effort involved in a stoppage on the railways the government simply took them over for long enough to grant substantial wage rises. Brief strikes in the coal areas resulted also in the mines being placed under the authority of the Secretary of the Interior, Harold Ickes. Ickes neatly summed up the invincible bargaining position conferred by labour participation in time of war: 'There are not enough jails in the country to hold these men,' he told Roosevelt, 'and, if there were, I must point out that a jailed miner produces no more coal.'[27] Eventually, in November 1943, the miners gained practically all of their demands, particularly a recognition of their travelling time to and from work, and an effective rise of $1·50 a day.

For all workers, the average weekly wage went up between 1939 and 1945 from $23·86 to $44·39. Trade union membership rose from under nine million to just short of fifteen million. But the only unalloyed example of the participation effect at work was the Servicemen's Readjustment Act of 1944, popularly known as the G.I. Bill, which entitled returning soldiers to unemployment insurance during the first year after the war, government loans for setting up homes or businesses, and educational grants for those wishing to enter colleges or undertake vocational training. The G.I. Bill was successful because it could be presented simply as a reward for genuine serving men, and was clearly dissociated from general schemes of welfare provision. None the less the whole case for such provision did make progress. War workers had to be housed, and, though, as we have noted, their conditions were often deplorable, the government did use the National Housing Agency set up in February 1942, to spend $2·3 billion on low-cost housing for migrant workers; it thus entered the housing business on a scale which would have been out of the question even in the palmiest days of the New Deal. The government also undertook responsibility for ancillary medical services and day-care nurseries, and instituted rent control for defence areas; by the end of the war 86 million tenants were benefiting from this highly popular measure. On the broader front participation in a united war effort by powerful interest groups (Republicans, businessmen, the medical profession) cut across any other attempts at the systematic extension of welfare provision. None the less, in the election of 1944, the Republican candidate Thomas Dewey, felt it wise to recognise what had changed during the war: acknowledging that 'it took a world war to get jobs for the American people' he pledged his party to the maintenance of the best of the New Deal, while administering it more efficiently.[28] The post-war politics of consensus were coming into being.

As the home of the more extreme manifestations of the Women's Liberation Movement, the United States has also been the subject of much argument over the precise significance and consequences of women's participation in the war effort. One extreme feminist line would insist that women were simply hired to do all kinds of jobs as required by military necessity, while being paid as little as possible and kept as far and as long as possible out of positions of responsibility; that they were encouraged to adopt a 'masculine image' while the war lasted; then, when the war was over, that they were firmly ejected from their new jobs and new responsibilities, and once again had the traditional 'feminine image' firmly thrust upon them.[29] Other issues crop up, such as whether working long hours in a steel works or ship yard can, in any sense, be termed 'emancipation'. The answers I suggest here must be very similar to the ones I offered with regard to the British experience.

First, there was no real abandonment of the feminine image during the war: whatever hard or responsible work women were performing, they were still, in novels, newspapers and films, despite circumstantial variations, essentially portrayed as home builders and boosters of male morale. There was much argument over what dress and grooming were suitable for the shop floor: film star Ann Sheridan supported the right of girls to wear sexy sweaters; but Veronica Lake, populariser of the flowing peekaboo hairstyle, patriotically changed to a less appealing style which would not invite her imitators to get their hair caught in factory machinery. Patriotism was not enough: Veronica Lake lost much of her sex appeal, and, significantly, much of her popularity.

The basic facts are clear enough. Between 1940 and 1945 the number of women workers rose from 12 million to 16·5 million, that is from 25·5 per cent of the domestic labour force to 36 per cent. It is perfectly true that in the first year of peace over two million women lost their jobs; in the end something like two-thirds of those who undertook war work remained in employment and the percentage of women in the labour force settled at about 29 per cent. Officially government policy, as announced by the War Labor Board on 25 November 1942, favoured equal pay for women engaged in the national effort; in practice it was always possible for employers to evade the spirit of this policy, and earnings among women production workers remained on average about 40 per cent below those of men. The conclusion is inescapable that the Second World War offered women opportunities normally unavailable in peacetime to improve their economic and social status, and to develop their own confidence and self-consciousness. In many cases these opportunities were firmly grasped; whether they would be extended depended very much on women themselves, for, without doubt, old attitudes, overpoweringly strong in 1941, were still influential in 1946. Whatever disgruntled Women's Liberationists might say, and however justified many of their complaints, it remains true that progress towards an enhanced status for women was made during the war, and continued to be made in the post-war years.

When we turn to the question of the black American, and his participation in the war effort, there is no story of steady progress to be told. In certain respects the objective material circumstances of most blacks (as of most whites) improved over the war period, and were maintained in conditions of post-war prosperity. But if there is one really significant change to be explained, it is the change from relative passivity in the 1930s to the conditions of 'Negro Revolt' which broke out openly in the 1960s and which still continues today; the 'Negro

Revolt', in turn, has certainly brought real gains, but so far, obviously, America's race problem is still a very long way from being solved. Central to the change is the phenomenon of black participation, both in the services, and in domestic industries.[30] But this must be taken in conjunction with the disruptive effects of a war which set off a migration towards the towns of the north and of California greater in scale than anything so far in the twentieth century; with the test effect of war which, at times, showed segregation to be clearly inefficient; and with the psychological implications of a war being allegedly fought on behalf of democracy against the most vicious racist régime the world had ever seen. The forces which made for an improvement in the status of the black man had to battle against counter-forces thrown up by the government's need, equally, to retain the support of interest groups – industrialists, white trade unionists, southern politicians – strongly hostile to the Afro-American.

With the experience and disappointment of the previous war fresh in the memory, and the outrageous contrast between Roosevelt's bid to make the country the 'Arsenal of Democracy' and the actual practice of racial discrimination sharp in the mind, certain black leaders moved into action almost as soon as the European war had broken out. Calls for an end to discrimination in the expanding American armed services were not immediately successful, but on the home front January 1941 saw the planning of what can, not unreasonably, be seen as one of the precursors of the movements of the 'Negro Revolt'.[31] The black trade-union leader, A. Philip Randolph announced a mass march on Washington to take place on 1 July. Instead of subtle negotiation this march would embody direct action. Instead of being confined to the black intelligentsia it would involve the masses of black workers. And it would exclude white men. Quite unashamedly the march was intended to cause the government the maximum amount of embarassment at a time when it was harassed by what it saw as its responsibilities in regard to the European war. All Roosevelt's attempts to have the march called off failed till he agreed to issue Executive Order 8802 (25 June 1941), which forbade discrimination in all defence industries and established a Fair Employment Practices Committee to investigate and attempt to deal with violations of this Order. The real benefits for the black man were not great. None the less a new element had been injected into the gathering struggle, which set higher objectives for the government, and encouraged the blacks, then, as the objectives were not achieved, angered them, while at the same time antagonising their opponents.

The new employment opportunities open to blacks meant that real

earnings in some cases rose by as much as ninety-eight per cent. On
the other hand the herding together of black families in run-down parts
of industrial cities increased the opportunity for militance and the
likelihood of violence; just how deplorable conditions in the rural south
were, was brought out by the fact that, even in the noisome city ghettos,
health and mortality statistics for black Americans actually improved.
For many blacks service, even in the segregated armed forces, meant
far higher living standards than they had ever enjoyed before. In December 1944 the last-ditch German offensive in the Ardennes found the
American combat units seriously short of men; black volunteers had to
be drafted in. Of still greater significance was the experience black
troops had of British and French civilians who sometimes treated them
with greater friendliness than they did white American soldiers.

On one level the most important events of the war period might seem
to be the race riots which took place in the summer of 1943 in Los
Angeles, Detroit and New York, and the outbreaks of white violence
against blacks which took place in 1946 (though not on anything like
the scale of 1919). Yet if, in some respects, antagonisms had been
sharpened, two other points also have to be noted. First, and most
important, black confidence and self-consciousness had been greatly
strengthened during the war. Apart from the obvious examples of this
in black newspapers for example, it can also be traced in other facets of
black culture: the whole Rhythm and Blues movement, it has been
argued, represented the new cultural consciousness of the post-war
black man.[32] Second, some white attitudes had changed: either white
men were more actively in favour of Civil Rights legislation than they
had ever been before, or at least they were aware as they had never
been before that the black man had grievances. In the immediate post-
war years there were developments: while the navy and air force were
in any case moving towards the ending of discrimination, and while the
army recognised the inefficiency of discrimination without being too
keen on doing anything about it, Roosevelt's successor as President,
Harry S. Truman, set up a Committee on Civil Rights. The Report of
this Committee, entitled *To Secure These Rights*, contains as neat a
statement of one important aspect of the participation theory as can
be found anywhere:

The record shows that the members of several minorities, fighting
and dying for the survival of the nation in which they met bitter
prejudice, found that there was discrimination against them even as
they fell in battle. Prejudice in any area is an ugly, undemocratic

phenomenon; in the armed services, where all men run the risk of death, it is particularly repugnant.[33]

But the Committee, and President Truman, went far beyond the purely military sphere, and Truman's Civil Rights Message of 2 February 1948 called for sweeping legislation, while Executive Order 9981 ended discrimination in the forces. For the time being, though, it was left to individual states and cities to pass their own anti-discrimination laws; federal action was halted by the new mood engendered by the Cold War and the rising tide of anti-Red feeling. But the movement towards Civil Rights was submerged not drowned; and meantime the frustrations of black men who had seen glimpses of better things increased. The scene was indeed being set for the 'Negro Revolt' of the 1960s.

## Psychological Aspects

In trying to assess the effects of the war on the Afro-American I have had to bring in the psychological dimension of war. We have already seen that to think of the war as bringing a new and complete national unity would be quite ridiculous. There were those who, as in Britain, declared that the war must usher in a new and better world; most of them were sincere, and the sentiments they expressed played at least a small part in the mix of ideas which helped to make collectivist social reform a little more acceptable in the United States. The North Carolina newspaper editor, Jonathan Daniels, in December 1941, set a tone which is perhaps more reminiscent of the Britain of the First World War than the Second World War:

> There never could have been a time when it was a greater privilege to be an American than now. The twenties are gone with self-indulgence. The thirties have disappeared with self-pity. The forties are here in which Americans stand on a continent as men – men again fighting in the crudest man terms – for ourselves and also for that destination in decency for all men of which our settlement, our spreading, was always a symbol. In an America grown magnificently male again we have a chance to fight for a homeland with the full meaning of homeland as a world that is fit to be the home of man.[34]

The echo of Lloyd George's 'homes fit for heroes' is striking; but it is worth noting, too, that in 1943 Daniels became the President's Administrative Assistant with special reference to racial affairs, that is, he was not a mere voice in cloud-cuckoo-land. More revealing, however, about an important aspect of the emotional climate engendered by the war, is the manner in which, in December 1941, the Chicago *Tribune*, a determined opponent of all American intervention abroad, changed its slogan from 'Save Our Republic' to 'Our Country Right or Wrong'. But a sharpening of patriotism could be to the severe disadvantage of minority groups. On the whole German- and Italian-Americans were not molested as German and other European elements had been in the previous war, but public opinion polls, Hitler's policies notwithstanding, revealed a marked increase in anti-semitism. Worst off of all were the Japanese-Americans, whose enforced deportation from the West Coast showed the strength of in-group hysteria evoked by the war. Private individuals, 'public opinion', officials, and public figures joined in the harassment. The Governor of Idaho offered his own solution: 'send them all back to Japan, then sink the island. They live like rats, breed like rats and act like rats.' [35]

However it would be wrong to end on that note. The war was an experience in American life which far surpassed that of 1917–18 though, sadly, such emotional set pieces as the invasion of Hitler's Fortress Europe had to be set alongside the fire bombing of Dresden and the atomic bombing of Hiroshima and Nagasaki. At all events, the war provided a rich vein to be worked by American writers for many years after it was over. The Pacific War against the Japanese was the basis of Norman Mailer's enormous and powerful *The Naked and the Dead* (1948); bombing missions on Italy and an American prisoner-of-war's experience of the Dresden fire raids, provide the personal and historical context for two unique novels which carry a stage further the creative insights into the real nature of modern war developed by European writers after 1919: Joseph Heller's *Catch 22* (1961), and *Slaughter House 5* (1969) by Kurt Vonnegut Jr.

## III   New Relationships

One weakness in Professor Polenberg's excellent *War and Society: The United States, 1941–1945* is its confinement to the terminal dates of the war. Evidently any real assessment of a war's social consequences must look to the years after the war. One difficulty with regard to the United States is that many of the developments fostered during the war were then submerged or diverted by further developments arising from the subsequent Cold War situation, a situation which, in itself, must merit some attention in any proper study of war and social change.

In contrasting the development of the United States after 1945 with that of Britain, we can distinguish some of the most important long-term consequences of the Second World War. First of all the war clearly established certain simple truths of geopolitical reality. A medium-sized power with little in the way of natural resources, such as Britain, could not hope to compete economically and politically with a large country rich in all kinds of natural wealth, such as the United States (or Russia). Nor could Britain hope to go on bolstering her position through possession of a far-flung and racially heterogeneous empire: the war had exposed the essential feebleness of Britain's grip on, for example, the Indian sub-continent, and participation in the war had brought a new self-awareness to the peoples of Africa and Asia. Even white Australia was revealed as belonging properly within the American rather than the British geopolitical sphere.

The United States moved at once into the peacetime affluence which was ultimately to characterise all the industrialised countries in the later post-war years; Britain, for the first half-dozen years or so, lived a poor relation's life of austerity and consumer shortages. Eventually affluence came to Britain as a part of the world-wide conditions in which the longer-term effects of the war were one, but not the sole, factor. Technology in all its aspects had been greatly affected by the war, the main upshot being that the United States in greater, and Britain in lesser, degree had a new and improved range of technologies at their disposal for social as well as military purposes. Principal among these were atomic energy, radar, rocket propulsion, jet propulsion, computerisation and automation, operational research, plastics, and new drugs. Britain, under the stresses of war, had not had the resources to develop to the full the potential of atomic power (nor of proximity fuses, the cavity magnetron, and penicillin); her secrets passed to the United States.

It can be argued that, in the area of military technology, the test effect of war had one particularly grave consequence. The United States in the 1930s was ill-armed, isolationist, afflicted by economic depression, and her businessmen, academics and scientists, in the best free-market tradition, operated independently of each other and of the federal government. During and after the war the United States moved into the era of the permanent arms economy, dominated by a 'military–industrial complex' in which government, industry and scientists co-operated in using vast sums of government money to maintain and develop the most sophisticated forms of technological warfare. Some commentators have claimed that the relatively high levels of employment of the post-war years have been dependent on this military expenditure, and that without it prosperity would collapse; and it is certainly not unreasonable to believe that the very existence of the 'military–industrial complex' inevitably tended to create pressure for an interventionist foreign policy (as, for instance, in Vietnam). On the economic point I remain unpersuaded. The pools of unemployment and squalor, and the occasional recessions apparent in recent U.S. economic history suggest that there is room for a rather different and altogether more conscious form of interventionism in economic affairs, and it is at least a tenable proposition that arms expenditure has diverted attention and potential resources from this. France and Germany, without military–industrial complexes on anything like the American scale, have proved economically healthier than the United States in recent years. For Britain the attempt to bump up arms expenditure on the outbreak of the Korean War in 1951 hinted at economic disaster, and, in the event, proved impossible to carry through. But technology, and, above all, the possession of nuclear weapons, certainly reinforced the United States' position (along with Russia) as a super-power.

On the surface at least Britain underwent much more in the way of guided change in the post-war years, with a Labour government committed to the establishment of a managed economy, a welfare state, and an attempt at social levelling. Yet, setting all value judgements aside, if we accept that the norms for later twentieth-century society are essentially defined by the United States (followed by West Germany) then it is in Britain that least change seems to have taken place. Certainly the war-time shake-up in social structure and social relationships was probably as great in the United States as it was in Britain. For the United States, as later in Germany, there was now a rich middle class together with a highly-paid class of manual workers who had achieved, or aspired to, middle-class standards. At the same time it was clear that where social peace had been maintained through the subjugation of minority groups, particularly black Americans, such peace had gone for good. While there was more deliberate experimentation in techniques of state management of the economy in Britain, the United States moved in a pretty straight line into the era of managed capitalism, with a mild government overview of an economy effectively dominated by vast (often supra-national) enterprises, which in turn, in keeping with the co-operative ethic of wartime, followed relatively benevolent policies towards their employees. Old-style progressive liberalism was dead; but its most constructive elements were embodied in the new politics of consensus. The post-war confrontation with Russia in some respects reinforced or resuscitated trends associated with the war itself: for example Russia's space 'first' of 1958 touched off an intense government interest in educational reform. It also provoked a form of hysteria probably greater than anything aroused during the war; and in other ways it cut across wartime developments. Thus in the 1950s the United States moved towards a much more pronounced political conservatism than did Britain, and also underwent the stultifying influence of McCarthyism, a more poisonous Red scare even than that of 1919.

On questions of life styles, patterns of behaviour, 'permissiveness' and so on, I can only reiterate the points already made in regard to West Germany. In the first fifteen years of peace, the United States was the trend-setter. That the war was only one influence among many, and eventually only a very minor one, is suggested by the curious way in which, from the early 1960s, Britain took over a significant trend-setting role of her own in pop culture. However the final, and most interesting change in the relationship of the United States to Europe occurred in the realm of the visual arts. Aided significantly by the Second World War flow of refugees from Europe, New York took over in the world of painting the role formerly occupied by Paris or Berlin: the first dominant new school of painting in the post-war world, abstract expressionism, was born in the United States.

Britain's experience of the Second World War is reminiscent of France's experience of the First World War. There has been much speculation about the effects on the British collective psychology of the 'loss of empire'. From today's perspective, while one is forcibly struck by how long it took politicians and industrialists even to realise that there had been a 'loss of empire', it is difficult to be sure that there has been any real effect at all on the mass of the British people. In many respects British society has not adjusted well to the contemporary world; but on the whole her recent history has been much happier than that of France after 1918. The United States' experience of the Second World War is in some respects reminiscent of British reactions to the First World War. Her material gains were much more real, and her power *vis-à-vis* other nations much greater. Her record since 1945 has not given great comfort to thoughtful Americans; but it has perhaps not been notably worse than that of Britain 1919–39.

*Notes and References*

1. A. M. Low, *Benefits of War* (1943).
2. H. Pelling, *Britain and the Second World War* (1970) p. 297.

3. A. Calder, *The People's War* (1969) p. 17. For a fuller statement of my own views see my article 'L'Impact de la Deuxième Guerre Mondiale sur les Britanniques' in *Revue d'histoire de la deuxième guerre mondiale* (April 1973).

4. I. L. Janis, *Air War and Emotional Stress* (1951) pp. 67–179; R. O. Gillespie, *Psychological Effects of War on Citizens and Soldiers* (1942) pp. 100–2; R. Ingersoll, *Report on England* (1940).

5. *International Journal of Psychoanalysis*, vol. 23 (1942) p. 28.

6. Ministry of Information, *Front Line* (1942) pp. 67–8.

7. e.g. *Fires were Started* and *London Can Take It* (both in the National Film Archive). Extracts from the *London Fire Service Film* can be seen in the Open University War and Society compilation, *Social Impact of World War II*.

8. H. Hamilton Fyfe, *Britain's War-time Revolution* (1944) pp. 105–6.

9. Janis, pp. 92 ff. Cp. Calder, pp. 225–7.

10. 'The Kids Perform', *British Movietone News*, 18 September 1939 (in the Movietone Archives, Denham).

11. The most striking single piece of evidence is *Our Towns* (1943), a report by the Women's Group on Public Welfare. The most thorough study is still R. M. Titmus, *Problems of Social Policy* (Official History of the Second World War: Civil Series, 1950) pp. 23–195.

12. Federation of British Industries, *British Industry* (May 1942) p. 136.

13. e.g. Ministry of Information film *Airwomen* (mostly showing the 'air women' serving in canteens); *British Movietone News*, 'The Rationing of Fashion' (24 December 1942), and 'Girls at War' (11 May 1945); and *War Pictorial News*, issue 98, 'A.T.S. Sewing School', (in Imperial War Museum and Movietone Archives).

14. Appendix to *Report on Pensionability of Unestablished Civil Service*, P.P., 1945–6, XII, Cmd. 6942.

15. *Ministry of Labour and National Service Report for 1939–1946*, P.P., 1946–7, XII, Cmd. 7225, pp. 4, 304–7.

16. D. Butler, *The Electoral System in Britain Since 1918* (1963) p. 184.

17. A. Marwick 'The Labour Party and the Welfare State in Britain 1900–1948', *American Historical Review*, LXXIII (Dec 1967).

18. R. C. O. Mathews, 'Why has Britain had Full Employment Since the War', *Economic Journal* (1968), pp. 555–69; Pelling, p. 300.

19. Examples are the Ministry of Information films, *Builders* (1942) and *A City Reborn* (1945), and the British Council film *Picture Papers* (1946); this last is actually about planning. (All in the National Film Archive).

20. William Miller, *A New History of the United States* (1958, 1970 edn) p. 351.

21. Richard Polenberg, *War and Society: the United States, 1941–1945* (1972) p. 4.

22. Quoted by Polenberg, pp. 83 and 73.

23. See Polenberg, p. 137.

24. Quoted by Polenberg, p. 12.

25. Polenberg, p. 13.

26. Cp. H. F. May, *The End of American Innocence* and p. 9 above.

27. Quoted by Polenberg, p. 164.

28. Polenberg, p. 209.

29. See, e.g. Betty Friedan, *The Feminine Mystique* (1963) esp. chap. 2.

30. See Neil A. Wynn, 'The Impact of the Second World War on the American Negro', *Journal of Contemporary History*, VI, 2 (Apr 1971), and his unpublished thesis 'The Afro-American and the Second World War' (Open University, 1973). Also see Richard M. Dalfiume, 'The "Forgotten Years" of the Negro Revolt', *Journal of American History*, LV, 1 (June 1968), and Polenberg, chap. 4.

31. Dalfiume, p. 93; Wynn, 'Impact', p. 42.

32. Wynn, unpublished thesis, pp. 198–204.

33. President's Committee on Civil Rights, *To Secure These Rights* (1947) p. 41.

34. Jonathan Daniels, 'The Hour of Elation' in *The Nation* (20 December 1941) reprinted in *America at War: The Home Front, 1941–1945*, ed. Richard Polenberg (1968) pp. 2–3.

35. Quoted by Polenberg, *War and Society*, p. 65.

# 6. The Second World War: France

## I  The Chagrin and the Pity of it

The French experience in the Second World War throws a pretty big spanner into the attempt at a systematic study of the relationship between modern war and social change. In international law France was at war with Germany throughout the period, since, technically, all that was concluded after France's defeat in May 1940 was an armistice. In a very real sense France was both at war, and not at war. At various times the energies of some of her people were, willy-nilly, enlisted in support of the German war effort; the energies of others among her people were engaged in trying to bring about Germany's defeat. In 1944 French territory suffered a second massive invasion, preceded and supported by heavy bombing; but this time the invasion was conducted by the Americans and British, and was aimed at removing the Germans from France.

Before attempting, in the context of their social significance, to outline the course of these bewildering developments, I want to see just where all this leaves us with regard to my four-tier model. Then, at the end of this section, I want to look at something of the reality of life in wartime France. The second section will discuss the longer-term social consequences of the war; and the final section, which rounds off the main part of this book, will discuss the relationship of wartime developments to the emergence of the European Economic Community.

### Four-Tier Model

Throughout the period that Britain feared the mounting of a sea-borne invasion from German-occupied France, the main French ports suffered

For Notes and References to this chapter, see p. 211 below.

from intensive British bombing. Between September 1940 and May 1941 Brest alone endured 78 separate air attacks. The intensive bombing of Le Havre over the same period resulted in a drop in population there of 50,000. The land battle around Dunkirk in May 1940 resulted in the destruction of 80 per cent of Dunkirk's housing; as late as November 1941, 60,000 of the town's 100,000 inhabitants had to take to the cellars in face of British air attacks. To all this must be added the disruptions of the *exode*, the massive movement of population in face of the German invasion, and then from Occupied to Unoccupied France. Severe physical destruction was renewed in the last stages of the war when, for instance, the old town of Caen was almost totally destroyed. Overall French deaths from Allied bombing amounted to at least 60,000, with 75,000 wounded.[1] The total of French civilian deaths (including air-raid victims, victims of land operations, and those shot or massacred by the Germans, the Vichy government or the Resistance) has been calculated at 160,000, but this probably includes an inflated figure for the executions carried out by the Resistance at the time of the Liberation (recent estimates put this at 12,000).[2] French soldiers fought and fell in the campaigns of 1939–40; outside France Frenchmen in uniform continued to fight in the Free French Forces and inside France in the French Forces of the Interior; Frenchmen from Alsace–Lorraine were forcibly enlisted in the German Army; French soldiers died in prisoner-of-war camps. Altogether, over the whole war, 250,000 soldiers of all categories were listed as dead or missing.[3]

From France Germany deported 776,000 workers, 100,000 political prisoners and 220,000 Jews: of these 200,000 perished. Within France the Germans employed, solely in the interests of their own military and economic effort, the equivalent of 5·2 million man-years over the four years of war. In addition to this, France lost to German prison camps the equivalent of 4·5 million man-years. Besides carrying out a systematic spoliation of all classes of French goods and materials, the Germans levied astronomically inflated 'occupation costs' – equivalent in 1940 to 10·9 per cent of the estimated total French National Income and rising to 36·6 per cent in 1943[4] – and actually at least ten times the real cost of the military occupation. It is not surprising that by 1944 French industrial production had dropped by more than half, and agricultural production by more than a quarter.[5]

France, in May 1940, failed the *test* of war. Or so many Frenchmen believed. On the Right, certain upholders of the Vichy régime set out to reorganise society so that, they hoped, France would never again be at such a disadvantage compared with Germany. Men of the Left, too, though powerless for the time being, felt confirmed in their belief in the need for a complete reconstruction of French society. All that apart, certain French institutions had simply collapsed; something would have to be put in their place. Inadequacy in high places had been glaringly revealed; now, and for the future, opportunity offered itself to new men. But for Frenchmen as a whole the biggest test of all was the complex and tragic situation presented by the war: if few were very brave, all were touched.

*Participation* is perhaps the most complex and elusive of all elements to be studied in a divided country such as France was. Participation in resistance to the conquering enemy compared say with serving in a conscript army, or with working longer hours in the factory for bonus wages, was the highest form that participation could possibly take – as the Resistance poet, Aragon, said, 'an outlaw is braver than a soldier, because he acts for himself'.[6] Just how far the rewards were proportionate is something we shall have to work out later. At the same time we shall have to ask how far participation in the official French collaborative effort with the Germans, or indeed direct participation in the German war effort, could also bring rewards.

For Russia, we have seen, the war was a colossal *psychological* experience; it was 'The Great Patriotic War'. For France, rather, the war was the great national humiliation, redeemed finally by the reality, and perhaps even more by the myth, of heroic resistance.

## Outline of Events

During March 1940 Daladier gave way to Reynaud as Prime Minister, and Reynaud, harking back to the previous war, brought Marshal Pétain, the hero of Verdun, in as Deputy Prime Minister (rather as Churchill was brought into the British government; Pétain, however, was already eighty-three). Gamelin was replaced as Commander-in-Chief by one of Foch's former staff, General Weygand; Clemenceau's right-hand man, Mandel, became Minister of the Interior; and a junior Great War officer, Charles de Gaulle, was appointed Under-Secretary for War. By late May 1940, after the French government had already moved to Tours and then to Bordeaux, France's military leaders were convinced – just as Germany's had been in September 1918 – that France must sue for an armistice. Prime Minister Reynaud, who disagreed, resigned to give way to Pétain. The armistice was signed on 22 June, and came formally into effect on 25 June.

Germany's policies towards her defeated adversaries varied, and a broad distinction can be made between countries which were annexed and countries which were simply occupied. Despite the depravity to which Nazism could sink, France was treated with relative leniency. At first only the northern half of France together with the entire Atlantic coast was occupied, leaving a remnant in the south west as Unoccupied France. However Alsace and Lorraine were wholly incorporated within Germany, the departments of the Nord and Pas-de-Calais were placed under the German military administration in Belgium, and a large area in the north east of France was declared a 'prohibited zone' in which German farmers were settled and to which French refugees were forbidden to return. The French government was to remain in existence, and would be responsible, in co-operation with the German occupying forces, for the administration of the entire country, and for meeting the costs of the occupation. It was free to sit in either Occupied or Unoccupied territory. Since Bordeaux was in the Occupied zone, Pétain decided for the resort town of Vichy, where the large number of hotels would provide the necessary government offices. Coming into existence on 11 July 1940, the Vichy régime at once endorsed the view that it was decadent French democracy which had failed the test of war, by establishing an authoritarian state in which the elective principle was abolished.

The four leading figures were Pétain himself, who began all his utterances in the regal form 'We, Philippe Pétain . . .', Weygand, Admiral Darlan, the naval chief, and the shrewd, but perhaps slightly naïve peasant politician, Pierre Laval, whose own justification for the establishment of the Vichy régime was that: '. . . parliamentary democracy whose greatest crime was to declare this war, lost the war; it must disappear and give way to an authoritarian, hierarchical, national and social régime.' [7]

In times of crisis, it is said, the French always turn to a hero-figure. Pétain (ably seconded by Laval) fulfilled this role. But at the same time another hero-figure took up the anti-Vichy, 'Free French' cry. On 18 June the former Under-Secretary for War, an exile in London, delivered his famous broadcast calling Frenchmen to 'Resistance' to the Vichy and Occupation régimes. In France itself probably the first and predominant sentiment was relief that hostilities had ceased. Certainly it was reasonable to argue that Pétain had taken the only sensible course open to him, and that, indeed, he had saved much for France. But although the Vichy régime was supposed to be responsible for the government of the entire country, in practice German policy turned the demarcation line between the two zones into a rigid barrier across which it was very difficult for individuals to pass, and which increasingly also formed an economic barrier.

As it happened, the Vichy zone contained such hotly left-wing areas as Lyons and Marseilles; and from the start there appeared, in both parts of France, elements of resistance to German rule and Vichy collaboration. Lyons attracted many Parisians, and its peculiar topography of steep, conspiratorial alleys helped to make it a kind of capital city for the Resistance. Here *Combat* was established under Captain Henri Frenay; while in Paris the Comité National de Salut Public was formed by a group of young scholars at the Musée de l'Homme. By the end of 1940 a number of underground newspapers were beginning to appear.

In November 1942 the geographical division of France came to an end. As a direct result of the Allied landings in North Africa, the German army on 11 November crossed the demarcation line to extend the occupation to the whole of France. There was now even less room for manoeuvre for the French government; and the government itself became in any case, for various reasons, more enthusiastic than before over the idea of active collaboration with the Germans. Russian successes in the east encouraged the passionate anti-Communists, who from the start had been an important mainstay of the Vichy régime, to become still more pronouncedly pro-German. Increasing Resistance activity encouraged repression, again often in collaboration with the Germans. In March 1942 quasi-Fascist elements formed the Service d'Ordre Légionnaire, which in January 1943 became the Milice Nationale. The *milice* became notorious as a bloody instrument of repression, operating hand-in-hand with the Germans against the Resistance. The common-sense, 'middle-of-the-road' justification for supporting the Vichy régime had disappeared with the events of November 1942: it could no longer be argued that support for Vichy was the only way to prevent all of France being occupied; nor, with the obvious change in the fortunes of war, could it be argued that since Germany was bound to win the war anyway it was better not to resist her. As negative reasons disappeared, neo-Fascist elements with strong positive reasons for collaborating with Germany came more and more to the fore.

None the less the notion that collaboration could still be in the interests of the bulk of the French people must not be dismissed out of hand. The German Ambassador responsible for political questions in France, Abetz, had been a sponsor of the Franco-German youth movement, a member of the Comité France–Allemagne, and had a French wife. Speer, though he believed the defeat of France to be 'necessary', was also strongly pro-French, and he found a kindred spirit in the Vichy Minister for Industry, Bichelonne. With Bichelonne, Speer was able to work out schemes whereby, contrary to Sauckel's wishes, French workers would remain in France, though working for the German war effort. Here was a curious side to the participation effect: efficient production from French labour was now so vital to the German war effort that it was possible to use this as a lever for preventing more French workers from being deported to Germany. Professor Milward puts the matter with his usual perceptiveness: 'The weakest point of the fascist idea of conquest was bound to be its relations with labour. The French workers struck at the insecure foundations of the whole edifice; they could not be compelled to work more productively. Labour problems had eventually to dominate all other aspects of the economic existence of the occupied powers.'[8]

Inevitably the Resistance groups in France were drawn from the Left rather than the Right. However, one cannot be too dogmatic, since so much depended on the individual; so much, even, on local circumstances. Where a man of the Left saw peace as a categorical imperative, he might well side with Vichy and the acceptance of an armistice with the Germans. Where a man of the Right put national pride as a categorical imperative, he might well throw in his lot with the Resistance. Most important were those Catholics – the 'social' Catholics – whose sense of Christian commitment led them to participate with Socialists and Communists in the Resistance to Vichy and the Germans: one of the best known of these was Georges Bidault, history teacher and crusading journalist from Lyons. In France, as elsewhere, the Communist Party started off in great disarray as a result of the German-Soviet pact. Only after the German invasion of Russia was the Communist Party able to assume an increasingly important role within the French Resistance. De Gaulle himself was certainly no man of the Left, and to begin with there was little contact between the Resistance movements in metropolitan France and de Gaulle's Free French movement. But by late 1942 de Gaulle was increasingly looking towards the Resistance as his only possible basis of support within France itself, while the Resistance, whatever the reservations of particular individuals and groups, came to see him as the symbol of unity and leadership.

By this time the main Resistance groups were: in the south, Combat, Liberation, and Franc-Tireur; and in the north, Organisation Civile et Militaire (O.C.M.), a right-wing organisation; Libération Nord, a mainly socialist organisation; and Défense de la France, largely composed of Paris students. Only one Resistance group covered both the north and south: this was the Front National founded by the Communists in 1941. The British government naturally hoped to enlist Resistance elements in the military struggle against Germany, and as early as July 1940 they set up the Special Operations Executive (S.O.E.), the 'Ministry of Ungentlemanly Warfare' as Churchill called it. From late 1940 S.O.E. agents were being sent to France (and to other countries) to make contact with Resistance groups; by the end of the war over a thousand British agents were operating in France. The question of the military significance of the Resistance is still a matter of debate among historians. The fashionable majority view is to discount its effects on the actual outcome of the war, though Professor M. R. D. Foot, among others, has consistently pointed out that, in contrast say with strategic bombing, the Resistance was remarkably effective in carrying out the destruction of key installations with the minimum loss of innocent life. Fortunately it is not necessary to enter into this controversy in this book; though it is my contention that the Resistance was of enormous social and psychological significance.

In May 1943 a Gaullist agent Jean Moulin was parachuted into France and a National Resistance Council (C.N.R.) was founded under his presidency to link together the major Resistance groups along with the political parties and trade unions operating in clandestine opposition to the Occupation government. The underground para-military forces were united under a single command as the French Forces of the Interior (F.F.I.). The terrible risks run by the brave members of these organisations were highlighted when in June Moulin was arrested by the Germans, and tortured to death. (Another martyrdom was that of the great French historian, Marc Bloch.) Demonstrating that it was neither Gaullist nor completely leftist, the C.N.R. itself chose Georges Bidault as president. However, at that very time de Gaulle visited Algeria, where on 3 June the Comité Français de la Libération Nationale (C.F.L.N.) was established to bring together the main military and political leaders outside France. From the start this organisation was dominated by de Gaulle.

Until the Allied invasion of Europe the underground military forces of the F.F.I. were under the political command of the C.N.R.; after D-Day, they were, by mutual agreement, to come under the control of de Gaulle's C.F.L.N. In the summer of 1943 it was also agreed between the C.N.R. and the C.F.L.N. that 'Liberation Committees' should be set up in each department of France. Although de Gaulle received only the most grudging support from President Roosevelt and the Allied leaders, and thus constantly ran the risk that his organisation might be supplanted by an Allied military government, these arrangements were to prove startlingly effective. On 3 June, three days before the Normandy landings began, the C.F.L.N. changed its name to the Provisional Government of the French Republic.

The first stages of the invasion proceeded far more painfully and slowly than had been expected; but then after a break-through at the end of July things moved much more rapidly than plans had allowed for. De Gaulle had the support of the Allied operational commanders, whose main concern was to have a satisfactory civilian government established as quickly as possible so that they could devote themselves to military matters; in July he gained the reluctant support of Roosevelt as the *de facto* civil authority. But de Gaulle's power was very far from monolithic. Against his advice, the Resistance in Paris rose against the German forces a week before the Allied armies could reach the capital. But it was de Gaulle who led the triumphal march down the Champs Elysées on 25 August, and the ceremony in Notre Dame Cathedral, when, as the B.B.C. live broadcast and the British newsreel material clearly reveal, he was subject to sniper fire from a few remaining Germans and German sympathisers – and one Japanese!

Meantime the retreating Germans had taken the entire Vichy régime with them and had installed it at Sigmaringen in southern Germany. Hence for the last year of the war the civilian authority in France was in the hands of de Gaulle's provisional government, while throughout the provinces, particularly in the south, local power was in the hands of Departmental Liberation Committees. For the time being participation in active Resistance was rewarded by civil and political power. None the less the real power still lay with the invading American and British forces. At this stage armed revolution was not in fact the policy of the Communist members of the Resistance; but even if it had been, it could scarcely have been carried out under the noses of the American and British armies.

*Life in France*

The recent four-and-a-half-hour film, banned from French television but shown to packed audiences in Paris, *Le Chagrin et la Pitié*, paints an unflattering picture of the way in which most Frenchmen were prepared to accept collaboration with the Germans. Back in 1958 the Hoover Institute published, in both English and French, a three-volume collection of 'documents' entitled *La Vie de la France sous l'Occupation* which suggested that although life was often hard, it was not as hard as it would have been had not the Vichy régime existed as a buffer between the Germans and the French people. The 'documents', however, consist

almost exclusively of later statements made by those associated with the
Vichy régime, and edited by Pierre Laval's daughter. They were subjected to devastating criticism in a book compiled by a group of French
historians and economists, *La France sous l'Occupation*.

Undoubtedly, given the systematic German plundering and the manner in which, as part of Germany's 'Fortress Europe' France was cut off
from outside supplies, living conditions were considerably worse than
those of the First World War. According to the official index prices rose
by 185 per cent between 1938 and 1944, but according to *La France
sous l'Occupation* the true rise was a six-fold one, while salaries and
wages, held steady to begin with, had risen only 63 per cent by 1944.[9]
The basic food ration never yielded more than 1200 calories a day, about
half what is needed to maintain healthy active existence. At the end of
1942 the bread ration was 1925 grams a week; that of meat varied,
depending on locality, between 180 and 125 grams; there were 70 to 100
grams of fat, 50 grams of cheese, and 4 to 6 kilograms of potatoes. The
sugar ration was 500 grams a month. The bread ration represented about
70 per cent of pre-war average consumption, though it had become the
staple food item (the fats ration was only 31 per cent of pre-war average
consumption and the meat ration only 18 per cent). Depending on
where a man lived, and on his business and family connections, these
rations could be augmented by supplies bought on the reduced free
market or through the flourishing black market. Those who lived on the
land were comparatively well-off; those who lived in big cities were
worst off. Cats and dogs, bark, roots and snakes were all searched for,
and eaten. Conditions in France perhaps cannot be equated with those
in Russia; but they were almost as bad, and for a longer period, as those
in Germany at the very end of the war. The signs of malnutrition were
clear enough, both in the physical appearance of Frenchmen, and in the
mortality statistics. The average rise in the crude mortality rate over the
war period was 11·6 per cent; but this blunt figure conceals the astonishing fact that in certain relatively well-off rural areas the death rate
actually dropped, whereas in certain other areas it rose by over thirty per
cent.[10] The overall infant mortality rate rose from 63 per thousand live
births in 1939 to 109 in 1945.

Under Vichy and the Occupation, Jews in France were, for the first
time since the Middle Ages, subjected to systematic persecution. Laval
claimed that he did his best to protect those who held full French citizenship, but only at the expense of hastening the progress of stateless
Jews towards the concentration camps.

Practically all commentators agree that the overwhelming majority of

Frenchmen, like the overwhelming majority of Germans, accepted the régime under which they were forced to live, though in the case of Frenchmen, without enthusiasm. The basic task was to get on with the hard business of keeping life going. For some aspects of some sorts of truth the pregnant phrases of the creative writer are better than the detail of a statistical survey. Here is the beginning of the anonymous preface to a famous short novel published secretly in February 1942:

> For three years France had lived under the mask of silence. Silence in the streets, silence in the home; silence because the German army parades at midday in the Champs-Élysées, silence because an enemy officer is living in the next room, silence because the Gestapo has spies everywhere, silence because the child dare not say that he is hungry, because the execution of patriots every evening makes each new morning another day of national mourning.[11]

## II  Social Consequences

Over a decade ago, Stanley Hoffman published a brilliant article entitled 'The Effects of World War II on French Society and Politics' in which he argued that instead of seeing the Vichy and Occupation régime as a uniformly reactionary force against which was posed its opposite, the Resistance and the Liberation régime, we should rather see Vichy and Resistance as 'co-operating' in a totally unintended way in bringing about social change in France.[12] In his own words, the theme of the Hoffman article was

> that in the period 1934–44 a political and social system which had gradually emerged during the nineteenth century and which had flourished in the period 1878–1934, was actually liquidated; that from 1934–40, this system, which I call the Republican synthesis, suffered severe shocks; that the events of 1940–4 turned these shocks into death blows, for a return to the previous equilibrium has been made impossible; and that many of the political, economic, and social forces which have carried post-war France increasingly farther from the pre-war pattern have their origins in the war years. What the next equilibrium will be like is hard to say, and France still [1961] seems far away from any. But it is in 1934 that movement began in earnest, and by 1946, when a political 'restoration' did in fact take place, the departures from the previous equilibrium were already considerable.

Essentially the two positive points which Hoffman makes about the 'Vichy revolution' are the setting up of new organisations for developing and controlling economic and social life together with a whole new anti-individualist and more interventionist attitude towards social and economic policy, and the emergence of more dynamic technocratic business and political leaders. Hoffman stresses what I call the 'un-guided' forces in history when he remarks that Vichy reforms often turned out quite different from what was intended, particularly since, in any case, the motives of Vichy politicians were mixed. The upholders of the New Order idea pressed for the sort of reorganisation of French life that Hitler claimed he had brought about in Germany. Other politicians felt it better to carry through their own reorganisation lest the Germans stepped in and took over complete control of the French economy. In any case the very facts of defeat and occupation forced the Vichy government to set up bodies to deal with the administrative restrictions forced upon France. Furthermore the problems arising from the physi-cal barrier of the German demarcation line forced French leaders to think of the economy nationally as they had tended not to do previously.

Hoffman lists four types of new organisation set up by the Vichy régime: 'Organisation Committees' within the world of business itself, on which the post-war Conseil National du Patronat Français was modelled; the Vichy government's Peasant Corporation, which provided the structure for the Liberations Confédération Générale Agricole (established in reaction against the Peasant Corporation) and the leader-ship for the Federation Nationale des Syndicats d'Exploitants Agricoles of post-war years; the workers' groups established within the Vichy Labour Charter, which continued to flourish in the post-war years; and finally the various professional organisations of lawyers, doctors, and so on, which were also preserved and consolidated in the post-war period. In theory at least, the Vichy Labour Charter recognised the just needs of the working classes, and the régime made much of its main contribution to social insurance policy, the institution of old-age pen-sions for retired workers. The new Vichy organisations, Hoffman claims, were put in the hands of a dynamic new generation of businessmen (partly, indeed as a result of pressure from the Germans, who were anxious to squeeze as much out of France as possible). The top figures he specially singles out for mention are – naturally, Bichelonne, whose 'administration initiated practices of co-operation which the Monnet plan institutionalised'; Aimé Lepercq, head of the Vichy Coal Mines Committee, who later became de Gaulle's Finance Minister; and Pierre Laroque, one of the main drafters of the Law of August 1940 which set up Vichy's Business Committees, who later 'built . . . the social security system of the Liberation'.

The Hoffman thesis, clearly, is overstated, as indeed the very prose style sometimes suggests: 'Vichy certainly did not create these bodies for purposes of industrialisation, economic modernisation, or education towards a less fragmented society. But after having been the transmission belts for Vichy's philistine propaganda or for the German war machine, such institutions could serve as the relays of the Monnet plan.' But there is validity in Hoffman's arguments that in the conditions of 1944–5 Resistance leaders simply had to turn to the existing machinery created by the Vichy régime, since there was neither time nor resource to create new structures, and that, in the end, war was a common, though bitter and traumatic experience, in which some of the *tests* to be surmounted affected everyone.

## Social Significance of the Resistance

Naturally the ideas put forward by Hoffman are most congenial to those who see the Vichy experiment as an understandable response to trying circumstances just as legitimate in its own way as the Resistance. They have little appeal for those whose special loyalty lies with the Resistance. While stressing once again that it is a major thesis of this book that it is the war situation itself, with all the unguided consequences which that implies, which usually has far greater significance than the ideological reactions of particular groups, I want to look at the case which can be made for the Resistance alone as a major agent of change. In the introduction to their valuable collection of documents, *Les Idées politiques et sociales de la Résistance*, Henri Michel and Boris Mirkine-Guetzevitch remark that while the Resistance continues to be famous for its sabotage and para-military activities, its social and political policies are largely forgotten.[13] The Michel and Mirkine-Guetzevitch collection establishes clearly enough the thoroughness and detail, as well as the character of Resistance social and political policies. After that, the two important questions are: were these policies put into practice; and, if so, was this due to the Resistance? (Or would they have been put into practice anyway?)

The most important single document is the Programme of the C.N.R. of March 1944, which shows both the mixture of influences behind the unified Resistance movement, and the strength of feeling for collectivist social reform. The programme begins by stressing the unity of purpose informing all the groups which made up the Resistance and their determination to remain united after the Liberation. The first clause is strongly Gaullist and nationalist in tone, calling for the establishment of de Gaulle's provisional government in order to restore national independence and the 'might, grandeur and universal mission' of France. The next two clauses announce the intention to punish traitors and collaborators and confiscate, or heavily tax, the gains of black-marketeers and others who have done well out of the war.

Clause 4 is concerned with political rights, yet, while calling for the establishment of universal suffrage, makes no special mention of votes for women: the call for a press free from foreign influence, and the insistence that the sanctity of the home and the secrecy of the postal services should be preserved, reflect the current situation, just as the demand for absolute equality for all citizens before the law is a response to the persecution of the Jews; leftist influence is clear in the demand that the press should also be free of moneyed interests.

It is with clause 5 that we come to the question of positive reform: divided into two sections, 'economic' and 'social', this clause is twice the length of the previous four taken together. The economic programme calls for the institution of a 'true economic and social democracy', involving the removal from the direction of the economy of the 'great economic and financial feudalisms'. The economy is to be organised rationally so as to secure the subordination of particular interests to the general interest, and (an interesting reference to some of the Vichy developments we have already discussed) is to be free from 'the professional dictatorship instituted in the image of fascism'. National production is to be developed in accordance with a national plan drawn up in consultation with representatives of all interests (including the workers). All sources of energy, all mineral wealth, the insurance companies and the big banks are to be 'returned to the nation'. Co-operatives are to be sponsored. Workers in general are to participate in the direction of the economy, and the direction and administration of individual enterprises is to be open to workers 'possessing the necessary qualities'.

The social programme calls for the right to work and the right to rest (the latter, of course, denied in German labour establishments); a guaranteed wage which would ensure for each worker and his wife security, dignity and the opportunity for a full life; the maintenance of purchasing power through a policy of fiscal stabilisation (nothing very socialistic about this, but strong echoes of the rampant inflation which had afflicted France throughout the war); and the recreation of an independent trade union movement, this time with a large say in the organisation of economic and social life. There should be a complete social security plan, guaranteeing the means of existence to all citizens who, for whatever reason, are unable to secure these by their own labour, together with guaranteed security of employment. The longest sub-clause of the whole section spells out the manner in which agricultural workers are to obtain the same rights as industrial workers: guaranteed farm prices, fair rents, opportunities of acquiring ownership of land, a scheme for providing modern farm equipment. Despite the very full terms of reference for the social security plan mentioned in an earlier sub-clause, adequate pensions for retired workers are included as a separate item. There is to be compensation for all war victims and victims of fascism. A further rather vague sub-clause calls for 'an extension' of the political, social and economic rights of native and colonial peoples. The final sub-clause, almost as long as the one on agricultural workers, deals with children and their education. The emphasis, perhaps, is meritocratic rather than socialist: the call is for 'the effective opportunity for French children to benefit from education and the best cultural environment, whatever the income of their parents, so that the best vocations shall really be accessible to all who have the necessary abilities, so that there will be a true élite, not of birth, but of merit, constantly renewed from below.'

Although it reflected many influences, and revealed immediate needs as well as longer-term policies, there was nothing necessarily inconsistent in this programme. Adapted to French circumstances it was remarkably similar to Labour's policies for Britain, and had clearly been partially influenced by the Beveridge Report, or, better, what the Beveridge Report was thought to stand for. De Gaulle certainly recognised the need for sweeping policies of change. In Algiers in 1943 he had said: 'If there are still Bastilles then let them get ready to open their doors.' The war situation in which he found himself, as Douglas Johnson points out, *forced* de Gaulle to be on the side of change.[14] Thus the Provisional Government did, quite unambiguously, put into effect the main features of that C.N.R. programme, going, in some respects, beyond anything that was done by the post-war Labour government in Britain. Certainly nationalisation of such major industrial concerns as Rénault was facilitated by their collaborationist record during the war; but (in contrast with what happened in Britain) the greater part of the insurance industry was also nationalised, as were the four major banks, with the others being placed under a supervisory commission. In 1946 the Monnet Plan launched France much further in the direction of efficiently managed state capitalism than any other country was prepared, or able, to go. A comprehensive Social Security programme, as laid down by the C.N.R., was inaugurated in October 1945 (it was behind Britain in health provision, but that, too, had been rather neglected in Resistance plans). The Provisional Government also gave votes to women, though this seems to have been less due to the brave participation of certain women in the Resistance than to the broad desire for a clean break with older French institutions and attitudes, and, in particular, Vichy's attempt to stress the virtues of the traditional family unit. (Sadly, the persistent image from the Liberation is of women having their heads shaven for 'horizontal collaboration'.[15]) *De facto* purges of the newspaper world ensured that, for a brief time, the press would indeed be 'free' in the manner desired by the C.N.R. But apart from the full restitution of trade unions, little was done about worker participation in the running of industry and the economy.

Beyond stressing democracy and universal suffrage, the C.N.R. programme had said nothing about the future French constitution. Here in fact there were very deep divisions within the Resistance. Close followers of de Gaulle, such as Michel Debré, had put forward plans for strong presidential government, while the Socialists and Communists continued to insist on the need to vest full sovereignty in an elected National Assembly. The 'social Catholics', who forged from their Resistance experience a new party, the Mouvement Republicaine Populaire (M.R.P.), hankered after something more akin to the British system. In a referendum held in October 1945 the French people overwhelmingly voted against any revival of the Third Republic; at the same time they elected a Constituent Assembly which was incapable of agreeing upon an alternative. After the election of yet another Constituent Assembly, France emerged with a form of government which was to show many of the characteristic weaknesses of the Third Republic (or, indeed, of Weimar, with whose history the Fourth Republic was to show certain remarkable similarities – though unlike Weimar, the Fourth Republic had to wrestle with colonial crises in Indo-China and Algeria). Some of the immense popular strength which the Socialists and Communists had acquired as a result of their prominence in the Resistance was frittered away in the debates over the constitution. None the less, in the first general elections of the new Fourth Republic in June 1946, the Communists received 26 per cent of the vote, the Socialists 21 per cent, with 28 per cent for the M.R.P. Already, however, the constitutional forms which the Socialists and Communists had done more than anyone else to establish ruled out the possibility of the strong executive which would be necessary if further sweeping reforms were to be carried through.

That, at any rate, is one of the reasons why Resistance-sponsored social reform, after spectacular successes in 1944 and 1945, achieved little more thereafter. The other two main reasons are also structural, and are to be found in the nature of the two major Resistance parties:

the Communists and the Gaullists. Finding that he was not carrying all before him as a great national leader, de Gaulle, in January 1946, withdrew from the centre of politics. His followers increasingly attracted a reputation for absurd neo-fascist postures. More serious was the fact that the obvious and most powerful party of the Left fell under the suspicion of being as much concerned with Russian, as with French interests. Britain, at least, had a powerful Labour party; while West Germany, thanks to the existence of the D.D.R., had no Communist party to speak of. But France had no powerful, united, trusted party of the Left. This situation, the fragmentation of the Resistance, left the way open for the return of the politicians of the old school, happy and at home in what was very much the old system under a new name. But the changes in French society were real and deep.

## Psychological Effects

Whereas in the First World War almost all Frenchmen, till 1917 anyway, had united against the foreign foe, war in 1939 and 1940 grossly aggravated the divisions already clearly apparent in the 1930s. The memory of the wartime nightmare seemed to endure much longer in France than in Germany, where, obviously there was even greater incentive to turn towards a fresh start. Yet, though it is true that the France which emerged from the war was unstable politically and divided ideologically, the common experience of war counter-balanced many of the divisive influences. 1918 had left problems unresolved, hopes unfulfilled, tensions sharpened; a shattered society in so many respects. Many other forces had to take effect before France moved into its present envied status as a country of high and balanced economic growth; and there is in any case much for a liberal to deplore in certain aspects of recent French history; but it may still be that the experiences of the Second World War provided French leaders with the mental set to overcome the obstacles bequeathed by the previous war.

The intensity of the war experience is well evidenced in French literature. Looking back now with a knowledge of developments since the 1950s, one would be most reluctant to make any generalisations about the overall effects of the war, but as far as the immediate post-war years are concerned the two most influential figures were undoubtedly Sartre and Camus. Camus always rejected the label 'existentialist', and Sartre's writings as an existentialist *tout court* had all been published before the war. Both men were *résistants*, and what their war-time and post-war writings implied was, within a broader perception of the irrationality and

absurdity of the world, the affirmation of social and political commitment. One route into what Liberation meant, and into the confusions and
weaknesses of the left in the immediate post-war years, is to be found in
Simone de Beauvoir's *The Mandarins*; both of the main male protagon-
ists are based on different aspects of Sartre's personality. Of the war
itself it has been said that *the* poet of the Second World War is Aragon.
The verse, especially in English translation, seems a little facile, but it
speaks powerfully of its time:

> What did I know about days of defeat
> When your country is a love forbidden
> When you need the voice of false prophets
> To bring lost hope to life again? . . .[16]

Best known of all (we studied it in my Scottish school around 1950) is
*Le Silence de la Mer*, the short novel published in February 1942 as the
first of his clandestine *Editions du Minuit* by 'Vercors' – the pseudonym
of Jean Bruller, an artist and writer of, hitherto, modest distinction. A
German officer is billeted on an old man (the narrator) and his niece.
The officer is handsome, a musician (the best of German culture) and an
admirer of the best in French, and even English (Shakespeare) culture.
He resented Germany's defeat in the previous war, but believes that
France and Germany must now be united. The old man warms a little
to the officer, but the niece treats him with unrelenting silence.

> His gaze fell on mine. I looked away. It lingered for a while on
> various points in the room and then turned again to the unrelentingly
> expressionless face of my niece.
> 'I am happy to have found here an elderly man who has dignity, and
> a young lady who knows how to keep silent. We have to overcome
> that silence. We have to overcome the silence of all France. I am glad
> of that.'
> Silently, with a grave and persistent expression in which there still
> lurked the remnant of a smile, he was looking at my niece, at her set,
> obstinate, delicate profile. My niece felt his gaze, and I saw her blush
> slightly, as a little frown formed gradually between her eyebrows. Her
> fingers plucked the needle rather too fast and too hard, risking a
> break in the thread.
> 'Yes,' went on his slow, droning voice. 'It's better that way. Much
> better. That makes for a solid union – for unions where both sides
> gain in greatness. . . . There is a very lovely children's story which I
> have read, which you have read, which everybody has read. I don't

know if it has the same title in both countries. With us it's called *Das Tier und die Schöne*. Beauty and the Beast....'[17]

Every evening thereafter the officer enters the living room and converses with the old man; the niece continues to treat him with implacable silence. Then the German, filled with high expectation, leaves for a trip to Paris. But there his fellow officers laugh at his ideas and tell him that Germany's one idea is the spoliation and destruction of France. On his return the officer does not enter the living room as usual, but knocks and waits to be invited in. The old man hesitates; the niece is silent as always. When it is clear that the German is about to retire to his own room without entering, the niece signals her distress to the old man, who invites the officer in. The officer explains how his ideals have been betrayed; he has asked for a posting to the front, and will leave for Russia the next morning. 'Adieu', he says; and finally the niece manages the one word she has ever spoken to him: 'adieu'. The next morning the officer has gone.

### Summary of Social Changes

During the war France was reduced in size and, till November 1942, effectively divided into two parts. At the end of the war she was restored to her full frontiers, which were now perhaps more secure than they had been at any time since the eighteenth century. There was little redistribution of industry during the war, and although some of her cities took heavy punishment, resulting in rebuilding in the modern brutalist style, on the whole the major rebuilding which has changed the appearance of so much of France, did not come till the 1960s, and can scarcely be attributed to the war. The most significant feature of France's demographic history since the war has been the substantial up-turn in the birth rate. If this can be linked to the war at all, then it must be linked to the new psychological outlook resulting from the war in which young couples were now prepared to have larger families.[18] These developments are all, on the whole, of rather less significance than comparable developments in Germany and Russia.

On the other hand, in the realm of economic structures and policies, the change in France was perhaps more radical than in any other of the countries studied in this book. Under the influence of the Monnet Plan and other aspects of managed state capitalism, which we can directly relate to the war, the stagnant society of the inter-war years gave place to a potentially booming economy.

There was wide agreement that the old bourgeois France collapsed in 1940; inevitably some elements of that old France crept back into the social structure as it re-established itself after 1945. None the less the position of that class was undoubtedly seriously weakened. More crucially, the working class, which had failed to consolidate its position after 1918, now quite definitely took its place as an accepted part of French society, and soon began to exhibit some of the same middle-class standards and aspirations as were to be apparent in West Germany. Working-class leaders had gained prestige for their part in the Resistance, and the working class as a whole, however ill-treated by the Germans, had shown, as we have seen, that in the end their co-operation was vital; the fact that the Germans never had the enthusiastic co-operation of the French working class was one factor hastening them towards defeat. French society in the 1930s had been markedly lacking in social cohesion. If one were to confine oneself to historical and polemical works on the Second World War one might well believe the bitterness and divisions of the 1930s, exacerbated by the events of 1940, to be permanent; but I have already suggested that I believe that the common experience of war, the necessity to rebuild, and the slow advent of prosperity have been stronger forces making for unity; though, of course, France continued to be politically a more unstable community than any of the other countries we have been studying.

The period of the Liberation and the provisional government took France sharply into a new era as far as social policies and ideas were concerned. The modest attempts of the Popular Front governments had been hotly contested; but the Social Security scheme of 1945 has remained unchallenged ever since. France at the end of the war was not suffering the extreme privation to be found in Germany. Her agricultural land was not laid waste as vast areas of Russia were; nor were her cities razed to the ground as were the German. None the less conditions of extreme austerity and indeed malnutrition persisted into the post-war years. Infant mortality rates, for instance, were still above the 1939 level in 1947. But as in all the other countries we have been studying, the Second World War was, in the perspective of time, to emerge as the watershed between the depressed conditions of the 1930s, and the more affluent conditions of the early 1950s onwards, even if the war was only one factor in a complex process which brought this about.

So too, in the matter of manners, customs and morals, France went through the same world-wide set of changes. Particularly relevant to France was the emergence in the war of social Catholicism, and the consequent weakening of Catholicism as a purely authoritarian doctrine bolstering older traditions of family morality. Paris is not France; and the intellectual coteries of the capital are not Paris: but in the cinema and in the novel France suddenly appeared to take the lead in new permissive styles, rather as Weimar had done after the previous war. During the 1920s Paris's primacy in the visual arts was already yielding to the challenge of Berlin; the rise of Hitlerism and the Second World War had, in turn, transferred this primacy to the United States. But in the arts generally, particularly in literature, music and the cinema, the Second World War seemed to have brought a new release of creative energies in France. In general, it was Paris once again which set the intellectual and artistic pace in the post-war years (in the cinema, she had perhaps to yield place to Italy, a country which had gone through many of the same sort of agonies as France, though in an even more extreme and bloody form).

Political structures seem always to be the last and the least to be affected by war. Perhaps events in Russia and Germany in the First World War and in Germany in the Second World War, do suggest that total and unambiguous defeat is a necessary precondition of real political change. Certainly the defeat of the Third Republic in 1940, and the defeat of the German-sponsored government in 1944, both provided the opportunity for a complete reconstruction. But the confused turn of events also muddied the issues. At the end, France was back in the role of a victorious power joining in the triumphant conquest of Germany. De Gaulle, though keen to develop a form of presidential government, was even more anxious to unite all Frenchmen. The Left, which had played the major part in the Resistance, was, in any case, hostile to strong presidential government. Thus, as both loser and victor, France carried on into the post-war years with political institutions which contained many of the weaknesses of those of the Third Republic. Some commentators have seen the defeat of the idea of presidential government, and the retirement of General de Gaulle, as a defeat for the Resistance by the older parties of the Third Republic. This view argues that the Resistance had its real triumph only with de Gaulle's *coup d'état* of 1958 when strong presidential government was in fact established.[19] This is stretching things a bit. One might equally argue that participation in the Resistance led inevitably to conspiracy, sabotage and a disrespect for established authority; and indeed, when France met her Algerian crisis, one of the leading conspirators against the duly elected French government was Georges Bidault, former President of the C.N.R. As with the other countries we have studied, external events after 1945 imposed their own imprint upon the confused aftermath of war. In France the crises in Indo-China and Algeria, which had such serious repercussions on domestic developments, were themselves, in part, related to the war.

## III   Beauty and the Beast: Economic Recovery and the Idea of a United Europe

The comparative study of the war experience of various countries can be a valuable way of illuminating differences in the societies studied; the war experience itself, in turn, can be illuminated by examining the subsequent history of these societies with particular reference to the two broad themes of European reconstruction and European integration. It would be quite unhistorical to see all developments in the post-war period as 'inevitably' tending towards the 'desirable' goal of European unification; and indeed even in the immediate aftermath of the accession to the E.E.C. of Britain and her associates, it is certanly not possible to speak of real unification as anything more than a distant possibility. None the less the various institutions of European integration, and the ideas and movements associated with them, are a central feature of our time.

The strongest drive towards European co-operation, if not unification, is to be found in relationships between France and Germany. The final test of war had shown just how utterly disastrous was the continuing conflict and rivalry between these two countries. Reconciliation did not arise, new-born and innocent, the moment hostilities ended; but in the Adenauer period, with the Federal German Republic in any case firmly facing in a westward direction, such a reconciliation became the keystone of European politics. The second powerful drive arose from the very destructiveness of the war: only through co-operation, particularly in the administration of American economic assistance, could recovery be speedily achieved; only through co-operation could industry be revived and the free flow of trade be restored. The sources of the third drive are to be found in the new positions assumed by the United States and Russia as they emerged from the war. To begin with, the United States, fearful that a divided, devastated, western Europe might fall easy prey to Russian influence, encouraged west European co-operation; and in face of the apparent reality of the Russian danger the European countries were pretty amenable. At the same time, and then with increasing credibility as recovery took place, the idea of unity was advocated within Europe as a means towards creating a third world-power which could achieve at least a rough parity with the two super-powers.

Before moving on to the fourth drive towards integration – the whole set of ideas arising from the war experience itself, particularly from, on the one hand, the New Order and collaboration, and, on the other, the Resistance – we should note that there were important forces making for unification which had less direct connections with the war. Far and away the most significant of these was the rapid expansion of modern large-scale technological, and technocratic, capitalism (in which certainly the war had marked an important stage). The failure of the League of Nations led at the end of the war to the establishment of the more down-to-earth United Nations: but European politicians were very conscious of the severe practical limitations upon such world-wide organisations, and regional associations, particularly if given a strong economic character, appealed to them as a sensible alternative. Finally, in the various countries different parties and different individuals had special political or personal reasons for supporting the ideal of European integration: to Adenauer, for example, it offered personal fulfilment, and for his Christian Democratic Party it offered a route to international respectability. There had, of course, been dedicated supporters of European federation since well before the war: none the less the significance of the war, direct and indirect, is difficult to deny.

Now let us look more closely at the ideologies of integration arising from the war experience itself; this drive, compared with the others I have listed, is both more closely related to the broader social movements that are our main concern in this book, and more complex and ambiguous. The clandestine publications of the various west European Resistance movements (in Belgium, the Netherlands and Italy as well as in France) are peppered with statements about the need for a true European unity, in contrast to the 'false' unity of the National Socialist New Order. 'Economic and social problems transcend national frontiers'; 'politics must no longer be confined within the narrow frontiers of separate states'; 'the peace of the world depends on the abandonment or the limitation of national sovereignties, the removal of monetary and customs barriers and military frontiers, the common development of resources, the establishment of universalism in education, the sciences, work and morals. . . .'[20] Writing sometime between September 1941 and September 1943, Michel Debré declared:

The economic crisis of 1929 proved to the world the uselessness of national action. . . . Each country isolated itself the better to share out the common misery. By intensifying poverty and unemployment this isolation contributed to bringing about the war. . . . 'France Alone', that was the false idea which could do us as much harm tomorrow as it did to us yesterday. . . .

Today no policy of national recovery can any longer be imagined outside of an international organization. . . . It is still possible for a nation to fail solely through its own faults. It can no longer save itself solely through its own merits. . . .

However, as Henri Michel has pointed out, the many statements take the form of declarations of principle, rather than detailed plans for European or international unification.[21] Resistance theorists ranged between those who looked far beyond Europe and those who talked of 'an economic federation for which the point of departure might be France, Belgium and the Netherlands'.[22] With regard to many French pronouncements the note of patriotic nationalism – as we saw in the C.N.R. Programme – is often more evident than any Europeanism or internationalism. Most significant for the future, perhaps, was the recurrent theme that France must occupy a special place in the Europe of the future. *Les Cahiers Français*, in September 1943, had seen 'coming from France, more than from any other country, the plans which will bring to the liberated peoples the hope of a European order of liberty and peace, since her own sufferings acquit her of any accusation of imperialism'. More subtly *Combat* (published in Algeria, issue of 12 December 1943) stated that, thanks to the Resistance, the peoples of Europe would wish to remake Europe 'in the spirit of 1789, applied to all nations'.

It would, therefore, be wrong to attribute to the Resistance a clear and definite contribution to the formulation of the institutions of European integration akin to the contribution which it undoubtedly made to the formulation of French post-war social policy. The Resistance statements rather should be seen as representing a new psychology in which certain sections of the peoples of Europe (as distinct from individual thinkers and politicians) were ready to accept some change in the traditional notions of national sovereignty. As early as November 1941 *Liberté* put forward what might be called the 'social' as distinct from the 'economic' or 'political' case for integration, together with the reservations which that implies:

Europe is the continent with the highest density of population, the smallest space, and 28 separate nations live there. With the international division of labour which has made each nation depend on the others, with the development of modern transport, these frontiers have become insupportable. They must be suppressed. But each people shall preserve its language, its *mores*, its customs, in the equality of peoples and races and in a fundamentally democratic manner.[23]

In so far as there was a National Socialist theory of the New Order, it was scarcely conducive to the development of genuine ideas of European unity; rather, as the Resistance said, it postulated 'a vast prison in which Germany would be the gaoler' so that 'the term "European" became as suspect as the term "honour" '.[24] However, as Professor Milward has so brilliantly shown, the necessities of war enforced a modification of the New Order in such a fashion as to lay much of the groundwork for future economic integration.[25] The managers and technocrats who came to the fore in the economic collaboration between France and Germany were not good Nazis or even good Vichyites, but, given the longer-term developments in international capitalism, the future was with them.

As early as September 1944 the Netherlands and Belgium–Luxembourg (long since united in an Economic Union), 'desiring, in the hour of liberation of the territories of the Economic Union of Belgium–Luxembourg and of the Netherlands, to create the most favourable conditions for the eventual establishment of an economic union and for the restoration of economic activity'[26] concluded the Benelux Customs Convention. Resistance activities had been quite well co-ordinated across the three countries; German destruction and pillage had been great; business interests in all three countries appreciated the possibilities of economic union; pretensions to independent national status were low.

Into the European arena the Russian government projected the distrust and fear which German occupation and barbarism had so recently intensified, and the aggressive chauvinism inspired by the 'Great Patriotic War'. For its part the U.S. government was now acting out the role of the great international power, while at the same time reflecting the heightened xenophobia and anti-Communism stirred up by the war. The United States' first major initiative was the remarkably generous and far-sighted programme of economic aid, always known, after the then Secretary of State, George Marshall, as the Marshall Plan. General Marshall's speech at Harvard on 5 June 1947 is a remarkably fair and open presentation of the motivation behind the Plan; it also reveals the way in which the Plan was expected to contribute to European co-operation:

The truth of the matter is that Europe's requirements for the next three or four years of foreign food and other essential products – principally from America – are so much greater than her present ability to pay that she must have substantial additional help or face economic, social, and political deterioration of a very grave character.

The remedy lies in breaking the vicious circle and restoring the confidence of the European people in the economic future of their own countries and of Europe as a whole. The manufacturer and the farmer throughout wide areas must be able and willing to exchange their products for currencies the continuing value of which is not open to question.

Aside from the demoralizing effect on the world at large and the possibilities of disturbances arising as a result of the desperation of the people concerned, the consequences to the economy of the United States should be apparent to all. It is logical that the United States should do whatever it is able to do to assist in the return of normal economic health in the world, without which there can be no political stability and no assured peace. Our policy is directed not against any country or doctrine but against hunger, poverty, desperation, and chaos. Its purpose should be the revival of a working economy in the world so as to permit the emergence of political and social conditions in which free institutions can exist. Such assistance, I am convinced, must not be on a piecemeal basis as various crises develop. Any assistance that this government may render in the future should provide a cure rather than a mere palliative. Any government that is willing to assist in the task of recovery will find full cooperation, I am sure, on the part of the United States Government. Any government which manoeuvres to block the recovery of other countries cannot expect help from us. Furthermore, governments, political parties, or groups which seek to perpetuate human misery in order to profit therefrom politically or otherwise will encounter the opposition of the United States.

It is already evident that, before the United States Government can proceed much further in its efforts to alleviate the situation and help start the European world on its way to recovery, there must be some agreement among the countries of Europe as to the requirements of the situation and the part those countries themselves will take in order to give proper effect to whatever action might be undertaken by this Government. It would be neither fitting nor efficacious for this Government to undertake to draw up unilaterally a program designed to place Europe on its feet economically. This is the business of the Europeans. The initiative, I think, must come from Europe. The role of this country should consist of friendly aid in the drafting of a European program and of later support of such a program so far as it may be practical for us to do so. The program should be a joint one, agreed to by a number, if not all, European nations. . . .[27]

Marshall Aid was welcomed in western Europe, where the Organisation of European Economic Co-operation was formed to administer it, and rejected – as expected – in Russia and the east European countries. The years 1947 and 1948 saw a number of developments which the western Governments saw as highly menacing, including the *coup d'état* in Czechoslovakia and the Berlin blockade.

The United States now took the initiative in establishing an explicit military alliance – the NATO alliance, concluded in April 1949 – between the United States and Canada, Britain, France, the Netherlands, Belgium and Luxembourg, Italy, Denmark and Norway. West Germany joined in 1955.

Over the years various individuals in Britain had seemed to favour European integration. In 1940 Churchill had proposed an Anglo-French Union; in March 1943 he declared his support for a Council of Europe, supported by ancillary institutions and a common military organisation. In January 1947, now in opposition, he launched the United Europe Movement. The British Labour government accepted the vague association implied in the West European Union, welcomed military co-operation, and, to a degree participated in the economic recovery programme. Britain had not been occupied; there had been no Resistance and no collaboration; in winning the war, the British government believed, it had established a 'special relationship' with the United States, and it had preserved its empire: thus few Britons, fully shared in the aspirations of European integrationists. (Churchill's preoccupations were essentially strategic.) The situation is highlighted by the establishment in May 1949 of the Council of Europe. British politicians could happily agree with its aim of achieving 'a greater unity between its Members for the purpose of safeguarding and realising the ideals and principles which are their common heritage and facilitating their economic and social progress'; and even more with its method, 'discussion of questions of common concern and by agreements and common action in economic, social, cultural, scientific, legal and administrative matters and in the maintenance and further realisation of human rights and fundamental freedoms'.[28]

Committed integrationists, such as Paul-Henri Spaak, the Belgian Socialist, hoped that the Council of Europe would mark a definite stage towards European Federation. While Britain remained aloof, further initiatives were taken in France, in particular by Robert Schuman, a

native of Lorraine who had been born a German citizen, and Jean
Monnet, author of France's post-war Monnet Plan. The 'Schuman
Plan' led, in April 1951, to the founding of the European Coal and
Steel Community. In essence this represented the twin forces of Franco-
German reconciliation, and co-operation in economic reconstruction.
The other members were Benelux and Italy; Britain remained aloof. The
route from there to the establishment of the Common Market in 1958
was by no means a straightforward one. Until the *coup d'état* of 1958
France was plunging deeper and deeper into political instability. For this
period, and even subsequently, the 'Beauty and the Beast' image seems
particularly apt; Germany, the former villain of Europe, all patience and
rationality: France, unstable and self-centred, having to be patiently
wooed. However by the mid-sixties, the Common Market, as a modern
mass capitalist regional association, was undoubtedly a success. For
most of the people within its borders, too, it meant higher living standards and greater mobility.

Victory had not gone to the 'goodies' of the Resistance, nor to the
'baddies' of Vichy and the New Order. If it lay with anyone from that
period it was with Speer, who in 1946 had been imprisoned as a war
criminal, and with Bichelonne, who had died in mysterious circumstances in Berlin late in 1944. But it also lay in part with those who had
envisaged a unity other than that imposed by Nazism.

## Notes and References

1. H. Amoureux, *La Vie des Français sous l'occupation* (Paris, 1961) pp.
   349–50. On the *exode* see J. Videlenc, *L'Exode de Mai–Juin 1940* (1957).
   Not all was total personal disaster as Richard Cobb (*Reactions to the
   French Revolution*, 1972, p. 59) points out in mentioning the '*professeur
   de philo* . . . who walked off westwards with a seventeen-year-old female
   pupil, leaving behind wife and family, and embarking on a five-year
   holiday'.
2. A. Piatiev, 'La Vie Economique de la France' in P. Arnoult and others,
   *La France sous l'Occupation* (Paris, 1959) p. 65. Peter Novick, *The
   Resistance Versus Vichy* (1968) pp. 202–8.
3. Piatiev, p. 65.
4. A. S. Milward, *The New Order and the French Economy* (1970) p. 273.
5. M. Cépède, 'Agriculture et Ravitaillement', in Arnoult, p. 83.
6. Quoted in Hannah Josephson and Malcolm Cowley, *Aragon: Poet of
   Resurgent France* (1946) p. 4.
7. Quoted by Peter Novick, *The Resistance Versus Vichy* (1968) p. 5. A
   very large number of posts in the Vichy government and administration, it may be noted, were filled by leading naval figures. One French

cardinal joked that he expected to be succeeded after his death by an admiral.

8. Milward, p. 297.
9. Piatiev, in Arnoult, p. 70.
10. Cépède, in Arnoult, p. 85.
11. *Le Silence de la Mer* (1942) preface.
12. Stanley Hoffman, 'The Effects of World War II on French Society and Politics', *French Historical Studies*, vol. II, no. 1 (spring 1961) pp. 28–63.
13. Henri Michel and Boris Mirkine-Guetzevitch, *Les Idées Politiques et Sociales de la Résistance*, preface. The programme of the C.N.R. is printed on pp. 215–18.
14. Douglas Johnson, *France* (1969) p. 73.
15. See the horrifying newsreel included in the Open University War and Society compilation *Women in Two World Wars*.
16. Quoted in Josephson and Cowley, p. 58.
17. Vercors, *Le Silence de la Mer* (1942) pp. 18–19.
18. Johnson, p. 92.
19. See, e.g., J. de Launay, *Le Dossier de Vichy* (1967) p. 287.
20. These, and the following quotations from Resistance statements are from Henri Michel, *Les Courants de Pensée de la Résistance* (1964) pp. 420–2.
21. Michel, p. 425.
22. A. Hauriou, *Le Socialism humaniste* (Algeria, 1944) p. 195.
23. Quoted by Michel, p. 421.
24. Ibid. p. 420.
25. Milward, p. 179.
26. Preamble to Benelux Convention printed in R.I.I.A., *Documents on European Recovery and Defence* (1949) p. 1.
27. Printed in R.I.I.A., *Documents on International Affairs, 1947–48* (1949) pp. 25–6.
28. Quoted in D. W. Urwin, *Western Europe since 1945* (1968) pp. 135–6.

# 7.  Problems and Conclusions

This book has attempted to indicate some of the areas where one or other, or both, of the two world wars played an important part in bringing about social change. Clearly I have been highly selective. The purpose of the main part of this chapter is to pinpoint issues which I might perhaps have included had I decided to write a book several times the length of this one, or which might, if ignored, be held to invalidate many of my generalisations. Essentially three types of problem arise if we subject my title to a final rigorous scrutiny. From the first part, 'War', the question arises, 'have I looked at enough wars, and, within the two to which I have confined myself, have I looked at enough countries?' From the second part, the question arises, 'have I, despite my systematic list of nine sets of changes, really exhausted all the implications of the phrase "Social Change"?' Finally, taking the title as a whole, 'have I really, with my perhaps too schematic methodology dealt adequately with all the subtle interactions between war and society?'

## Other Countries and Peoples

Many of the points made with regard to Russia in the First World War, and some of those made in regard to the Kaiser's Germany, apply to Austria–Hungary. Above all, war tested the viability of her ramshackle multi-racial empire, while at the same time military participation on the part of the subject nationalities hastened their independence. Italy in both wars presents a specially complicated and tortured case, and one which needs very careful study: but the disruptions and psychological implications of the First World War are apparent enough in the emergence of fascism at the end of the war. Resistance as participation is a key phenomenon in the Second World War;[1] as it is, of course, throughout Europe. Belgium in 1914 had a foretaste of the sort of calamitous occupation which affected Holland, Denmark and Norway, and almost

For Notes and References to this chapter, see p. 224 below.

all of eastern Europe in the Second World War. Only Sweden, along with Switzerland, Spain and Portugal managed to remain neutral and territorially inviolate in both wars.

At first sight it might seem that my theories are shattered by the history of those countries which, though remaining neutral, none the less underwent the same broad social changes as belligerent countries; on closer inspection the problem simply dissolves. In some degree or another, war did impinge on the several neutral countries of the First World War, and on occupied Denmark and neutral Sweden in the Second World War. Even in spheres where the direct impact of war was slight, or non-existent, as with regard to *participation* within the neutral countries in the Second World War, these countries found that, after the war was over, they were inescapably part of the new social, intel-lectual, economic and political structures created elsewhere by war. (Broadly, this applies to Switzerland, though, revealingly, women still did not have the vote there in 1972; Spain has remained a backwater.) Sweden in the First World War enjoyed a boom in the production of her high grade steel, and endured a blockade more complete than that of any other country save Germany.[2] Norway in the same war suffered des-truction of her shipping greater, in proportion to her shipping resources, than any other country, and in absolute terms second only to the United Kingdom.[3] In 1921 Sweden *followed* most of the major belligerent countries in granting universal manhood suffrage and votes for women; even although there had been no participation effect, Sweden was now *joining* a new political and social order created elsewhere by the exper-ience of war. In the Second World War Sweden was inevitably affected by the international dislocations of war; she was subject to severe press control (to prevent the voicing of strong anti-German sentiment); and she was torn by arguments over where participation in the national interest properly lay.

Of special interest is the range of psychological reactions to be found in the various countries which succeeded in, or desired to, remain neutral when everywhere else the tides of patriotism were flowing high. This is not a subject which can be explored here; it is however worth comparing this calm Royal Message which King Christian of Denmark addressed to the nation on the outbreak of the 1914–18 war, with the jingoistic effulgences so prevalent in other countries:

At no time more than the present has there ever been demanded a greater sense of responsibility, both in the individual and in the whole nation.

Our country stands in friendly relations to all nations. We feel confident that the strict and equal neutrality which has always been maintained as the foreign policy of our country, and which now also will be unhesitatingly maintained, will be respected by all.

This is the common view of the Government and of all responsible and sensible people, and we trust that no one by an untimely display of feelings, by rash demonstrations, or in any manner will violate the dignity and peace which it is of vital importance to maintain in order to create confidence in the attitude of our country. Everyone now has his responsibility and his duty. We feel convinced that the seriousness of the moment will be reflected in the actions of all Danish men and women.

God save our country

CHRISTIAN R.[4]

Given the situation in Schleswig–Holstein, it was none too easy for all the Danes to keep cool. Much greater moral and emotional issues arose during the Second World War: for many Danes it was a great relief when the Germans ceased to be 'guests' allegedly keeping open their supply lines to conquered Norway, and in August 1943 took over formal occupation of the country. All occupied countries shared in the same difficult and complex experience, though non-Jewish west Europeans were not to suffer quite the same hideous barbarities as east Europeans. Werner Warmbrunn's authoritative account of occupied Holland brings out well the way in which ordinary life had to go on being lived amid the nightmare of war and occupation, and the terrible moral dilemmas which faced Dutch individuals and groups.[5] Rolf Schuursma's classic compilation film *Anton Mussert 1934–1945* brings out the pathetic nature of the relationship between Holland's own fascist leader and the German conquerors. Above all the diary of a German-Jewish girl, whose parents had sought refuge in Holland before the war, written while she was cooped up in a secret hiding place, expresses the universal tragedy of the era of aggressive National Socialism. At the age of fifteen Anne Frank could reflect that peoples everywhere, not just Nazi leaders, were guilty of the violent impulses which had created the present holocaust.[6] The Allied invasion of Europe was already well under way when the secret hiding place was raided by the Gestapo; German defeat was only two months away when Anne Frank died in the concentration camp at Bergen-Belsen.

Asiatic and African countries raise further special considerations of their own, yet again the broad applications of the model seem to fit. The parallel between the Japanese economic miracle after the catastrophe of defeat, and the German one, is almost too obvious to need stressing. Obviously there are many intriguing differences of environment and tradition to be worked out. For example it seems that the outbreak of war and the unchallenged ascendancy of Japanese militarism meant a definite reaffirmation of the inferior role traditionally occupied by women; yet the post-war years, whatever differences from western practices still remained, saw an undoubted improvement in the status of Japanese women.

The defeats inflicted by the Japanese on British, French and Dutch imperialism, and their attempts to enlist the participation of the colonial peoples in the apparently anti-imperialist struggle, had enormous repercussions in the post-war years. Discussing the emergence at the end of the war of the modern national state of Indonesia (in place of the former Dutch East Indies), W. H. Elsbree mentions several contributory factors, all of which can be readily fitted into my four-tier model. First, there is 'the *disruption* of life occasioned by the war' (my italics) and 'the overthrow of the old colonial system'. Then the test of war (as I would put it) had other specific results: the new civil and military organisations, the new forms of communication and transport, and the education system created by the Japanese; the breaking down of the isolation of the villages; and the development under the occupation of a more determined and centralised nationalist movement. Up to a point the Japanese encouraged both 'political participation' and nationalism among the Indonesians. Finally the psychological climate during the war was ripe for the spread of nationalist ideas to a wider audience.[7]

The key idea of participation can be applied to the wartime experiences of colonial peoples throughout the world. Again this is a topic which would repay detailed examination, but, whatever other circumstances were also involved, there is a clear link between the Second World War and the self-assertive and successful colonial nationalist movements of the post-war years. (As indeed there was a link between the First World War and the emergence of the self-assertive white Commonwealth.) Thinking back to the previous chapter we might, in particular, note how wartime events in Indo China and Algeria brought on a period of acute crisis for post-war France.

## Other Wars

The kindlier critics of my theories have tended to remark that though all very well in their way, and indeed all that one could expect from a specialist in twentieth-century history, they have no relevance at all to earlier periods. Indeed it has been said that my theories apply only to *total* war. As a matter of fact much, rather technical, debate has raged over how exactly one should use the phrase 'total war'. Berenice Carroll has rightly pointed out that there are two aspects to the question, depending on whether you are on the giving or the receiving end.[8] I have talked of Hitler being engaged in 'blitzkrieg war', as distinct from total war, though of course the blitzkrieg was total enough as far as the Poles, for instance, were concerned. Military theorists today regard total war as implying the use of strategic nuclear weapons, and distinguish it from 'general war', 'limited war', and 'revolutionary war'. My usage is that of a social historian. In general terms I have spoken of the two World Wars as total wars, but I have made distinctions between those periods of time when a society had not yet given itself over fully to total war, and those when the full impact of total war was being felt. Used in this way 'total war' means: a war involving whole populations; a war in which organisation of the domestic front becomes as important as organisation of the military front; a war into which is thrown every resource of science and technology, and every resource of propaganda: an 'all-out' and 'all-embracing' war. But the phrase is also often used for emotional and propagandist purposes. It was not till Clemenceau came to power in 1917 that a French Prime Minister openly promised to wage total war ('guerre intégrale');[9] and Goebbels's famous speech threatening the Allies with total war ('totalen Krieg') was not made till 18 February 1943.[10] Probably there is more than a semantic difference between 'integral' and 'total'.

Rather, then, than ask the blanket question, was a particular war a total war, or a limited war, or a revolutionary war, I believe it is much more fruitful to ask the particular questions which arise from my model; and I believe that that model can indeed be applied to all periods of human history. The questions to ask are: to what extent did a certain war bring about *destruction* and *disruption*; in what ways did it *test* existing institutions; how far, if at all, did underprivileged groups *participate*; and in what ways was the war a *psychological* experience. Where the answers are 'not much' or 'not at all', then we have something of an explanation of why that particular war was not accompanied by much social change. In the Middle Ages wars were largely fought by the privileged members of society – the knights and their superiors, who beat the hell out of the non-participating peasantry of both sides, trampling their crops into the ground. In other words, through non-participation the peasants made losses, not gains; this, in fact, is a negative validation of the participation aspect of the theory. Actually, as much recent work on the Hundred Years' War for example, has shown, the story is often much more complicated than that, and elements of participation and social change can be detected.[11]

But what about other wars in the twentieth century, particularly wars since 1945? Do civil wars, and guerrilla wars come within the scope of the theory? The answer is the same as the one I have just given for pre-twentieth-century wars. Guerrilla wars obviously reveal many parallels with the resistance movements, whose relationship to social change has already been discussed. Civil wars certainly raise specially complicated questions; here more than ever it is vital to obey the first principle that one cannot begin to understand the impact of war on any given society till one understands the nature of that society as it existed on the eve of war. The very fact of civil war breaking out suggests that there are deep inadequacies within the structure and institutions of the existing society. Society has already 'failed the test': what follows is largely destruction; though that in turn can ultimately bring the reconstructive effect of the disaster syndrome into play.

But perhaps even more interest attaches to the recent wars in which the United States has been engaged. Professor Carroll's point is important here: obviously from the point of view of the North Vietnamese on the receiving end of American napalm and defoliation canisters the Vietnam War was pretty nearly total war (though American strategists, and those who equate total war with nuclear war, would disagree); but from the point of view of the historian of American society, neither the Korean War nor the Vietnam War was total. The Vietnam War had no very direct *destructive* effect on American society (apart from the high cost of the non-productive technology of war), though it was undoubtedly *disruptive*. In that the military–industrial complex was already in being, it did not directly test the United States' capacity to develop a war economy, though it did reveal the near-impossibility of defeating a highly-committed enemy in a far-off country; it also revealed weaknesses in the processes of American decision-making, and, in setting up a whole new series of stresses and strains, it severely tested the cohesion of American society. Since the United States had military conscription continuously from 1948 to 1973 one might well expect a considerable *participation* effect. In a highly selective system a disproportionate share of the actual fighting fell on the shoulders of black Americans. Did the black community therefore make gains? The fact that one cannot give an unhesitating 'yes' highlights the point I made in Chapter 1, and which has been cropping up implicitly throughout the book: it is not so much *military* participation (i.e. in uniform) as wartime participation that is important. To talk at all of participation is to suggest a sense of involvement as between society as a whole and individual sections of it. A subject which therefore needs to be examined very fully is: how far was there a feeling in American society that the black soldier was participating in a national cause, and how far did the black soldier himself feel this? I have no answers. All I am saying is that the nature of participation has to be very carefully scrutinised; and further, I am suggesting that black participation in Vietnam was in some way qualitatively different from black participation in the Second World War, and that this helps to explain the lack of social gains resulting from the Vietnam war. The *psychological* effects were undoubtedly very great, creating serious and bitter divisions in American society. How far, also, did they intensify violence in American society? Traditionally the theory has always been that external war siphons off internal violence. While, clearly, that has not been the case in regard to the Vietnam War, it is also not possible to draw a direct correlation between internal violence and the war.[12] Equally, there is no empirical foundation for statements associating internal violence in the various European countries with the absence of general war.

To illuminate further the way in which my theories fit with regard to 'small' or 'limited' wars, it is worth looking at the relationship of the Korean War to British society. The destructive effect (cost of the new arms programme) was high, and this in turn had a high social cost. There was little or no participation effect, nor was the war much of a psychological experience. The test effect was strong; but it tended to bring collapse rather than change. All the weaknesses of Labour in office were sharply exposed, as was the absence at that time of a competent second generation of political leadership. Health service charges were imposed, followed by resignations from the government, with Harold Wilson complaining of 'the first cutting-into our social services which we have built up over these past years, and which represent a system in which all of us rightly take great pride'.[13] As a minor compensation the Treasury was forced by the Korean crisis to improve its methods of gathering economic information. On the whole, then, this 'limited' war, with a very small participation element, had mainly regressive effects on social change.

## Other Aspects of Social Change

Two topics to which I have not given more than passing reference are pacifism, and military organisation and civil–military relations. Within my definition of social change, pacifism falls under parts of the two final headings in my list, 'intellectual attitudes' and 'political ideas'. It merits either the brief treatment I have given it, or else the separate and full treatment it has received from many other distinguished writers. It is hard to generalise over whether two world wars have increased or decreased pacifist feeling in the various countries. Probably the most important development is the growth of 'peace research', linking the philosophical or ethical wish for peace with scientific efforts to work out how this might be achieved. Two world wars, and the other conflicts since 1945, have taught men to be less optimistic about human behaviour and more rational in their study of it.

Arguably, military organisation and civil–military relations – which I have taken as falling under the heading of 'political institutions' – ought, as matters of considerable significance in social development, to be singled out for separate treatment. Yet, oddly enough, the wars of the twentieth century have not brought great changes in military organisation and its relationship to society, always excepting the emergence after the Second World War of the military–industrial complex in America. Certainly the traditional liberal contention that wars always result in the aggrandisement of military power must be approached with caution.[14] In certain respects the military authorities were already very powerful on the eve of the First World War: it was the inflexibility of their plans, and their insistence that, at the first hint of crisis, they must be put into operation which finally precipitated general war in August 1914.[15] However certain principles were widely accepted: matters of policy and general strategy should be determined by the civilian authority; the detailed military execution of these policies should be left to the military authorities. The aim was to avoid both complete independence from the civil government on the part of the military (which might in turn lead to military dictatorship) and complete control of the army by the civil government (which could also lead to dictatorship). Before 1914 these principles were most fully observed in the United States, Britain, and, to a marginally lesser degree, France; in Germany the military had rather more influence over politics; while in Russia the separation of function between military and civilian élites had gone less far than in the more industrialised countries.

In France in the First World War it was very much a case of the wheel coming full circle. Expecting a short war, the civilian authorities allowed General Joffre to exercise what was practically a military dictatorship up till late 1915. Thereafter, thanks to the pressures of total war and the need to enlist the co-operation of all civilians, and to his own lack of success in the battle field, Joffre had to accept a steady restoration of parliamentary authority. Clemenceau, at the end of the war, re-established a near-dictatorship, but it was a civilian dictatorship. In the inter-war years there were grumbles of discontent from the army (particularly at the time of the Popular Front government), but in the main it remained properly subservient to the civil authority. In Britain, the civil–military balance was scarcely altered, despite the much-publicised squabbles between generals and politicians: Lloyd George could adopt various devices to limit Haig's powers, but he did not dare to sack him. In the Second World War the complaints that were raised were not of a military usurpation of civilian authority, but that Churchill, as civil leader, interfered too much in military matters (in fact there were severe practical limits on Churchill's powers).

For Russia and Germany the Second World War began with the political dictators in both countries exercising considerable power over the professional soldiers (though the status and prestige within society of the German army was again at least as high as in the Kaiser's day). In Russia the very exigencies of war returned much power to the soldiers; in Germany the destruction of the National Socialist régime resulted in the creation (in the Federal Republic) for the first time of a civil–military relationship in which the army was quite clearly subordinate to the civilian authority, while at the same time free from day-to-day interference in professional matters. The most interesting case is that of France, where the events of the Second World War undoubtedly played a part in creating a situation whereby the army felt sufficiently independent of civil society to assist in de Gaulle's *coup d'état* of 1958, and to attempt another one in 1961. The grave conflict of loyalties during the war and the manner in which vengeance was taken on Vichy officers at the end of the war, called in question the whole principle of unswerving obedience to the civil authority; in the last campaigns of the war, the old professional army found itself isolated and distrusted by Resistance fighters and the F.F.I.[16] But these developments are due to the particular way in which the test of war affected the institutions of the Third Republic, exposing the weaknesses of the civil authorities, not to any drive to military oligarchy inherent in war itself. Furthermore the actual events of 1958 and 1961 had their immediate origins in the colonial crises of Indo-China and Algeria.

This is not to say that everything in the garden is lovely: the nature of civil–military relations must always continue to be a matter for concern and scrutiny. Questions of power apart it is broadly true that massive

participation in two world wars brought soldier and civilian closer together than ever they had been in the nineteenth century,[17] though the
sharp bitterness felt by many who served in the First World War against
those who stayed at home is another consideration to add to the special
developments in France in the Second World War. Since the Second
World War soldiering has become increasingly professional, increasingly
specialised, and increasingly remote from civilian life; but this is as much
a result of technological change as of war as such. And, in turn, it is a
development mediated by the fact that higher educational standards for
professional soldiers help to restore contact with civilian society: soldiering moves towards being a job, or profession, like any other.

## War and Society

Every skirmish with history involves a degree of falsification. On the
whole I have had to treat war as an external phenomenon producing
certain reactions in given societies, though at the very beginning I did
deliberately include some brief reflections on the causation of war. For
war, of course, is not an external phenomenon: wars spring out of
human society; and just as societies can be changed by the experience of
war, the nature of war itself is shaped by existing levels of technology
and social organisation. For the purposes of analysis I have, with qualifications, posited a one-way flow: war's impact on society. A true picture
would not so much be of a two-way flow, but of constant flux. But then
that is history. And that is why the hard edges of my analysis have so
often been blurred by the realities of history as it actually happens.

There is another problem: the danger of falling into the trap of *post
hoc ergo propter hoc*. Without war, societies change. The comparison
one has to make therefore is not simply between post-war society and
pre-war society, but between post-war society and the situation that
society would have reached at the same point in time had there been no
war. My claim is that it is my very method of analysis that makes this
kind of discrimination feasible.

## Conclusions

I am, therefore, fairly pleased with the help afforded by that method in
attacking quite sizeable problems. However, anyone with a theory
should tread warily. One is rather in the position of the unmarried girl
who is on the pill; one may have doubts, but one doesn't want to waste
the damn thing. If the theory has been too obtrusive I am still hopeful
that the material covered and the comparisons revealed are in themselves

of interest. What does clearly emerge is that Andreski's term M.P.R. (Military Participation Ratio) is unsatisfactory. True, in this sort of conceptualisation we are dealing with the whole class or group from which the military participants were drawn, not with the individual participants themselves. But it should be stressed just how sordid, bloody and frightening individual participation in war could be:

> The air in the tunnel was foetid; I'd rather have stayed in the open, even to die. Outside you risked a bullet; here, you could go mad. There was a pile of sand-bags up to the vault, and this was our refuge; outside the storm went on, the hammering of shell of all types. Above our heads, under the thundering vault, there were a few filthy electric bulbs casting a shadowy light, with clouds of flies circling round them. They buzzed on, irritatingly, and landed on you; even if you struck at them they would not get off. Men's faces glistened, and the tepid air was sickening. You lay on muddy sand, fixed to a rail, your eyes on the vault, or you lay face down, rolled into a bundle. These stunned men waited, slept, snored, dreamt, and moved only when someone trod on their feet; water and urine trickled through; and there was an animal stench, mingled with saltpetre, chloroform, sulphur, choride, of excreta and corpses, of sweat and filth, which made you retch. No one could eat, and at best some tepid and frothy coffee-water from a tin could be used to calm the universal fever. Other first-aid posts could not even offer relative quiet: a very young corporal arrived, with both hands torn off at the wrist, and he looked at the hideous red stumps with wild despair.[18]

When we talk of the emancipation of women, we should not forget that a vote won might well coincide with a husband or son lost. However the substantive point to be made about M.P.R. is that, on the whole, the benefits accruing to those who actually served in uniform were usually more limited than the ones accruing to those who, in one way or another, participated in the war effort on the home front: that is why Military Participation gives a wrong slant, and why the simple term 'participation' is to be preferred.

Which of the World Wars had the more profound consequences? On the level of 'guided' political change it can at least be said of the Second World War that it resulted in the destruction of Nazism; whereas it is sometimes difficult to see just what the First World War was fought for at all. None the less when it comes to 'unguided' social change, it is the 'futile' Great War of 1914–18 which has the greater significance. The search for watersheds in history is a treacherous one; yet if ever there was a case for using that tired old metaphor, it occurs in regard to the First World War. Much of the explanation for this lies in the psychological realm, and in what I have referred to as 'The Great Analogue of War'. The First World War was an experience to which people made constant reference, a discontinuity out of which they kept extrapolating explanations and justifications, an experiment in which they sought lessons and precepts, and a catastrophe on which they could blame the misfortunes of themselves and the world. The Second World War, immensely more destructive though it was, never quite had this force. Another factor qualifies the social significance of the Second World War. Already, since 1945, we have gone through a rather different discontinuity: the advent of affluence, which, though indirectly related to the war, has itself set off a whole chain of social change. The changes of the Second World War have thereby been cast into the shade.

To study war is not to glorify or condone it. War indeed – the Western Front, German occupation policies, Dresden, and such a dreadful amount more – is a nightmare. But still one seeks through a defined area of study to understand a little more of man's relationship, within the dimension of time, to his social and physical environment. Studying man and society in war, we see how often the changes which actually take place are totally at variance with the deliberate intentions of political and other leaders. At the same time we see that it is necessary to plan, as the British, fitfully, planned during the Second World War, to organise, as even the Americans managed to organise at the height of both wars, to respond reflectively to changing situations, as the French, by the skin of their teeth, did in the First World War, and to resist circumstances and apparent *force majeure*, as did members of the Resistance. We do make our own history, though not usually quite in the way we intended.

## Notes and References

1. There is a good, brief, perhaps slightly too enthusiastic summary in D. W. Urwin, *Western Europe since 1945* (1968) pp. 1–26. Note also, especially the title (borrowed from Churchill), Valentine Selsey, *Italy Works her Passage* (1945). Also in English there are: Italian Foreign Ministry, *The Italian Contribution to the War of Liberation against Germany* (1946); Pietro Badoglio, *Italy in the Second World War* (1948); and Max Salvadori, *Brief History of the Patriotic Movement in Italy 1943–1945* (1954). Still better is Roberto Battaglia, *Storia della Resistanza Italiana* (1964).
2. E. Hecksher in E. Hecksher *et al.*, *Sweden, Norway, Denmark and Iceland in the World War*, Carnegie series (1930), p. 5.

3. W. Keilhau, ibid.
4. Quoted by Einer Cohn, ibid., pp. 416–17.
5. Werner Warmbrunn, *The Dutch under German Occupation 1940–1945* (1963) pp. 99–120, 264–82.
6. *The Diary of Anne Frank* (English edn, 1950) p. 233. For the *Mussert* film see 'Notes on the Use of Archive Film Material'.
7. W. H. Elsbree, *Japan's Role in South-east Asian Nationalist Movements 1940–1945* (1953) p. 167.
8. Berenice A. Carroll, *Design for Total War* (1968) pp. 9–36.
9. Marc Ferro, *The Great War* (1973) p. 151.
10. The best and most revealing source is the German newsreel *Deutsche Wochenschau* (27 February 1943), Imperial War Museum (GWY 392/1).
11. See Kenneth Fowler (ed.), *The Hundred Years' War* (1971); K. B. McFarlane, 'War, the Economy and Social Change', *Past and Present*, 22 (Dec 1962); and M. M. Postan, 'The Costs of the Hundred Years War', *Past and Present*, 24 (Apr 1964).
12. See Robin Brooks, 'Domestic Violence and America's Wars', and 'International War and Domestic Turmoil', by Raymond Tanter, in *The History of Violence in America*, ed. Hugh D. Graham and Ted R. Gurr (1969).
13. *House of Commons Debates* (23 April 1951).
14. Gordon Wright first supports this contention, then finds he has no evidence to substantiate it: *Ordeal of Total War, 1939–45* (1969) p. 244.
15. A short book which makes the point most effectively is L. C. F. Turner, *Origins of the First World War* (1970).
16. See John Steward Ambler, *The French Army in Politics 1945–1962* (1966) pp. 56–82.
17. Morris Janowitz (ed.), *The New Military* (1967) pp. 5–6.
18. French lieutenant at Verdun, quoted by Marc Ferro, *The Great War* (1973) p. 91.

# Notes on the Use of
# Archive Film Material

The idea that historians should use archive film just as they use other types of primary source is no longer a very revolutionary one, though it remains true that there are still many serious technical difficulties which prevent scholars, teachers, and students having ready access to film material. Most of the early discussions of the use of film to the historian originated from non-historians whose primary professional concern was with film. The real break-through probably came when historians themselves began to take a serious interest in the subject. For many years now a number of institutes on the continent have been carrying out specialised historical analysis of film material: the Institut für den Wissenschaftlichen Film, Göttingen; Stichting Film En Wetenschap, Utrecht; Historisk Institut, University of Copenhagen; and Danmarks Laeverhøjskole, Copenhagen. In France a perhaps rather broader view of the uses of film has been taken for some years. Marc Ferro made use of film evidence in his classic study of the Russian Revolution, and he helped to make the French television compilation film '1917'. The Comité International d'Histoire de la Deuxième Guerre Mondiale has also taken a close interest in film material, and organised a conference on Resistance film at Padua in 1971. In Britain the Slade School at University College London, the British Universities Film Council, the Inter-Universities Film Consortium, the Imperial War Museum, certain individuals at the University of Oxford, and the Open University have all been involved in attempts to make film material more readily available to scholars and students. In the United States, too, a Historians' Film Committee has recently been formed, and it publishes the quarterly, *Film and History*. Over the past half-dozen years four important conferences have been held in London to discuss various aspects of the uses of film to the historian, in addition to one in Utrecht, one in Göttingen, and the one at Padua. In 1970, furthermore, the massive and prestigious Anglo-American Conference of Historians, organised by the Institute of Historical Research in London, included a session on Film and the Historian. The Historical Association has a Film Committee, and its journal, *History* includes a Film section edited by Professor J. A. S. Grenville.

My concern here is to describe the use I have made of film in my researches on war and social change in the twentieth century. Thus I shall be dealing with the uses of film to the researcher rather than the uses of film as a teaching medium; and I am not concerned now to go further into the literature of the subject, though at the end of these notes I do include a short list of the main articles in the field.

Because it is more difficult, and more expensive, to study film than to study any other kind of source material, it is specially advisable to do all possible paper work and planning of research in advance. Many film archives, it is true, are extremely badly catalogued, and many contain cans of film which are not labelled at all or are wrongly labelled. My own detailed researches have been conducted exclusively in the British film archives and here I have depended heavily for preliminary paper work on the pioneer registering of film material started by Lisa Pontecorvo, and continued by Frances Thorpe and her colleagues at the Slade Film School. In the end, obviously, there is no alternative to going and sitting for hours and hours viewing material in the archives; but it is extremely valuable to have some lead into the material.

Once the initial hurdles have been overcome, and they are big hurdles, film, as I see it, is to be studied by the historian in accordance with exactly the same principles that he brings to bear on all of his sources. I simply do not go along with those historians who argue that film is somehow more dishonest, or more trivial, than any other type of source. It is true that in choosing his angles and his shots the cameraman filters reality from the start; more critically, producers and editors, in the way in which they cut shots together, can come very close to faking reality. When commentary and music are added, the distortion seems to go still further. For me these are not crucial problems. No primary source is absolutely objective. Every primary source was created by some human being, or group of human beings, for special purposes of their own, usually far removed from the purpose for which the later historian uses the source. In criticising and interpreting any source, the historian has to be sceptical, cautious, and he has to bring to bear the whole range of his expertise. He must always ask, how did the source come into being;

for what purpose; who were the people who created it; and so on. Obviously, one can only make use of film if one understands the technicalities and the tricks of film making; but then every branch of historical study calls for particular ancillary skills: the medieval historian for instance must master the disciplines of palaeography. Equally, too, only the historian who is a thorough master of the period he is studying will be able to get the most out of the film documents.

It must be said about film, as it must be said about any primary source, that the historian seldom gains one piece of information, or one type of insight, from one source alone. The work of the historian is essentially cumulative. It most usually happens that, after immersing himself in a vast range of sources, it is when he comes across some new piece of evidence that suddenly all that he has already learned fits into place, and he is ready to formulate a new idea or a new insight, or simply to produce a new concrete fact. The general value of film to the twentieth-century historian is that, because it is a slightly different type of source, it is specially good at making him reflect again upon his other evidence. But film too has more specific uses.

Many historians working with film material put most stress on film as a particularly important source in the special study of propaganda and the formation of social and political attitudes. This is a particularly important topic in wartime, as we have seen, and undoubtedly one of the most important uses of archive film for the historian lies in this very area. In the hands of governments film became a very potent source of propaganda and manipulation of opinion; and even where there was no direct control by governments, film helped to spread the attitudes of wealthy and influential ruling groups within society. Nicholas Pronay has pointed out the way in which, by the 1930s, newsreel films had come to assume the attitude-forming role of the popular press. In studying any document, the historian derives from it both 'witting testimony' – that is to say the overt message of the document, the deliberate intention of whoever created it, and 'unwitting testimony' – what the document reveals to the trained historian about assumptions, contemporary conditions, and other matters which it was no part of the intention of the original deviser of the document to convey. This use of film in the study of propaganda and the formation of opinion is part of the 'witting testimony' of film evidence. The study of this witting testimony is the first specific use of archive film to the historian.

But for the historian the 'unwitting testimony' is usually much more interesting. However much filtering has been done by the cameraman, however much reality has been distorted by cutting, editing, and many other devices, it is still possible for the historian to deduce from the film evidence facts about past situations which indeed he might well find it hard to derive from any other source. The most important aspects of unwitting testimony are:

1. *Environment.* If we are to ask whether an older world perished in the holocaust of the First World War; or whether the world of the late forties and early fifties was totally different from that of the thirties: then it is as well to view as much film material as possible of the different periods in order to form a clear impression of what exactly the environment of the period studied was like. If, in a comparative study, we are to understand the different geographical characteristics, the different urban styles, of different countries, then film is very helpful.

2. *Life styles and patterns of behaviour.* As I have argued in my text, one of the best ways of seeing just what had changed over the period of the First World War is to look at the film material. The world of the Kaiser and the Tsar comes through in the early silent films as it does in no other source. Writing of children working an eleven-and-a-half hour day in Petrograd just before the revolution, Marc Ferro has remarked that: 'Film has preserved these tragic adolescents, crawling in mines with a chain round their ankles, drawing a cart of ore.' (*The Great War*, p. 170).

3. *Portraiture.* Film frequently shows us more of the real character of past individuals than any other source can. I have referred specifically in my text to Goebbels's 'total war' speech. For an understanding of Hitler, too, film is an indispensable source; as it is also for the gentler politicians of democracy.

4. *The 'crash course' function of archive film.* If we want to know immediately what some technological, or specialist, operation was really like, film can more readily give us a 'crash course' in this experience than any other possible type of source. For instance, exploitation of the knowledge of how to make penicillin was one of the scientific consequences of the Second World War; film of the process of developing the penicillin mould gives a new insight into this well-known fact. Similarly with the many other scientific and technological developments associated with the two wars.

5. *The concrete reality of particular situations.* If the historian is to deal in the actual and the concrete, as he must, instead of becoming enmeshed in verbal mystique and fancy, then film is a vitally helpful source. Concentration Camp film was shown at the Military Tribunal at Nuremburg; as one of the executive trial counsel, Thomas J. Dodd, remarked, such film 'represents in a brief and unforgettable form an explanation of what

the words 'concentration camp' imply'. (I.M.T., *Trial*, II, p. 286).

6. *The ethos of the times.* Such a phrase may, rightly, be regarded as a dubious one, analogous to that other historian's standby, 'the climate of the age'. Yet it is a fundamental task of the historian to see a past age 'from the inside' as it were, on its own terms, as contemporaries saw it, rather than as the historian with the advantage of hindsight sees it. In a useful rephrasing one might use James Joll's term 'the unspoken assumptions' – the things people in a past age took for granted about themselves and their environment, but which it is very difficult for the historian to latch on to. Film has a particular value here, especially when it becomes a central medium of communication as in the 1930s. A good example occurs in some of the British propaganda cartoon films of the First World War. Here war is portrayed over and over again as sport continued by other means. Constantly the British Tommy is administering the knock-out to the Kaiser. It is this sporting imagery, concealing the true horror and sordid bloodshed of the trenches, which helps to explain the way in which the British people were prepared to put up so cheerfully with the long agony.

In general I would make a broad distinction between newsreels on the one hand, and made documentaries on the other. It is true that many newsreels were in fact compiled from older shots, often stock shots, and therefore in this sense come near to the documentary. Still, in the main there is an immediacy, a nearness to 'actuality' about newsreel, which one does not find in the more self-conscious, composed documentary. On the whole, given that the historian accumulates his view from a large number of single pieces of evidence, I have found newsreels of greater value than documentaries, though every now and again a single documentary does give one a rather breathtaking insight: this is the case, for instance, with *The Warning* made with government support for showing to British audiences early in 1939; this documentary gives a deliberately shocking view of the horrors which war will bring.

If documentaries can be regarded as very roughly analogous to magazines and periodicals, and newsreels to popular newspapers, feature films are roughly analogous to novels and plays. Like novels and plays they can tell a good deal about the attitudes of the period in which the film was made. But they have to be handled very delicately. On the whole one has to absorb the flavour and quality of the total work, whereas one can often get quite a lot from very short pieces of newsreel. Some documentaries are very heavily fictionalised; and some feature films, particularly in the early days, have a very strong educational, or propagandist message, which almost brings them back into the realm of the

documentary. The Marie Stopes's film, *Maisie's Marriage*, mentioned in Chapter 3, falls exactly within this borderland. Here quite short sequences, such as the birth-control one I mentioned, can be very illuminating. But for grasping a whole web of tangled attitudes and assumptions, there is no substitute for seeing the whole film.

It should perhaps be said, finally, that researching in the film archives can be just as tedious as carrying out research in more conventional sources. One has to wade through masses of pretty useless, and often boring stuff, in order to come across the odd piece of significant film.

In the Annotated Bibliography I refer mainly to secondary sources and to printed collections of documents. In the same way I am now going to list here those compilation films of archive material which are at least available for hire or purchase. Some are very much analogous to a simple collection of film documents; others are more like a good secondary source and aim to tell a rounded and complete story. But all contain valuable items of archive material which form not just a supplement, but an added dimension to the study of War and Social Change. (The University of Birmingham publishes a comprehensive *Survey of History Films for Hire* covering all sorts of films on all sorts of topics and periods; more directly relevant is the Imperial War Museum's brochure, *Film Loans*.)

## List of Archive Compilation Films

### A. *Inter-University History Film Consortium*

British Universities Historical Studies in Film:
1. 'The Munich Crisis' (John Grenville and Nicholas Pronay).
2. 'The End of Illusions – from Munich to Dunkirk' (John Grenville and Nicholas Pronay).
3. 'The Spanish Civil War' (Paul Addison, Owen Dudley Edwards and Tony Aldgate).

In general these films aim at being comprehensive statements on their respective subjects, rather than at the 'collection of documents' approach, but they contain much fascinating material.

### B. *EMI – Pathé*

'The Emancipation of Women' (Richard Dunn, Arthur Marwick and Lisa Pontecorvo)
Falls between the comprehensive, and the 'collection of documents' approach.

## C. *Granada TV Films*

'Cities at War':
  'Leningrad "The Hero City" '
  'London "The First City" '
  'Berlin "The Doomed City" '
In the traditional television compilation style, but again contain much
interesting material.

## D. *Thames Television*

'The First Casualty' (John Terraine and Peter Morley)
Interesting film, though not a great deal of straight archive film material.
'The World at War' (Jeremy Isaacs)
Traditional compilation style at its very best.

## E. *Visual Programme Systems Ltd*

'Peace-Making 1919'
Some interesting material, though rather confusingly presented.

## F. *Stichting Film En Wetenschap*

'Anton Mussert' (Rolf Schuursma)
The classic biography of the Dutch Fascist Leader made in a very
careful 'collection of documents' fashion.

## G. *The Open University*

'War and Society' (Arthur Marwick, Edward Hayward, Nick Levinson,
Lisa Pontecorvo and Des Murphy)
1. 'Archive Film and the Study of War and Society' (Arthur Marwick, Nick Levinson)
2. 'The Origins of World War I' (Arthur Marwick, Edward Hayward)
3. 'Social Impact of World I, 1914–1918' (Arthur Marwick, Edward Hayward)
4. 'Social Consequences of World War I, 1914–1930' (Arthur Marwick, Edward Hayward)
5. 'Women in Two World Wars' (Arthur Marwick, Edward Hayward)
6. 'The Conduct of War 1914–1945' (Brian Bond, Nick Levinson)
7. 'The Organisations of Peace' (Arthur Marwick, Edward Hayward)

8. 'The Effect of World War I on Russia and Germany' (Harry Hanak, Edward Hayward)
9. 'The Social Impact of World War II, 1939–1945' (Arthur Marwick, Nick Levinson)
10. 'Strategic Bombing of Germany' (Noble Frankland, Edward Hayward)
11. 'The Nazi New Order' (Alan Milward, Edward Hayward)
12. 'The Resistance' (M. R. D. Foot, Edward Hayward)
13. 'The Social Consequences of World War II, 1939–1950' (Arthur Marwick, Nick Levinson)
14. 'The Impact of World War II on Indonesian Nationalism' (Donald Watt, Nick Levinson)
15. 'The Afro-American and World War II' (Neil Wynn, Nick Levinson)
16. 'Guerrilla Warfare in Algeria' (Clive Emsley, Edward Hayward)

These compilations are orientated very definitely towards the 'collection of documents' approach.


## Some Publications on the Uses of Archive Film

Tony Aldgate, 'British Newsreels and the Spanish Civil War', *History* (Feb 1973).

British Universities' Film Council, *University Vision No. 1*, Feb 1968 (articles by John Grenville, Lisa Pontecorvo, etc.).

British Universities' Film Council, *Film and the Historian*, ed. Liz-Ann Bawden (proceedings of the first British Conference on 'Film and the Historian').

Thorold Dickinson, 'Discovering Unreleased Newsreels', *Times Higher Education Supplement* (15 June 1973).

Sir Arthur Elton, 'The Film as Source Material for History', *Aslib Proceedings* (Nov 1955).

Marc Ferro, '1917 History and the Cinema', *Journal of Contemporary History* (1968).

Marc Ferro, 'Le Film, une Contre-Analyse de la Société?', *Annales* (1973).

John Grenville, *Film as History* (1971).

International Scientific Film Association and Encyclopaedia Cinematographica, *Bulletin of the Research Film Section* (Dec 1971): *Research Film* (ed. G. Wolf and R. Robineaux).

J. B. Krieger, 'The Historical Value of Motion Pictures', *The American Archivist* (Oct 1968).

Arthur Marwick, 'Video-History', *Listener* (1 May 1969).

C. L. Mowat, 'Film', *Great Britain Since 1914* (1971) pp. 163–70.

Open University, *War and Society: Archive Film Compilation Booklet* (Arthur Marwick, Lisa Pontecorvo, and Edward Hayward, 1973).

Nicholas Pronay, 'British Newsreels in the 1930s' Part I, 'Audiences and Producers', and Part II, 'Their Policies and Impact', *History* (Oct and Dec 1971).

C. H. Roads, 'Film as Historical Evidence', *Journal of Society of Archivists*, III, 4 (Oct 1966).

# Annotated Bibliography

These notes are designed for the general reader and undergraduate who is interested in the comparative and conceptual approach followed in this book.

## A.    General

Some of the most important books have already been discussed in the text or notes for Chapter 1, and I shall not repeat here titles mentioned there. There is an interesting essay on 'War and the Historian' by John Bowditch in *Teachers of History*, ed. H. Stuart Hughes (1954). The leading British military historian, who has always stressed the importance of the social implications of war, is Michael Howard. See his *Soldiers and Governments* (1957), *The Theory and Practice of War* (1965), and his *Studies in War and Peace* (1970). Note also Alfred Vagts, *A History of Militarism* (1959); R. E. Dupuy and T. N. Dupuy, *Encyclopaedia of Military History* (1966); Alastair Buchan, *War in Modern Society* (1966); and Correlli Barnett, *Britain and her Army* (1970). A distinguished opponent of the idea that war might foster social change is John U. Nef; see his book, *War and Human Progress* (1950).

Useful studies from the Social Sciences which I have not mentioned in Chapter 1 are (roughly in the order of their usefulness to me personally): Willard Waller (ed.) *War in the Twentieth Century* (1942); Leon Bramson and G. W. Goethals, *War: Studies from Sociology, Psychology, Anthropology* (new edn, 1968); Martha Wolfenstein, *Disaster* (1957); W. H. Form, C. P. Loomis and S. Nosow, *Community in Disaster* (1958); Rex A. Lucas, *Men in Crisis* (1960); L. Berkowitz, *Aggression* (1962);

w.s.c.—9*

J. B. Carthy and F. J. Abling, *The Natural History of Aggression* (1964); John Cohen, *Human Nature, War and Society* (1946); Stanley Hoffman, *The State of War* (1965); James Burnham, *Total War* (1940). For matters taken up briefly in my conclusion, the following are very useful: M. Janowitz, *The Professional Soldier* (1951); M. Janowitz (ed.), *The New Military* (1967); S. P. Huntington (ed.) *The Soldier and the State* (1957), and (ed.) *Changing Patterns of Military Politics* (1962); and S. E. Finer, *The Man on Horseback: The Role of the Military in Politics* (1962).

General works covering geography, population and so on are (in alphabetical order): Robert E. Dickinson, *Germany: a General and Regional Geography* (1961); Folke Dovring, *Land and Labor in Europe* (1960); R. Easterlin, *Population, Labor Force and Economic Growth* (1962); D. V. Glass, *Population Policies and Movements* (1967); George Walter Hoffman, *A Geography of Europe* (1961); International Labour Organisation, *The Displacement of Population in Europe* (1943); Eugene M. Kulischer, *Europe on the Move: War and Population Changes 1914–47* (1948); M. R. Reinhart and A. Armengaud, *Histoire generale de la population mondiale* (1961); Theodore Shabad, *Geography of the U.S.S.R.* (1951); United Nations, *Displacement of Population: Studies and Reports* (1943); W. S. and E. S. Woytinsky, *World Population and Production* (1953).

Also note two other I.L.O. publications: *Approaches to Social Security* (1942); and *The War and Women's Employment* (1946).

For the creative arts in general, an invaluable supplement to my book is to be found in the twentieth-century sections of John Ferguson (ed.), *War and the Creative Arts* (1972).

## B.    The First World War

Marc Ferro's brilliant textbook, *The Great War* (first published in France in 1967) is now (1973) available in English. Marvellously unconventional in its treatment, it does in the end concentrate rather heavily on the more obvious military and political issues, with especial emphasis on revolution; it does not really concern itself with the kind of social developments I have tried to discuss in this book. John Williams, *The Home Fronts: Britain, France and Germany 1914–1918* (1972) brings together much intriguing information and is a useful guide to some of the literary sources.

For Russia the most useful book in this connection, though little is explicitly said about the war, is C. E. Black (ed.), *The Transformation of*

*Russian Society* (1960). But most books on Russia tend, naturally enough, to be orientated towards the revolutions, rather than towards the war itself. Michael Florinsky, *The End of the Russian Empire* (1931), and George Katkov, *Russia 1917* (1967), I have already discussed in the opening chapter. Marc Ferro's majestic study of *The Revolutions of 1917* (first published in France in 1967) is now also available in English translation (1972). Other useful accounts are W. H. Chamberlin, *The Russian Revolution* (1935); J. Carmichael, *A Short History of the Russian Revolution* (1966); N. N. Sukhanov, *The Russian Revolution, 1917*, ed. J. Carmichael (1955); E. H. Carr, *The Bolshevik Revolution* (1950); L. Schapiro, *The Communist Party of the Soviet Union* (1960); A. Ulam, *Lenin and the Bolsheviks* (1966); and Lionel Kochan, *Russia in Revolution* (1966). Lionel Kochan's *The Making of Modern Russia* (1962), also has some interesting reflections on the effects of war. Two useful collections of documents are Robert Browder and Alexander F. Kerensky (eds.), *The Russian Provisional Government* (1961); and Frank A. Golder (ed.), *Documents of Russian History* (1927). Alec Nove's immaculate *An Economic History of the U.S.S.R.* (1969), contains interesting material on the First World War. Out of the Carnegie Series I have found the following most useful: Paul N. Ignatiev, *Russian Schools and Universities in the World War* (1929); T. B. Struve, *Food Supply in Russia During the War* (1930); and Alexis N. Antsiferov, *Russian Rural Economy During the War* (1930). Insights of a rather different type can be gleaned from: Leon Trotsky, *History of the Russian Revolution* (1932–3); John Read, *Ten Days that Shook the World* (1919); Bernard Pares, *My Russian Memoirs* (1931); Sir Alfred Knox, *With the Russian Army 1914–17* (1921); and B. Gurko, *Memoirs and Impressions of War and Revolution in Russia 1914–17* (1918).

For Germany, Gerald Feldman's *Army Industry and Labor* (1966) is in a class by itself, a brilliant example of the new approach to the study of war and society discussed in Chapter 1. R. H. Lutz has edited two substantial collections of documents, *The Fall of the German Empire*, two volumes (1932), and *The Causes of the German Collapse* (1934). H. P. Hanssen's *Diary of a Dying Empire* (also edited by R. H. Lutz, 1955) is fascinating, though given the Danish bias of its author, it has to be taken with some caution. In the Carnegie Series, Mendelssohn Bartholdy's *The War and German Society: the Testament of a Liberal* (1937) is admirably summed up in that sub-title; much more useful is Leo Grebler and Wilhelm Winkler, *The Cost of the World War to Germany and Austria–Hungary* (1940). G. Bry, *Wages in Germany 1870–1945*

(1960) is indispensable. Three sound, but rather conventional economic histories are: W. F. Bruck, *Social and Economic History of Germany, 1888–1938* (1938); Sir John Clapham, *Economic Development of France and Germany* (1936); and Gustav Stolper, *The German Economy, 1870–1940* (1940). Much emphasis has been directed towards the German army, and also, of course towards the revolution. Useful books here are: Arthur Rosenberg, *Imperial Germany: The Birth of the German Republic, 1871–1918* (1970); Gordon Craig, *The Politics of the Prussian Army* (1955); F. L. Carsten, *The Reichswehr and Politics, 1918–1933* (1966), and *Revolution in Central Europe, 1918–1919* (1972); A. J. Ryder, *The German Revolution of 1918* (1967). Two more specifically political studies are A. Joseph Berlau, *The German Social Democratic Party 1914–1921* (1949); and Carl Schorske, *German Social Democracy* (1965). See also Rohan Butler, *The Roots of National Socialism* (1941). An excellent general textbook which has many shrewd reflections on the effects of the First World War is Koppel Shub Pinson, *Modern Germany* (1966). There is interesting autobiographical material in P. Scheidemann, *Memoirs of a Social Democrat* (1929); and interesting biographical material in James Joll, *Intellectuals in Politics* (1960), including an essay on Rathenau, Klaus Eckstein, *Matthias Erzberger and the Dilemma of German Democracy* (1959); J. W. Wheeler-Bennett, *Hindenburg, The Wooden Titan* (1936); and J. P. Nettl, *Rosa Luxemburg* (1969).

For France, the best starting point is probably to be found in the Carnegie Series. Among the volumes available in English, Charles Gide, *Effects of the War on French Economic Life* (1923), Arthur Fontaine, *French Industry During the War* (1926), and Pierre Renouvin, *The Forms of War Government in France* (1927), all bring out the effects of war quite strongly. G. Olphe-Galliard, *Histoire economique et financière de la guerre* (1923), and M. Augé-Laribé, *L'Agriculture pendant la Guerre* (1925) are also very useful, as are the separate individual studies in French of the various main French towns: for example Henri Sellier's book on Paris, or P. Courteault's book on Bordeaux. Shepherd B. Clough, *History of National Economics* (1939), stresses the influence of the war in furthering measures of State control. Also very important are Val Lorwin, *The French Labor Movement* (1954), and Gordon Wright, *Rural Revolution in France* (1968); there is also a brilliant survey in Gordon Wright's textbook, *France in Modern Times* (1962). D. W. Brogan, *The Development of Modern France* (1940) includes quite a full account of the First World War; and J. P. T. Bury, *France 1814–1940* (4th edn, 1969), is a good straightforward textbook. Finally, though not directly relevant to most of the main concerns of my book, one must mention Jere C. King's authoritative *Generals and Politicians: Conflict between France's High Command, Parliament and Government, 1915–1918* (1951). To that I should also add that no one should attempt to study France in the First World War without reading Henri Barbusse's *Under Fire* (first published in 1916) which is briefly discussed in my text.

For Britain I must inevitably refer to my own study *The Deluge: British Society and the First World War* (1965, and subsequent editions). To this can now be added Alan Milward's useful bibliographical pamphlet, *The Economic Effects of the World Wars on Britain* (1970). Paul Guinn has an excellent chapter on 'The War on The Home Front 1914–18' in the admirable *A Guide to the Sources of British Military History*, ed. Robert Higham (1971). Paul Barton Johnston has published a detailed and scholarly study of the planning of British reconstruction 1916–19, *Land Fit for Heroes* (1968); for my taste, however, like Philip Abrams's article 'The Failure of Social Reform 1918–1920', *Past and Present*, no. 24 (Apr 1963), it concentrates too exclusively on 'guided' social change; and both follow quite closely R. H. Tawney's pioneer essay, 'The Abolition of Economic Controls, 1918–21', *Economic History Review*, XIII, no. 1 (1943). Susan Armitage, *The Politics of Decontrol of Industry* (1970), is sensible and modest, but again concentrates on 'guided' change. *Essays in Labour History, 1886–1923*, ed. Asa Briggs and John Saville (1971), contains important essays by Philip Bagwell, James Hinton and Royden Harrison. An up-to-date economic history which brings out the effects of the war is D. Aldcroft and H. W. Richardson, *The British Economy* (1969). The best summary is still contained in the two relevant chapters of A. J. P. Taylor's *English History 1914–1945* (1965). S. L. Hynes, *The Edwardian Turn of Mind* (1968), argues that social change took place *before* the First World War; so does Donald Read, *Edwardian England* (1972); and the relevant chapter of A. F. Havighurst's reliable textbook, *Twentieth-Century Britain* (2nd edn, 1966), is also a useful antidote to the 'Marwick' line. John Terraine, *Impacts of War* (1970), is a fascinating and original work; and the best introduction to the realities of trench life is contained in Charles Carrington, *Soldier from the Wars Returning* (1965). Useful books in the Carnegie Series can be traced in my book, *The Deluge* (1965). Five more than usually interesting contemporary sources which might otherwise be missed are: Clive Bell 'The Artist and War', *International Journal of Ethics*, XXVI (Oct 1915); C. R. W. Nevinson, *Modern War Paintings* (1917); Cyril Leeson, *The Child and the War* (1917); Ivor Nicholson and Lloyd Williams, *Wales: Its Part in the War* (1919); and

Mark Gertler, *Mark Gertler: Artists of Today, Number 1* (1925).

Not to be missed in any study of the United States and the First World War are Henry F. May, *The End of American Innocence* (1959), which argues that social change took place *before* the war; and W. E. Leuchtenberg, 'The New Deal and the Analogue of War' in *Change and Continuity in Twentieth-century America*, ed. John Braeman, R. H. Bremner and Everet Walters (1966). Also see W. E. Leuchtenberg's general textbook, *The Perils of Prosperity* (1958). There is some good material on the war in Arthur S. Link, *American Epoch* (1966). S. D. Morison, H. S. Commager, and W. E. Leuchtenberg, *The Growth of the American Republic*, vol. II (6th edn, 1969), contains an excellent chapter on the war. Jack J. Roth (ed.), *World War I: a Turning Point in Modern History* (1967), is interesting, but does not quite live up to the promise of its title. *Documents of American History*, ed. H. S. Commager (1963), is useful for brief extracts from primary material; and Frank Freidel and Norman Pollock, *American Issues in the Twentieth Century* (1968), is a collection of documents and readings. Of all the books in the Carnegie Series J. M. Clark, *Costs of the War to the American People* (1931), is one of the most level-headed. John B. McMaster, *The United States in the World War* (1918–20), and F. L. Paxson, *American Democracy and the World War*, 3 vols (1936–48), are not much use. For the war's effects on the black American, the article 'The Wilson Administration and the Wartime Mobilization of Black Americans', by James L. and Harry N. Scheiber, *Labor History*, x, 3 (Summer 1969), is indispensable. J. H. Franklin, *From Slavery to Freedom: History of the American Negroes* (1956) contains much information but is rather impressionistic. E. J. Scott, *Negro Migration* (1920) is a useful contemporary account. See also H. S. Commager, *Struggle for Racial Equality* (1967). For the effects of war on ideas and social policy, the following are useful: Zachariah Chafee, *Free Speech in the United States* (1942); Clark A. Chambers, *Seed Time of Reform* (1963); Charles B. Fawcey, *The Crossroads of Liberalism* (1961); Christopher Lasch, *American Liberals and the Russian Revolution* (1962); and Roy Lubove, *The Struggle for Social Security 1900–1935* (1968).

Another useful book in the Carnegie Series is E. F. Hecksher (ed.) *Sweden, Norway, Denmark, and Iceland in the World War* (1930).

This is probably the place to mention that out of both world wars the French produced very detailed learned journals. For the First World War there is the *Revue d'histoire de la guerre mondiale*. I am afraid that, in looking at the immensely detailed articles in this journal, I am often reminded of Kruschev's scornful comparison of a dissertation on 'Partisan Operations in the Bellorussian Forests during the Patriotic War' to one on 'The Ecology and Economic Importance of the European White Stork, the Black Stork and the Common Grey Heron in Bellorussia'.

## C.  The Second World War

Gordon Wright's *The Ordeal of Total War 1939–1945* (1969) is a splendid textbook which makes a real effort to deal with questions of social change.

For Russia, two works of meticulous scholarship stand out immediately: Alexander Dallin, *German Rule in Russia 1941–45* (1957); and John A. Armstrong (ed.) *Soviet Partisans in World War II* (1964). C. E. Black, *The Transformation of Russian Society* (1960) is again very useful, but some of the essays in A. Inkeles and K. Geiger, *Soviet Society* (1961) have more than a whiff of the Cold War about them. Two journalists have written valuable accounts incorporating first-hand information: Alexander Werth, *Russia at War* (1964), and J. Champenois, *La Peuple Russe et la Guerre* (1947). Alec Nove's account (already mentioned) supersedes the rather unreliable *L'Economie de Guerre de l'U.R.S.S. dans la periode de la Grande Guerre nationale 1941–1945* (1948), by N. Voznessenski. There are some perceptive points to be gleaned about the war from J. P. Nettl, *The Soviet Achievement* (1967); and there are some interesting personal reminiscences in M. MacDuffie, *Red Carpet* (1955).

For Germany, essential starting points are Alan Milward, *The German Economy at War* (1965), and A. and V. Toynbee (eds.), *Hitler's Europe: The Royal Institute for International Affairs Survey of International Affairs for 1939–1946* (1954), together with the accompanying two volumes of documents. Two much-mined primary sources are the Reports of the International Military Tribunal, *The Trial of the German Major War Criminals* (1946–51), together with the *Proceedings and Documents* (1947), and the many *Reports of the United States Strategic Bombing Survey*. Views of Germany at war are perhaps a little too coloured by Albert Speer's volume of reminiscences published in English as *Inside the Third Reich* (1970), but it is a valuable source none the less. For the bomb attacks on Germany the standard work is Sir Charles Webster and Noble Frankland, *The Strategic Air Offensive Against Germany*, 4 vols (1961). Noble Frankland has written a shorter more popular account, *The Bombing Offensive Against Germany* (1965). Also see H. Rumpf, *The Bombing of Germany* (1960). There is material on Germany in the two invaluable Social Science studies, I. L. Janis, *Air War and Emotional Stress* (1951), and F. C. Iklé, *The Social Impact of Bomb Destruction* (1958). Life in wartime Germany as seen by an opponent of the Hitler régime who lived throughout the war in Sweden is described in M. Seydewitz, *Civil Life in Wartime Germany* (1945). G. Bry on *Wages in Germany* (1960) is again very useful, and can be supplemented by the Marxist account of J. Kuczynski, *A Short History of Labour Conditions Under Industrial Capitalism*, vol. 3, part II, *Germany Under Fascism* (1944). Other aspects of the German wartime experience are summarised in G. Ritter, *The German Resistance* (1958), J. S. Conway, *The Nazi Persecution of the Churches 1939–45* (1968), and The International Labour Office, *The Exploitation of Foreign Labour by Germany* (1945). For the social condition of Germany on the eve of the war, the following are useful: D. Schoenbaum, *Hitler's Social Revolution: Class and Status in Nazi Germany* (1967); C. W. Guillebaud, *The Social Policy of Nazi Germany* (1941); and Jill McIntyre (now Stephenson), 'Women and the Professions in Nazi Germany' in *German Democracy and the Triumph of Hitler*, ed. A. J. Nichols and Eric Mathias (1971). Berenice Carroll, *Design for Total War: Arms and Economics in the Third Reich* (1968) is a pungent book in its own right, though not quite central to my concerns. Similarly, William Carr, *Arms, Autarky and Aggression* (1972), is useful though not directly relevant. For the structure of the Germany which emerged from the war, Ralf Dahrendorf, *Society and Democracy in Germany* (1967), is a most useful study by a sociologist. For a traditional, but perceptive historian's account, the final chapters of Golo Mann, *History of Germany since 1870* (1968), are very helpful. Of the many published diaries and reminiscences, *The Goebbels Diaries*, ed. Lewis P. Lockner (1948), and W. Prüller, *Diary of a German Soldier* (1965), are specially revealing. Finally, there is an interesting thesis, made abundantly plain in the title, in John D. Montgomery, *Forced to be Free: The Artificial Revolutions in Germany and Japan* (1957).

For Britain, the most comprehensive study is Angus Calder, *The People's War* (1969). One important chapter in Henry Pelling's briefer *Britain and the Second World War* (1970) is devoted to the question of war and social change. See also the relevant chapter of my *Britain in the Century of Total War* (1968), and also my article 'L'Impact de la Deuxième Guerre mondiale sur les Britanniques', in *Revue d'histoire de la deuxième guerre mondiale* (April 1973). A unique primary source lies in the files of Mass Observation, now housed at the University of

Sussex; for the undergraduate, many of the published Reports of Mass Observation are fairly readily available. Two published diaries of special interest are H. Hamilton Fyfe, *Britain's Wartime Revolution* (1944), and J. L. Hodson, *The Home Front* (1944); other rather interesting primary material is to be found in the *Annual Reports* of the Arts Council and in the magazine *Current Affairs*, published by the Army Bureau of Current Affairs. On the economic side, R. C. O. Mathews 'Why Has Britain Enjoyed Full Employment Since the War?', *Economic Journal* (1968) is indispensable; while Alan Peacock and Jack Wiseman, *The Growth of Public Expenditure in the U.K.* (1961), and the relevant chapter in Sidney Pollard, *The Development of the British Economy, 1914–1950* (1960), are very useful. For scientific developments there are Margaret Gowing's brilliant *Britain and Atomic Energy* (1964); Hilary and Steven Rose, *Science and Society* (1969); and Guy Hartcup's rather limited *The Challenge of War* (1970). Ian Hamilton (ed.) *Poetry of War 1939–1945* (1965) is well chosen.

With the publication of Richard Polenberg, *War and Society: America 1941–1945* (1972), American historiography has suddenly caught up with the war and society studies being conducted in other countries. It inevitably supersedes the two popular accounts, John Brooke, *The Great Leap* (1966), and Richard R. Lingeman, *Don't You Know There's a War On?* (1958), though it can still be supplemented by Polenberg's own collection of documents and readings, *America at War* (1968). A more recent popular account is Geoffrey Perrett, *Days of Sadness, Years of Triumph* (1973). In addition to the general histories already mentioned, William Miller, *A New History of the United States* (new edn, 1968), has some important points to make about the Second World War. The special question of the black American has been fully explored by Neil Wynn in his Open University Ph.D. thesis, 'World War II and the Afro-American', and in his two articles 'The Impact of World War II on the American Negro', *Journal of Contemporary History*, VI, 2 (Apr 1971) and 'Black Attitudes Towards Participation in the American War Effort 1941–1945', *Afro-American Studies*, III, 1 (June 1972). See also Richard M. Dalfiume, 'The "Forgotten Years" of the Negro Revolution', *Journal of American History*, LV, 1 (June 1968), and J. S. Olson, 'Organised Black Leadership and Industrial Unionism: the Racial Response, 1936–1965', *Labor History*, X, 3 (Summer 1969). Other special topics are touched on in H. K. Girvetz, *From Wealth to Welfare: The Evolution of Liberalism* (1957); R. H. Bremner, *From the Depths: The Discovery of Poverty in the United States* (1956); American Social Science Research Council, *Studies in Social Psychology in World War II* (1949–50); and

Betty Friedan, *The Feminine Mystique* (1964). There are some stimulating essays in Hugh D. Graham and Ted R. Gurr (eds.), *The History of Violence in the United States* (1969). Lewis Smith, *American Democracy and Military Power* (1951) provides an introduction to an important topic arising directly from the war; but perhaps the most influential book is Michael Kidron, *Western Capitalism since the War* (1968); *The Naked and the Dead* and *Catch 22* are mentioned in my text; the hero of *Mr. Sammler's Planet* by Saul Bellow is governed by the brooding horror of his experiences of the Second World War.

The standard authority for France in Hitler's Europe is the book with that very title (*Frankreich in Hitlers Europa*) by Eberhard Jäkel, also available in French, though unfortunately not yet in English. There is also Alan Milward's very important study, *The New Order and the French Economy* (1970). For Vichy there is Robert Aron, *Vichy Régime* (1958), though this has met with a good deal of criticism; and a collection of short extracts from documents, linked with quite extensive commentary, *Le Dossier de Vichy* (1967), by Jacques de Launay. Robert O. Paxton, *Parades and Politics at Vichy* (1966), studies the officer corps as a social group. Geoffrey Warner, *Pierre Laval and the Eclipse of France* (1968) is a brilliant study of more than merely biographical interest. The two sides of wartime France are brought together in Peter Novick, *The Resistance Versus Vichy* (1968), and also, of course, in that stimulating and seminal article, 'The Effects of the World War II on French Society and Politics' by Stanley Hoffman, in *French Historical Studies*, I (Apr 1961). The doyen of French Resistance historians is Henri Michel whose books include, at one end of the scale, *Bibliographie Critique de la Résistance* (1964) and at the other the short *Histoire de la Résistance* (1958). Particularly valuable are his *Les Courants de Pensée de la Résistance* (1964), and the volume of documents edited in collaboration with Boris Mirkine-Getzovitch, *Les Idées Politiques et Sociales de la Résistance* (1954). These belong to the important series 'Esprit de la Résistance', which also includes: M. Baudot, *L'Opinion Publique sous l'Occupation* (1960); J. Vidalenc, *L'Exode de mai-juin 1940* (1957); Marie Granet and Henri Michel, *Combat: Histoire d'un Mouvement de Résistance* (1958); Renée Hostache, *Le Conseil national de la Résistance* (1958); and André Mazeline, *La Résistance dans le Départements de l'Orme* (1957). The standard authority on the British involvement with the Resistance is M. R. D. Foot, *S.O.E. in France* (1968); Professor Foot's book on the *European Resistance to Hitler* is also eagerly awaited. Hannah Josephson and Malcolm Cowley (eds.), *Aragon: Poet of Resurgent France* (1946) is a useful guide. Vercors, *Le Silence de la Mer*

(1943) must be read, even if nothing else is. There is some somewhat unsatisfactory documentation in the three volumes of *French Life under the Occupation* (1958) published by the Hoover Institute of Stanford University. Much more impressive is the collection of essays written in reply, *La France sous l'Occupation* (1959) ed. P. Arnoult and others. H. Amoureux, *La Vie des Français sous l'Occupation* (1961) is a popular account, but it contains important information. Alexander Werth, *France 1940–55* (1960) is a good general survey. Henry W. Ehrmann has written on *Organised Business in France* (1958), and on *French Labor: Popular Front to Liberation* (1947). Also useful in the latter connection are George Lefranc, *Les Experiences Syndicales en France de 1939 à 1950* (1950), and Val Lorwin, *The French Labor Movement* (1954). Aspects of French society as it emerged from the war, are studied in: Edward Earle (ed.), *Modern France* (1951); Catherine Gavin, *Liberated France* (1955); François Goguel, *France Under the Fourth Republic* (1952); International Labour Office, *Labour–Management Cooperation in France* (1950); Herbert Luethy, *The State of France* (1955); Dorothy Pickles, *French Politics: The First Years of the Fourth Republic* (1953); O. R. Taylor, *The Fourth Republic of France* (1951); and J. S. Ambler, *The French Army in Politics 1945–1962* (1966). W. A. Robson has an interesting comparative study of 'Nationalised Industries in Britain and France' in *American Political Science Review*, XLIV (June 1950). Other insights into post-war France are contained in Simone de Beauvoir's novel, *The Mandarins* (first published in English in 1957).

For countries just mentioned in passing in my concluding chapter, the following may be used: J. Andenaes, O. Riste and M. Skodvin, *Norway and the Second World War* (1966); Pietro Badoglio, *Italy in the Second World War* (1948); J. B. Cohen, *Japan's Economy in War and Reconstruction* (1949); W. H. Elsbree, *Japan's Role in South-East Asian Nationalist Movements 1940–1945* (1953); Italian Foreign Ministry, *The Italian Contribution to the War of Liberation against Germany* (1946); Alan Milward, *The Fascist Economy in Norway* (1972); A. A. Pallis, *Problems of Resistance in the Occupied Countries* (1960); Royal Institute of International Affairs, *Japan in Defeat* (1945); G. Valentine Selsey, *Italy Works her Passage* (1945); and W. Warmbrunn, *The Dutch under German Occupation 1940–1945* (1963). A moving document which can never really become hackneyed is Anne Frank, *Anne Frank: The Diary of a Young Girl* (1952).

For European reconstruction and movements towards integration, the following are useful: J. Freymond, *Western Europe since the War* (1964); S. R. Graubard (ed.), *A New Europe?* (1964); H. Stuart Hughes,

*Contemporary Europe: A History* (1966); A. J. May, *Europe Since 1939* (1966); Royal Institute of International Affairs, *Documents on International Affairs 1945–1951* (1945–51); Royal Institute of International Affairs, *Documents on European Recovery and Defence* (1949); and D. W. Urwin, *Western Europe Since 1945* (1968). M. M. Postan, *An Economic History of Western Europe 1945–1964* (1967), is indispensable.

For various aspects of the Second World War there is again a detailed French journal, *Revue d'histoire de la deuxième guerre mondiale*. Most useful to the student probably, are certain special numbers on particular topics or countries, as for instance: no. 43 on Russia, no. 54 on the French Occupation, no. 55 on the Resistance and Liberation in France, and no. 81 on France in general.

# Index

Abetz, German Ambassador to
France 189
abstract expressionism 182
Adenauer, Konrad 135, 136, 144,
205, 206
aftermath of Second World War
134–49; relief work 134; East and
West Germany 131–6; frontiers
137–8; displaced persons 138;
population movements 142
Agricultural Adjustment Act
(U.S.A.) 99
*Air War and Emotional Stress*
(Janis) 154
*All Quiet on the Western Front*
(Remarque) 85
Allied Maritime Transport
Council 72
All-Russian Congress of Soviets 101
Alsace–Lorraine 5, 186, 188
*American Democracy and the
World War* (Paxson) 7
American Federation of Labor 74,
172
Andreski, Stanislaw 223
anti-semitism 99, 104, 107, 112,
142–3
anti-trust legislation (U.S.A.) 167
*Anton Mussert 1934–1945* (film)
215
Appalachian 'captive' coal mines
172–3
Aragon, Louis 187, 201
*Archive Film in the Study of War and
Society* 115
archive film material, notes on use of
226–30
Army Bureau of Current Affairs 158
*Army, Industry and Labor in Germany
1914–1918* (Feldman) 10
arts and the First World War 83–6

arts and the Second World War 133,
146–7, 164, 179, 200–2, 204
Arts Council 164
Asquith, H. H. (Earl of Oxford and
Asquith) 65, 66
Atlantic, battle of the 157
atom bombs 2, 166, 179
Auschwitz concentration camp 112
Austria–Hungary 6, 24, 213: and
outbreak of First World War 4–5

Barbusse, Henri 83, 86
Barnett, Correlli 7
Baruch, Bernard M. 68
Battle of Britain 153
Bauer, German Social Democrat 48
Beauvoir, Simone de 201
Beckmann, Max 85
Belgium 87, 213: invasion of
(1914) 5, 57
Benelux Customs Union 208, 211
Beria, L. P. 130
Berlin 139: bombing of 115–17;
blockade 210
*Berliner Tageblatt* 32, 33
Bernstein, Eduard 44
Bethmann-Hollweg, Theobald von
31, 33
Beveridge, Sir William
(Lord Beveridge), and
Beveridge Report 158, 198
Bevin, Ernest 171
Bichelonne, Vichy Minister for
Industry 189, 195, 211
Bidault, Georges 190, 192, 204
birth control, discussion of 94
blitzkrieg 109, 217
Bloch, Marc 192
Blum, Léon 99
Blumenfeld, R. D. 60

Bolsheviks, the   6, 18, 33, 34, 36,
  39–40, 45, 102. *See also* Russian
  Revolution
bombing raids   2, 179: early British
  raids on Germany   109–11; blitz
  on London   110; 'precision
  bombing'   110, 120; 'area bombing'
  110, 114, 120; British and American
  offensives from 1942   114–18. *See
  also* atom bombs
Bonn, as capital of West
  Germany   139
Brecht, Berthold   147
Bremen, bombing of   115
Brest, bombing of   186
Brest-Litovsk, Treaty of (1918)
  24, 40, 46
Briand, Aristide   54, 55
Britain: in 1914   15; government
  20; Liberal legislative programme
  21; Labour party   21; women's
  suffrage movement   21, 77;
  urbanisation   21
    and First World War   57–61,
  221: outbreak of war   5, 57, 60;
  military efforts   57; casualties   58;
  economic consequences   58–9;
  dislocation of trade   59;
  interruptions to social progress
  59–60; restrictions   60; bombing
  60–1
    test of war: control of railways
  64; munitions crisis   65; coalition
  government   65; increase of
  bureaucracy   65; Lloyd George
  government   66; rationing   66;
  state interference   67; liquor
  control   69–70
    participation: trade unions   74;
  Labour members in government
  74–5; skilled workers   76; votes for
  women   76
    social legislation   90–2:
  unemployment insurance   90–1;
  education   91; health   91; housing
  91; real wages   92
    between the wars   95, 98:
  'National Government'   98–100;
  unemployment   100; medical
  provision   100
    and Second World War   151–65,
  221: 'phoney war'   152–3;
  Churchill's government   153;
  Dunkirk evacuation   153; Battle of

Britain   153; blitz   153–6;
  evacuation of civilians   156–7;
  austerity   157; social reform
  proposals   157–8; strikes   158;
  colour problem   159; position of
  women   159–61; hospital system
  161; management of economy   161;
  higher wages and shorter hours
  162–3
    election of Labour government
  163: welfare state   163; full
  employment   163–4; revival of the
  arts   164; comparison with U.S.A.
  180–2; and European integration
  210; 'special relationship' with
  U.S.A.   210
*Britain in the Century of Total War*
  (Marwick)   10
British Restaurants   157
Brookes, John   166
Bruller, Jean, *see* 'Vercors'
*Burgfrieden* ('fortress truce')   25, 29
Byrnes, James F.   172

Caen, destruction of old town   186
Cagoulards, the   99
*Cahiers Français, Les*   207
Calder, A.   151–2, 161
Camus, Albert   146, 200
Capek, Karel   86
Carnegie Endowment for International
  Peace   8
Carroll, Berenice   217, 218
casualties in First World War   2,
  166, 186
*Catch 22* (Heller)   179
causes of war   3–6
Centre Party (Germany)   19, 29, 32,
  43, 148
Chaffee, Zachariah   8
*Chagrin et la Pitié, Le* (film)   192
Chamberlain, Neville   153
Champenois, Jean   124
Channel Islands   151
*Cheka*, the   101
Cherwell, Lord   114
*Chicago Tribune*   179
Christian, King of Denmark   214–15
Christian Democrats (West Germany)
  148, 206
Churchill, (Sir) Winston   3, 7, 114,
  133, 153, 157, 158, 187, 191, 220,
  221: on First World War   1–2

Civil Rights in U.S.A., movement towards 177-8
civil wars 218
Clark, John M. 80
Claveille memorandum 66
Clemenceau, Georges 55, 66, 217, 221
Cold War, the 148, 178, 179
Cologne, bombing of 115
*Combat*, Resistance newspaper 189, 207
Comité Français de la Libération Nationale (C.F.L.N.) 191-2
Comité France–Allemagne 189
Comité National du Salut Public 189
Commission Internationale de Ravitaillement 72
Committee on Civil Rights (U.S.A.) 177-8
Common Market, the 211. *See also* European Economic Community
Common Wealth Party (Britain) 157
Communism 103, 148, 199: in Russia 45, 98, 101, 133; and French Resistance 190, 192
concentration camps 112, 121-3: Official Report on 122-3
Confédération Générale Agricole 195
Congress of Industrial Organizations (U.S.A.) 172
Conseil National du Patronat Français 195
*Consequences of the War to Great Britain* (Hirst) 7
contraception, discussion of 94
Council for the Encouragement of Music and the Arts (C.E.M.A.) 164
Council of Europe 210
Council of People's Commissars 101
Coventry, bombing of 153, 154
Croix de Feu 99
*Current Affairs*, journal 158, 159
Czechoslovakia, Communist *coup d'état* in 210

Dahrendorf, Ralf 141-2
*Daily Express* 60
*Daily Mirror* 158
Daladier, Édouard 76, 99, 187
Daniels, Jonathan 178
Danzig, Free City of 87
Darlan, Admiral 188
Debré, Michel 199, 206-7
de Gaulle, General Charles 187, 195, 199: broadcast from London (June 1940) 188; and the Resistance 190, 191; and the C.F.L.N. 191; and Roosevelt 191, 192; and the liberation of Paris 192; and social change 198; withdrawal from centre of politics 200, 204; *coup d'état* (1958) 204, 221
Delbrück, Clemens von 28
Delbrück, Hans 32
*Deluge, The: British Society and the First World War* (Marwick) 10
Democratic Party (U.S.A.) 167-8
Denmark 213-15
destructiveness of war 11, 38, 57-63, 90, 114, 123, 132, 136, 161, 166-8, 217, 218
Detroit race riots (1943) 177
Dewey, Thomas 174
displaced persons 138
disruptions of war 11, 37, 39, 50, 52-63, 109, 113, 119, 129, 161, 166-8, 176, 213, 216-18
Dominicus, Chief Burgomaster of Berlin 32
Donitz, Admiral 121
*Don't You Know There's a War On* (Lingeman) 166
Dortmund, destruction in 134
Dresden, bombing of 2, 120, 121, 146, 179, 223
*Duma*, the 18, 34: summoned in 1915 36; 'Progressive Bloc' 36-8; dissolved 37; in 1917 37-8
Dunkirk: battle and evacuation 153, 186; bombing 186
Düsseldorf, bombing of 115

East Germany, *see* German Democratic Republic
Ebert, Friedrich 43, 48
*Economic and Social History of the Great War* (Carnegie Endowment volumes) 8
'economic' view of social effects of war 9
*Economist, The* 7
Edinburgh International Festival of Music and Drama 164
Education Act (1918) (Britain) 60
*Edwardian Turn of Mind, The* (Hynes) 9
Eisner, Kurt 42, 43
*Elements of Reconstruction,* (*The Times* articles, 1916) 6

Eliot, T. S. 85
Elsbree, W. H. 216
Employment Act (1946) (U.S.A.) 169
*Employment Policy* (White Paper, 1944) 162
*End of American Innocence, The* (May) 8
*End of the Russian Empire* (Florinsky) 10
Erhard, Ludwig 140
Erzberger, Matthias 32
Eupen 87
*Europe Since Napoleon* (Thomson) 10
European Coal and Steel Community 211
European Economic Community (E.E.C.) 205. *See also* Common Market
evacuation 118, 124, 156–7
*Evacuees, The* (ed. Johnson) 156
existentialism 200

Fair Employment Practices Committee (U.S.A.) 176
Falkenhayn, General von 30
Falls, Cyril 6
fascism 95
*Fascist Economy in Norway* (Milward) 9
February Revolution (Russia) 31, 36, 38. *See also* Russian Revolution
*February Revolution, The* (Katkov) 10
Fédération Nationale des Syndicats d'Exploitants Agricoles 195
Federation of British Industries 157–8, 161
Feldman, Gerald 10
*Feminine Mystique, The* (Friedan) 160
*Feu, Le* (Barbusse) 83, 86
Fisher, H. A. L., and Fisher Education Act 91
Fite, G. C. 8
Fitzgerald, Scott 85
Florinsky, M. T. 10
Foch, Marshal Ferdinand 187
Foot, M. R. D. 191
Ford, Henry 69
four-tier model 11–14, 50, 56, 79, 136–7, 161–5, 185–7, 216, 217
Four Year Plan (Germany) 108, 119

France 5, 24, 95, 98–100: in 1914 15–16, 19, 21–2; government 19; political parties 19, 21; centralisation 19, 20; Socialists 19, 21; women's suffrage movement 21
and First World War 52–6, 220–1: invaded territory 52; mobilisation 52–3, industrial and political crises 54; austerity in 1917 54; labour unrest 55; 'mutinies' 55; casualties 55; loss of production 55; social problems 56
test of war: control of railways 64–5; increase of bureaucracy 65; shipping tonnage 65–6; maintenance of trade 66; mixed economy 66; liquor control 69; social welfare provision 70; weakness of political structure 71–2
participation: trade unions 74; labour representation 75; skilled workers 75–6; peasantry 76; position of women 76–7
economic consequences of war 87–8; social legislation 90; housing 90; eight-hour day 90; family allowances 90; unemployment provisions 90
and Second World War 185–211, 221: war till May 1940 187; defeat in 1940 195–7; Occupied and Unoccupied France 188; Vichy régime 186, 188–90, 192–7; Resistance movement 186, 187, 189–92; Germans move into Unoccupied France (1942) 189; elements of collaboration 189; Germans and French workers 189; C.F.L.N. 191–2; Liberation Committees 191, 192; Allied invasion of France 191–2; Provisional Government 192; Liberation of Paris 192
bombing by British 185–6; civilian casualties 186; military casualties 186; deportations to Germany 186, 189, 190; loss of production 186; rationing and prices 193; black market 193; mortality rate 193; persecution of Jews 193

social consequences of the war 194–204; C.N.R. programme 196–9; Social Security programme (1945) 198, 203; votes for women 198–9; Constituent Assembly 199; Fourth Republic 199; psychological effects 200–2; post-war conditions 203; Indo-China crisis 204, 216, 221; Algerian crisis 204, 216, 221

economic recovery and idea of United Europe 205–11; relations with Germany 205, 211; *coup d'état* of 1958 204, 211, 221

*France sous l'Occupation, La* 193

Francis Ferdinand, Archduke, assassination of 4–5

Franco-Prussian War 5

Frank, Anne 215

Frankfurt, since Second World War 139

*Frankfurter Zeitung* 33

Free French Forces 186

*Free Speech in the United States* (Chaffee) 8

Freikorps, the 43, 49

Frenay, Captain Henri 189

French, Sir John (Earl of Ypres) 58

French Forces of the Interior (F.F.I.) 186, 192, 221

French Revolution, the 44

Freud, Sigmund 93

Friedan, Betty 160

Friends' Relief Service 134

Fry, Roger 85

full employment 163–4

Gamelin, General 187

gauleiters 108, 119

General Strike (Britain) 95

geographical consequences of First World War 86–7

*German Catastrophe, The* (Meinecke) 121

*German Economy at War, The* (Milward) 9

German Democratic Republic (D.D.R.) (East Germany) 136, 141–3, 200: economy 140

German Federal Republic (West Germany) 135–6, 143–5, 181, 182, 199, 203, 205, 221: economy 139–40; two party state 148

Germany 4, 5, 16: in 1914 16–21; government 18–19; Prussian predominance 18; political parties 19; trade unions 19; social welfare legislation 19–20; women's suffrage movement 21; urbanisation 21

'Fortress Truce', August 1914–November 1917 25–33; emotional impact of war 25; support of Social Democrats 25–6; hatred of the enemy 26; emergency legislation 27–8; scarcities 28, 30; restrictions and controls 28–9; workers and employers 29; national minorities 29; 'Turnip Winter' (1916–17) 30; 'Hindenburg programme' of 'war socialism' 30; grievances and social tension 30–1; strikes and food riots 31; and February Revolution 31; and Stockholm conference 31–2; demands for negotiated peace 32–3; government changes 33; and October Revolution 40

Revolution 40–9: strikes in 1918 40–1; failure of offensive in West 41–2; signs of breakdown 41–2; alteration of constitution 42; mutiny in fleet 42; revolution in Munich 42; Workers' and Soldiers' Councils 42, 43; abdication of Kaiser 42–3; Ebert's Government 43; Weimar Republic 43, 48; Spartacists put down 43; Bavarian Republic destroyed 43; comparison with Russia 43–5; Constitution of August 1919 45–6

between the wars 46–9, 87–8, 95, 103–8: settlement after 1919 46; loss of manpower 47; disruption and inflation 47; recovery 47; frontiers with Poland 87; economic consequences of war 87–8; National Socialism 103–8; economic policy 108

the Second World War: September 1939 to spring 1942 108–12: blitzkrieg 109, 111; rationing and shortages 109; control of labour 110; British bombing 109–11; invasion of

Germany – (contd)
  Russia   109–10, 112;
  anti-semitism   112
    spring 1942 to spring and
  summer 1944   112–20: casualties
  in Russia   112; battle for
  Stalingrad   112–13; labour
  situation   113–14; bombing of
  Germany   114–18; evacuation
  facilities   118
    final phase   120–3: food
  supply   120; plot to assassinate
  Hitler   120; underground factories
  121; People's Army   121; scorched
  earth policy   121; collapse of
  National Socialist state   121;
  concentration camps   121–3
    after the war: food shortages
  134, 135; West and East Germany
  135–6; war casualties   138
Gestapo, the   105, 112, 118, 121, 215
Gibbs, N. H.   7
Goebbels, Josef   105, 113, 114, 118,
  217
Goering, Hermann   108, 109, 119
Gompers, Samuel   75, 80
G.P.U., the   101
Grass, Gunther   147
Gray, H. L.   9
Great Britain, see Britain
Great Leap, The (Brookes)   166
Groener, General   29, 43
Guchkov, A. I.   36
guerrilla wars   218
Guillebaud, C. W.   106


Haber, Fritz and fixation of nitrogen
  28
Haig, Sir Douglas (Earl Haig)   58,
  221
Hamburg, bombing of   2, 115–16
Hanover, since Second World War
  139
Harlem Renaissance, the   79, 83
Harris, Sir Arthur   114
Heller, Joseph   179
Hemingway, Ernest   85
Henderson, Arthur   74
Hertling, Count von   33
Hess, Myra   164
Himmler, Heinrich   113, 119
Hindenburg, Field-Marshal Paul von
  105: and Hindenburg programme 30

Hiroshima, atom bomb on   2, 166,
  179
Hirst, F. W.   7–8
Hitler, Adolf   5, 39, 103–9, 111–13,
  118–21, 123–5, 142, 145–7, 153, 179,
  204: comes into power   105;
  Führer and Chancellor   105; 'New
  Order'   108, 205, 206, 208, 211;
  assassination plot   120; suicide 121
Hoffman, Stanley   10–11, 100, 194–6
holidays with pay   102, 107
Holland   213: German occupation
  215
Hoover, Herbert   67, 68
Housing Acts (1919) (Britain)   60, 91
Hugenberg, Alfred   28
Hurwitz, Samuel J.   9
'Hymn of Hate'   26
Hynes, S. H.   9

Ickes, Harold   173
Idées Politiques et Sociales de la
  Résistance, Les (Michel and
  Mirkine-Guetzevitch)   196
Iklé, F. C.   117, 154
Independent Socialists (Germany)
  26, 30, 41, 43, 44
Indonesia   216
in-group feelings   79, 81–2, 133, 134,
  179
Instincts of the Herd in Peace and War
  (Trotter)   79
Institute for Sexual Science (Berlin)
  93
International Journal of Psychoanalysis
  154
International Labour Office   89

Janis, I. L.   154
Japan   216
Japanese-Americans, treatment of
  179
Jeffers, Williams   170
Joffre, Marshal   53–5, 220–1
Johnson, B. S.   156
Johnson, Douglas   198
Jouhaux, Léon   75
Joyce, James   84, 85
Junkers, the   18, 106

Kadets, the   18
Kafka, Franz   85
Kandinsky, Vasily   85
Kapp putsch   46

Katkov, George 10
Kerensky, Alexander 38, 39, 45
Keynes, J. M. (Lord Keynes), and
  Keynesian economic theories 162,
  169
Kitchener of Khartoum, Earl 57
Klee, Paul 85
Konody, P. G. 84
Korean War, the 181, 218: effect on
  Britain 219
Kornilov, General 39–40
Kulischer, Eugene 142

Labour Party (Britain) 74–5, 82;
  Government (1945) 163, 181, 198,
  210, 219
Lake, Veronica 175
Lampson, Mrs I. P. 81–2
Lancaster bombers 114
Landtag (Prussian state parliament)
  18
Laroque, Pierre 195
Laval, Pierre 188, 193
League of Nations 6, 46, 73, 206
Le Havre, bombing of 186
Lenin, Vladimir Ilyich, and
  Leninism 39–40, 47, 101, 102, 107,
  142
Leningrad 139, 143: defence of
  124–6, 134
'Leningrad' symphony (Shostakovich)
  133
Leparcq, Aimé 195
Leuchtenberg, W. E. 10, 95–6
'liberal' view of social effects of war
  7–9
Liberté 207
Liebknecht, Karl 43
limited war 217
Lingeman, Richard R. 166
liquor control 69–70. See also
  prohibition
Lissauer, Ernst 26
Lloyd George, David (Earl
  Lloyd-George) 40, 66, 71, 178, 221
London, 'blitz' on 110, 125, 153–6
London Fire Service Film 155
Lorenz, Konrad 3
Los Angeles race riots (1943) 177
Lübeck, bombing of 114
Ludendorff, General von 30, 42
Luxemburg, Rosa 43
Lvov, Prince 33–4, 37, 39
Lyons and the Resistance 189

McAdoo, William G. 67–8
Macaulay, Lord 93
McCarthyism 182
MacLeish, Archibald 167
Magic Mountain, The (Mann) 86
Mailer, Norman 179
Maisie's Marriage (film) 94
Malenkov, G. M. 130
Malmedy 87
Mandarins, The (de Beauvoir) 201
Mandel, Georges 187
Mann, Golo 145
Mann, Thomas 85, 86
Married Love (Stopes) 94
Marshall, General George, and the
  Marshall Plan 208–10
Marx, Karl 44, 101
Marxism and Marxists 26, 40, 132,
  147
Mata Hari 55
Mathews, R. C. O. 163
Max of Baden, Prince 42, 43
May, Henry F. 8–9
Meinecke, Friedrich 32, 127, 146
Memel 87
Mensheviks, the 18, 34, 36, 38
Michael, Grand Duke 38
Michaelis, Georg 28, 33
Michel, Henri 10, 196, 207
Military Participation Ratio (M.P.R.)
  23, 222. See also participation
Miller, William 165–6
Milner, Lord 6
Milward, Alan 9, 190, 208
Ministry of Health Act (1919) (Britain)
  91
Mirkine-Guetzevitch, Boris 196
Molotov, V. M. 130
Monnet, Jean, and the Monnet plan
  195, 196, 198, 202, 211
Monts, Count von 32
Moscow in Second World War 124–
  7
Moscow Underground 102
Mothers' Aid (U.S.A.) 89–90
Moulin, Jean 191
Mouvement Republicaine Populaire
  (M.R.P.) 199
Müller, Dr August 33
Munich revolution (1918–19) 42, 43

Nagasaki, atom bomb on 2, 166, 179
Naked and the Dead, The (Mailer)
  179

Nash, Paul   83
National Defense Mediation Board
   (U.S.A.)   173
National Gallery wartime concerts
   104
National Health Service (Britain)
   161
National Housing Agency (U.S.A.)
   174
National Labor Relations Act (U.S.A.)
   99, 100
National People's Party (Germany)
   48
National Recovery Administration
   (U.S.A.)   99
National Resistance Council (C.N.R.)
   (France)   191: programme (1944)
   196–9, 207
National Socialism, *see* Nazism
National War Labor Board (U.S.A.)
   169, 172, 175
NATO   210
Naumann, Friedrich   48, 82, 95
Nazism and National Socialist régime
   5–6, 43, 95, 98, 103–10, 112–14, 117–
   21, 129–30, 143, 144, 146 148, 188,
   205, 206, 211, 215, 221, 222:
   economic planning   9;
   revolutionary character   97, 103;
   one-party State   105; S.A. and S.S.
   105; reduction of unemployment
   105–6; social welfare   107;
   anti-semitism   107; New Order
   108, 205, 206, 208, 211
'Negro Revolt' in U.S.A.   175–6, 178
Nelson, Donald   169
Neuve Chapelle, battle of   57
New Deal, the   90, 95, 98–100, 165,
   167, 168, 174
New Economic Policy (Russia)   47
*New Order and the French Economy,
   The* (Milward)   9
*New Republic*   167
New York race riots (1943)   176
Nicholas II, Tsar   37, 38: abdicates
   38
Nivelle, General Robert   54, 55
N.K.V.D. (People's Commissariat of
   International Affairs)   101
Norway   213, 214: German
   occupation   215
Noske, German Social Democrat   42,
   43
Nove, Alec   130

Nuremberg Laws (1935)   107
Nuremberg Tribunal   121, 122, 144

October Revolution (Russia)   33, 40,
   45
Octobrist party (Russia)   18, 36
Office of Economic Stabilization
   (U.S.A.)   169, 172
Office of Price Administration (U.S.A.)
   169
Office of War Mobilization (U.S.A.)
   169
O.G.P.U.   101
Old Vic wartime tours   164
Oliver, F. S.   80
*opolchenya* (workers' brigades)   124
*Opponents of War 1917–18* (Peterson
   and Fite)   8
*Ordeal of Total War, The* (Wright)
   10
Organisation for European Economic
   Co-operation (O.E.E.C.)   210
Orlov, Admiral   102
Owen, Wilfred   84

P.51 Mustang long-range fighter   120
pacifism   62, 63, 220
Pankhurst, Sylvia   31
Paris   204: liberation of (1944)   192
Parti Populaire Français   99
*participation*   12–13, 36, 37, 40, 73–9,
   90, 110–11, 119, 123, 132–3, 137,
   162–3, 166, 170–8, 187, 213, 214, 216,
   217
Passchendaele campaign   58
Pasternak, Boris   133
Paxson, Frederick L.   7
peace research   220
Pearl Harbor, Japanese attack on   166
Peasant Corporation (Vichy)   195
Pelling, Henry   157, 161, 163, 165
pension schemes (U.S.A.)   90
Pétain, Marshal Philippe   55, 187, 188
Peterson, H. C.   8
Petrograd Soviet   38
*Peuple Russe Pendant La Guerre*
   (Champenois)   124
Poincaré, Raymond   53
Poland, reconstitution of   86;
   frontiers with Germany   87; Nazis
   and Polish Jews   112
Polenberg, Richard   166, 179
Polish Corridor   87
Polish minority in Germany   29

Politburo, the  101
pop culture  182
Popular Front (France)  99, 100, 203,
   221
Post-Impressionists, the  84, 85
Potsdam Conference (1945)  138
*Pravda*  103, 128
*Prince Regent Leopold*, hunger strike
   on  31
Progressive Party (Germany)  19, 43
prohibition: movement in U.S.A.  21,
   62–3; imposed in Russia  35
propaganda  81
psychological experiences of war  13,
   40, 50, 79–83, 95, 111–12, 120, 123,
   133–4, 137, 166, 170, 176, 178–9,
   200–2, 213, 214, 217

racial discrimination  176–8: ended
   in U.S. forces  178
railways, control of  64
Randolph, A. Philip  176
Rasputin, Grigoriy  36, 37
Rathenau, Walter  28, 118
Red Cross, the  78
*Reichstag*, the  18
Remarque, Erich Maria  85
Renouvin, Pierre  72
Republican Party (U.S.A.)  167–8,
   171, 174
Resistance movement in France  186,
   187, 189–92, 196, 204–7, 211, 221,
   223: underground newspapers
   189; left-wing members  190, 192,
   204; Catholic members  190, 199;
   main groups  190; and British
   agents  191; C.N.R. and F.F.I.
   191, 196–9, 207; social significance
   196–200
revolutionary war  217
Reynaud, Paul  187
Rhythm and Blues movement  177
Ribot, Alexandre  55
Roberts, J. M.  148–9
Robson, W. A.  11
Rodzyanko, chairman of Duma  328
Roosevelt, President Franklin D.  68,
   95–6, 99, 171–3, 176–8, 191, 192
Rostock, bombing of  114
Ruhr, the, bombing of  115
*R.U.R.* (Capek)  86
Russia  4, 5, 16, 24, 205, 208: in
   1914  14, 16–18, 20: Tsarist
   autocracy  18; *Zemstvos* and

Municipalities  33–4; patriotic
   enthusiasm  34; mobilisation  34,
   35; fall in production  34, 35;
   'voluntary organisations'  36, 38;
   War Industries Committee  36;
   strikes and middle-class demands
   36; summoning of Duma  36
   Revolution  37–40: Petrograd
   under military command  38;
   widespread strikes  38; soldiers go
   over to workers  38; Provisional
   Government  38, 39; end of
   monarchy  38; Soviets  38, 39;
   peasants take over estates  38–9;
   Kerensky's Government  39;
   Lenin's part  39, 40; Kornilov's
   attempted *coup*  39–40; October
   Revolution  40, 45; negotiations
   with Central Powers  40; Treaty of
   Brest-Litovsk  40; Bolsheviks
   assume power  45
   Civil War  47; 'War
   Communism'  47; New Economic
   Policy  47; privation and
   starvation  49; social welfare
   provisions  50
   between the wars  95,, 101–3:
   Communism  101; secret police
   101; Stalin's 'second revolution'
   101; real wages  102;
   industrialisation  102; prestige
   projects  102; health provision
   102; housing  102; Soviet
   Constitution (1936)  102; wave of
   terror  102
   and Second World War  123–34,
   221: comparison with Germany
   123, 129–30; annexation of
   neighbouring states  123; German
   invasion  109, 110, 112, 123;
   defence of Leningrad  124–6, 134;
   food shortages  125; hardships in
   Moscow  126–7; loss of territories
   127; loss of production  128–9;
   statistics of wartime production
   130–1; State Committee of Defence
   130; participation  132–3; women
   workers  132; mobilisation of
   resources  132–3; partisan activities
   133; in-group feelings  133–4
   after the war, 135, 145–6: war
   casualties  138; economy  140–1;
   social structure  141;
   anti-semitism  142–3; social

Russia – (contd)
welfare 143; confrontation with
U.S.A. 181–2; space 'first' (1958)
182
Russian Revolution 6, 10, 37–40.
See also February Revolution and
October Revolution
Russo-Japanese War 18

S.A. (Sturm Abteilung) 105
Saarland 46
Sadler's Wells Opera Company 164
Sartre, Jean-Paul 200–1
Sauckel, Nazi Labour minister 113,
119, 190
Scheidemann, Philipp 43, 48
Schlieffen plan 52
Schoenbaum, David 106
Schuman, Robert, and the Schuman
plan 210–11
Schuursma, Rolf 215
Schweinfurt, bombing of 116
science and technology 12, 13, 47,
68–9, 180
Scott, Emmett 78
'Scottish Renaissance' 83
Second World War, The (Churchill)
7
Service d'Ordre Légionnaire 189
Servicemen's Readjustment Act (G.I.
Bill) (1944) (U.S.A.) 174
sex, war, and 'permissiveness' 50, 93–
4, 143–4, 182, 204
Seydewitz, Max 110
Shakhovskoy, Prince 34
Sheridan, Ann 175
Shop Council Act (1944) (Germany)
49
Shostakovich, Dmitri 133
Shotwell, J. T. 8
Silence de la Mer, Le ('Vercors')
201–2
Sinclair, Upton 87
Slaughter House 5 (Vonnegut) 179
Slavophobia in Germany 104
Smith–Connally Act (1943) 173
social consequences of war 6–14:
'tory' view 6–7; 'liberal' view
7–9; 'economic' view 9;
'sociological' view 9–10; use of
metaphors 10–11; four-tier model
11–14
Social Democratic party (Germany)
19, 25–6, 33, 42–4, 48, 148

Social Impact of Bomb Destruction,
The (Iklé) 154
Socialist Revolutionaries (Russia) 18,
36–8
'sociological' view of social effects of
war 7, 9–10
Somme, battle of the 58
Soviet Constitution (1936) 102
Soviets 38, 39
Spaak, Paul-Henri 210
Spain 214
Spanish Civil War 146
Spartacists 26, 43
Special Operations Executive (S.O.E.)
191
Speer, Albert 111, 116–19, 121, 140,
169, 189, 211: extension of his
influence 118–19
S.S. (Schutz Staffeln) 105, 112, 113,
118, 119
Stalin, Josef, and Stalinism 101, 102,
107, 123, 126, 129–31, 133, 147–8:
'cult of personality' 130
Stalingrad, battle for 112–13
State Intervention in Britain (Hurwitz)
9
Steel Workers Organizing Committee
(U.S.A.) 172
Stinnes, Hugo 28
Stockholm international socialist
conference (1917) 31–2
Stopes, Marie 94
Strategic Bombing of Germany, The
(film) 115
Stravinsky, Igor 84, 85
Sunday Times 124
Supreme Court (U.S.A.) 99–100
Supreme Economic Council (1919) 72
Sweden 214
Switzerland 214
synthetic rubber, new American
industry 170

Temple, Archbishop William 158
Terraine, John 7
test of war 12, 35, 38, 39, 63–73, 110,
118, 119, 129–32, 136–7, 166, 168–71,
176, 180, 186–7, 217
Third Man, The (film) 7
Third Republic (France) 95
Thomson, David 10
Tiburtius, Dr, German labour expert
29

*Times, The* 6

*Tin Drum, The* (Grass) 146–7

*To Secure These Rights*, Committee on Civil Rights Report (U.S.A.) 177–8

Todt, Fritz 118

'Tory' view of social effects of war 7–8, 80

total war 217, 220

totalitarianism 95, 103, 106

trade unions: in Germany 19, 106; in U.S.A. 74, 172–4; in France 74, 191; in Britain 74, 158

Trades Union Congress (Britain) 80, 82

Troeltsch, Ernest 32

Trotter, Wilfred 79

Trudoviks, the 34

Truman, President Harry S. 177–8: Civil Rights Message (1948) 178

Tukhachevsky, Marshal 102


unemployment: in the 1930s 100; in Germany 105–6; in U.S.A. 168, 181

unemployment insurance 90–1

Union of Municipalities (Russia) 34

United Automobile Workers (U.S.A.) 172

United European Movement 210

United Mine Workers (U.S.A.) 172

United Nations 206

United States 24, 47, 205: in 1914 14–15, 17–18; nation of immigrants 17–18; government 20; socialist and 'Progressive' movements 21; women's suffrage movements 21, 77; urbanisation 21; WASPS and Planters 22

    and First World War 61–3: and western Allies' war needs 61; mobilisation 61–2; military service 62; casualties 62; anti-German hysteria 62; liquor control 62–3; and 'progressivism' 63, 71

    test of war 67–8: state action 67; supply and support of Allies 67; government interference 67–8; control of railroads 67–8; food administration 68

    participation: trade unions 74; labour representation 75; position of women 77; black participation 77–9; social legislation 89–90; real wages 92

    between the wars 95, 98–100: New Deal 90, 95, 98–100, 163, 167, 168, 174; unemployment 100

    Second World War 165–79: cost of war 166; casualties 166; destruction and disruption 167–8; abeyance of anti-trust laws 167; child labour 167; war industry problems 168; war as test 168–71, 176, 180; production boom 169; conversion to war effort 169–70; wartime agencies 169; mixed war economy 169–70; new synthetic rubber industry 170; change in civil–military relations 170–1; power of the President 171; participation 171–8; labour policy 171–2; trade unions 172–4; strikes and industrial discontent 172–3; wage increases 173; G.I. Bill 174; housing 174; women's participation 174–5; black Americans and the war effort 175–8; racial discrimination 176; blacks in armed forces 177, 178; race riots (1943) 177; white violence (1946) 177; movement towards Civil Rights 177–8; psychological impacts 178–9; treatment of minority groups 179; Japanese-Americans 179

    new relationships 179–82; comparison with Britain 180–2; military technology 180; military–industrial complex 180–1, 220; confrontation with Russia 181–2; the visual arts 182; and Korean War 218; and Vietnam War 218–19

urbanisation 21


venereal diseases, discussion of 93–4

'Vercors' (Jean Bruller) 201–2

Versailles, Treaty of 46, 86–9, 138, 144

Vichy régime 186, 188–90, 192–7, 211, 221: Organisation and Business Committees 195; Labour Charter 195

*Vie de la France sous l'Occupation, La*, collection of documents 192–3

Vietnam War  218–19
Viviani, René  53, 54
Vonnegut, Kurt, jr  175
Voroshilov, Marshal  130

*War and Social Reform, The*
  (Worsfold)  7
'War and Society' films  115
*War and Society: The United States
  1941–1945* (Polenberg)  179
war crimes  144
War Industries Committee (Russia)
  36
War Industry Board (U.S.A.)  67, 68
War Labor Administration (U.S.A.)
  75
War Manpower Commission (U.S.A.)
  169
War Production Board (U.S.A.)  169
War Purchase and Finance Council
  72
*Wartime Control of Industry* (Gray)
  9
War Wheat Corporation (Germany)
  28
Warmbrunn, Walter  215
WASPS (White Anglo-Saxon
  Protestants)  22
Weber, Max  26

Weimar Republic  43, 85, 141–2, 199,
  204
Welfare State, the  163, 181
Welles, Orson  7
Werth, Alexander  124–8, 134, 143–4
West European Union  210
West Germany, *see* German Federal
  Republic
Weygand, General Maxime  187, 188
*While Germany Waits* (film)  134
Wilhelm II, Kaiser  26, 31–3, 110,
  221: abdication  42–3
Wilson, Harold  219
Wilson, William B.  75
Wilson, President Woodrow  42, 61,
  67, 68, 77
Women's Liberation Movement  174,
  175
women's suffrage movement  21
Woodward, E. L.  82
Workmen's Compensation (U.S.A.)
  90
*World Crisis, The* (Churchill)  3, 7
Worsfold, W. Basil  6–7
Wright, Gordon  10

*Zemstvos* (rural districts)  18, 33, 34,
  45: Union of  33–4
Zhdanov  147